Pocket
PARIS

TOP EXPERIENCES · LOCAL LIFE

D0388738

JEAN-BERNARD CARILLET,
CATHERINE LE NEVEZ, CHRISTOPHER
PITTS, NICOLA WILLIAMS

Contents

Plan Your Trip 4

Jardin des Tuileries (p78)
MAREMAGNUM/GETTY IMAGES ©

Explore Paris 35

Worth a Trip

Survival Guide 203

Special Features

COVID-19

We have re-checked every business in this book before publication to ensure that it is still open after the COVID-19 outbreak. However, the economic and social impacts of COVID-19 will continue to be felt long after the outbreak has been contained, and many businesses, services and events referenced in this guide may experience ongoing restrictions. Some businesses may be temporarily closed, have changed their opening hours and services, or require bookings; some unfortunately could have closed permanently. We suggest you check with venues before visiting for the latest information.

Paris' Top Experiences

MARINA1A/SHUTTERSTOCK ©

Climb the Eiffel Tower (p38)

Explore the Musée Rodin (p40)

View Paris from the Arc de Triomphe (p54)

Discover artistic treasures at the Louvre (p68)

HERACLES KRITIKOS/LONELY PLANET ©

DENNISVDW/GETTY IMAGES ©

Wonder at the Sacré-Cœur (p94)

Delight at the Centre Pompidou (p112)

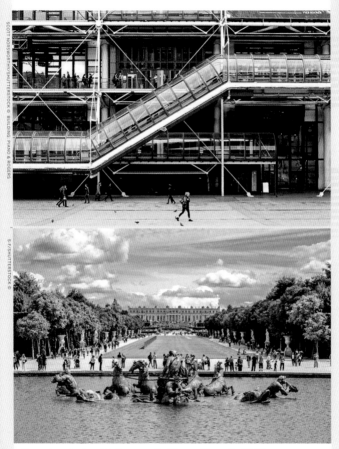

SCOTT NORSWORTHY/SHUTTERSTOCK © BUILDING: PIANO & ROGERS

S-F/SHUTTERSTOCK ©

Dazzle at the Château de Versailles (p198)

Marvel at the masters in the Musée d'Orsay (p176)

PHOTO.UA/SHUTTERSTOCK ©

MYKOLASTOCK/SHUTTERSTOCK ©

Relax in the Jardin du Luxembourg (p178

Admire Notre Dame (p138)

Stroll through the Père Lachaise (p134)

Dining Out

France pioneered what is still the most influential style of cooking in the Western world and Paris is its showcase. Colours, textures and garnishes are impeccabley arranged everywhere from simple restaurants to haute cuisine establishments. Paris is the crossroads for France's regional produce and flavours.

Evolving Trends

In addition to classical French fare, look out for cuisines from around the globe. Neobistros offer some of Paris' most exciting dining options. Generally small and relatively informal, they're run by young, talented chefs who aren't afraid to experiment. Exclusively vegetarian and vegan establishments are increasing, as are places offering gluten-free dishes.

Dining Times

Petit déjeuner (breakfast; usually a baguette with butter and jam, and strong coffee) is seen as a mere precursor to *déjeuner* (lunch; the traditional main meal, starting around 12.30pm). Most restaurants open for *dîner* (dinner) around 7pm or 7.30pm. Some high-end restaurants close at weekends, and many places close in August.

Menus

Restaurants usually serve a *plat du jour* (dish of the day) at lunch (and occasionally at dinner), as well as *menus* (fixed-price meals) of an *entrée* (starter), *plat* (main course) and *fromage* (cheese) or dessert or both. These offer infinitely better value than ordering à la carte. Meals are often considerably cheaper at lunch than dinner.

Best Classic Bistros

Le Bistrot Paul Bert Legendary address with perfectly executed classic dishes. (p125)

Chez Dumonet The quintessential Parisian bistro experience, lace curtains and all. (p191)

Le Cassenoix *Terroir* specialist footsteps from the Eiffel Tower. (p47)

ALEXANDROS MICHAILIDIS/SHUTTERSTOCK ©

Café de la Nouvelle Mairie
Latin Quarter favourite for seasonal cuisine. (p162)

Best Neobistros

Richer Brilliant-value bistro fare but no reservations, so arrive early. (p81)

Le Servan Daily changing creations near Père Lachaise. (p124)

Clover Watch the chefs in the combined dining space–kitchen. (p191)

Best Gastronomic Experiences

Septime A beacon of modern cuisine. (p122)

Restaurant AT Abstract-art-like masterpieces made from rare ingredients. (p161)

Frenchie The bijou bistro that redefined Parisian dining. (p81)

Best Sweet Treats

Jacques Genin Assembled-to-order *millefeuilles*. (p122)

Cédric Grolet Opéra
Queues down the street for these elaborate creations. (Pictured above; p81)

Ladurée The original creator of the lighter-than-air macaron. (p62)

Top Tips for Parisian Dining

• Midrange restaurants will usually have a free table for lunch (arrive by 12.30pm); book a day or two in advance for dinner.

• Reservations up to one or two months in advance are crucial for lunch and dinner at popular and high-end restaurants. You may need to reconfirm on the day.

• Service is always included: a *pourboire* (tip) on top of the bill is not necessary, though rounding the bill up is common.

Bar Open

For Parisians, drinking and eating go together like wine and cheese, and the line between a cafe, salon de thé (tearoom), bistro, brasserie, bar and even a bar à vins (wine bar) is blurred, while the line between drinking and clubbing is often nonexistent – a cafe that's quiet mid-afternoon might have DJ sets in the evening and dancing later on.

Coffee

If you order *un café* (a coffee), you'll be served a single shot of espresso. A *café allonge* is lengthened with hot water, a *café au lait* comes with milk and a *café crème*, lengthened with steamed milk, is the closest to a latte. Local roasteries such as Belleville Brûlerie and Coutume prime cafes citywide for outstanding brews made by professional baristas, often using cutting-edge extraction techniques.

Beer

Paris' growing *bière artisanale* (craft beer) scene is going from strength to strength, with an increasing number of city breweries. An excellent resource for hopheads is www.hoppyparis.com.

Wine

Wine is easily the most popular beverage in Paris and house wine invariably costs less than bottled water. *Les vins naturels* (natural wines) contain little or no sulphites.

Cocktails

Cocktail bars are undergoing a resurgence; many hip restaurants pair cocktails with food. Paris Cocktail Week (www.pariscocktailweek.fr) takes place in late January.

Best Coffee

Beans on Fire Collaborative roastery and cafe. (p130)

La Caféothèque Coffee house and roastery plus in-house coffee school. (p130)

Coutume Café Artisan roastery with a flagship Left Bank cafe. (p49)

Honor Outdoor coffee bar in an elegant rue du Faubourg St-Honoré courtyard. (p64)

TUPUNGATO/SHUTTERSTOCK ©

Best Cocktails

Bar Hemingway Legendary cocktails inside the Ritz. (p83)

Le Mary Céleste Innovative cocktails in the hip Haut Marais. (p127)

Baby Doll Concoctions and decor inspired by French musician Serge Gainsbourg. (p84)

Django Order the Reinhardt cocktail at this former guitar shop. (p101)

Tiger Gin specialist with 130 varieties. (p195)

Wine Bars

Au Sauvignon Original zinc bar and hand-painted ceiling. (Pictured above; p192)

Le Baron Rouge Unpretentious neighbourhood hang-out. (p128)

Augustin Marchand D'Vins Atmospheric decor and excellent wines. (p192)

Best Pavement Terraces

Scilicet Right on the Seine with a spectacular Parisian panorama. (p83)

Maison Maison The perfect Seine-side terrace in warm weather. (p81)

Shakespeare & Company Café Live the Parisian Left Bank literary dream. (p165)

Drinking Like a Local

○ Although most places serve at least small plates (and often full menus), it's normally fine to order a drink if you're not dining.

○ The French rarely go drunk-wild and tend to frown upon it.

○ For clubbing events, visit www.sortira-paris.com: click on 'Soirées & Bars', then 'Nuits Parisiennes'.

Treasure Hunt

Paris has it all: broad boulevards lined with international chains, luxury avenues studded with designer fashion houses, grand department stores and lively street markets. But the real charm lies in strolling the city's backstreets, where tiny speciality shops and quirky boutiques are wedged between cafes, galleries and churches.

Fashion

Fashion shopping is Paris' forte. Parisian fashion is about style and quality first and foremost, rather than status or brand names.

A good place to get an overview is at the city's famous *grands magasins* (department stores).

Markets

The city's street markets are social gatherings for the entire neighbourhood. Nearly every little quarter has its own street market at least once a week (never Monday) where tarpaulin-topped trestle tables bow beneath fresh, cooked and preserved delicacies. *Marchés biologiques* (organic markets) are increasingly sprouting up across the city. Many street markets also sell clothes, accessories, homewares and more.

The website www. paris.fr/pages/ les-marches-parisiens-2428 lists every market by *arrondissement* (city district), including speciality markets such as flower markets.

Gourmet Shops

Food and drink shops make for mouthwatering shopping. Pastries might not keep, but you can take home (customs regulations permitting) chocolates, jams, preserves and French cheeses. Many of the best *fromageries* (cheese shops) can provide vacuum packing.

Best Department Stores

Le Bon Marché Paris' oldest department store, designed by Gustave Eiffel. (Pictured above; p196)

Galeries Lafayette Has a magnificent stained-glass

VLASYUK INNA/SHUTTERSTOCK ©

dome, and a Champs-Élysées outpost. (p87)

Le Printemps Fabulous fashion, cosmetics and French food and wine. (p88)

La Samaritaine Seine-side landmark reopened in 2020. (p88)

Best Concept & Design Stores

Merci Fabulously fashionable and unique: all profits go to a children's charity in Madagascar. (p132)

Empreintes Emporium showcasing some 6000 French artists and designers. (p132)

L'Exception Fashion, homewares, books and more from over 400 French designers. (p88)

O/HP/E Designer homewares, stationery and cosmetics. (p109)

Best Gourmet Shops

La Grande Épicerie de Paris Glorious food emporium. (p196)

Place de la Madeleine Single-item specialist shops and famous caterers. (p86)

La Manufacture de Chocolat Alain Ducasse's bean-to-bar chocolate factory. (p133)

La Dernière Goutte Wines from small, independent French producers. (p195)

The Best Tip for Shopping

● Paris' twice-yearly *soldes* (sales) generally last four weeks, starting around mid-January and again around late June.

● Most shops offer free (and very beautiful) gift wrapping – ask for *un paquet cadeau*.

● Non-EU residents may be eligible for a TVA (*taxe sur la valeur ajoutée*; value-added tax) refund.

Museums

If there's one thing that rivals a Parisian's obsession with food, it's their love of art. Hundreds of museums pepper the city, and whether you prefer classicism, impressionism or detailed exhibits of French military history, you can always be sure to find something new just around the corner.

Planning Your Visit

Most museums close one day a week, generally Monday or Tuesday; many open late one or more nights a week – usually the least crowded time to visit. You'll also save time by purchasing tickets online where possible. Remember that the cut-off for entry to museums is typically half an hour to an hour before the official closing times (including times listed in this guide). Audio-guides are sometimes included with admission but often incur an extra charge.

National Museums

If you can, time your trip to be here on the first Sunday of the month, when you can visit the *musées nationaux* (national museums; www.rmn. fr) as well as a handful of monuments for free (some during certain months only). Temporary exhibitions still incur a charge.

City Museums

You can visit the permanent collections of most *musées municipaux* (city-run museums; www.paris. fr) for free any time. Temporary exhibitions incur a charge.

Best Can't-Miss Museums

Louvre The one museum you just can't miss. (p68)

Musée National Picasso An incomparable overview of Picasso's work and life. (p118)

Musée Rodin Rodin's former mansion and its rose gardens contain his masterworks. (p40)

Best Modern & Contemporary Art

Musée National d'Art Moderne The country's national modern- and contemporary-art museum, located within the striking Centre Pompidou. (p112)

Atelier des Lumières Paris' first digital art museum. (p118)

Collection Pinault – Paris Major 2020-opening contemporary-art museum. (p80)

Musée d'Art Moderne de la Ville de Paris Paris' modern-art museum spans the 20th century to the present day. (p61)

Palais de Tokyo Temporary exhibitions and installations. (p61)

Best Impressionist Collections

Musée d'Orsay France's national museum for impressionist and related artistic movements is a must. (p176)

Musée de l'Orangerie Monet conceived a stunning cycle of his *Water Lilies* series especially for this building. (Pictured above; p78)

Musée Marmottan Monet The world's largest Monet collection occupies a former hunting lodge. (p46)

Money-Saving Tips

○ Save time and money by investing in a Paris Museum Pass or Paris Passlib' (which includes public transport) to bypass (or substantially reduce) ridiculously long ticket queues.

○ Look out for museum combination tickets.

○ EU citizens under 26 years get in for free at national monuments and museums.

Architecture

Baron Haussmann's overhaul, which made way for boulevards lined by neoclassical buildings, still defines Paris today. After the art nouveau movement, additions centred on French presidents' bold grands projets (legacy projects). For an architectural overview, visit the Cité de l'Architecture et du Patrimoine (p58).

Haussmann's Renovation

Paris' appearance today is largely the work of Baron Georges-Eugène Haussmann. Under Napoléon III, Haussmann completely rebuilt swathes of Paris between 1853 and 1870, replacing chaotic narrow streets (easy to barricade in an uprising) with arrow-straight, wide thoroughfares, including the 12 avenues radiating out from the Arc de Triomphe.

Rising Skyline

The controversial construction of the 1970s eyesore Tour Montparnasse (undergoing major renovations from 2020 to 2024) prompted a clampdown on skyscrapers. However, due to Paris' lack of housing space, the city council approved raising height limits to 180m in some areas. Advocates include Pritzker Prize–winning French architect Jean Nouvel.

Best Art Nouveau Splendours

Eiffel Tower Paris' 'iron lady' is art nouveau at its best. (p38)

Abbesses metro entrance Hector Guimard's finest remaining metro entrance. (p97)

Brasserie Bofinger Dine amid art nouveau brass, glass and mirrors in Paris' oldest brasserie. (p124)

Musée d'Orsay The former railway station (built in 1900) that houses this monumental museum justifies a visit alone. (p176)

Galeries Lafayette Glorious department store topped by a stunning stained-glass dome. (Pictured above; p87)

BOTOND HORVATH/SHUTTERSTOCK ©

Le Carreau du Temple This old covered market in Le Marais is now a cutting-edge cultural and community centre. (p115)

Best Presidential Grands Projets

Centre Pompidou Former president Georges Pompidou's now-beloved cultural centre sparked furore when it was unveiled in 1977. (p112)

Louvre glass pyramid IM Pei's pyramid, instigated by former president François Mitterrand, likewise created an uproar in 1989. (p68)

Opéra Bastille Mitterrand's costly *projets* include the city's second, state-of-the-art opera house. (p130)

Bibliothèque Nationale de France Another Mitterrand vision, the national library's four towers are shaped like half-open books. (p173)

Best Jean Nouvel Buildings

Musée du Quai Branly President Jacques Chirac's pet *projet,* designed by Nouvel. (p44)

Institut du Monde Arabe The building that established Nouvel's reputation blends modern and traditional Arabic elements with Western influences. (p158)

Fondation Cartier pour l'Art Contemporain Stunning contemporary art space. (p187)

Best Contemporary Structures

Lafayette Anticipations Contemporary art, design and fashion space transformed in 2018 by Rem Koolhaas. (p120)

Cinémathèque Française Frank Gehry designed this postmodern stunner housing two cinema museums and presenting screenings. (p173)

Forum des Halles Central shopping mall now topped by a giant rainforest-inspired canopy. (p80)

Fondation Louis Vuitton Fine-arts centre by Frank Gehry, topped by a giant glass 'cloud'. (p61)

History

Paris' history is a saga of battles, bloodshed, grand-scale excesses, revolution, reformation, resistance, renaissance and constant reinvention. But this epic is not just consigned to museums and archives: reminders of the capital's and the country's history are evident all over the city

Early Beginnings

Paris was born in the 3rd century BC, when the Parisii tribe of Celtic Gauls established a fishing village in the area. Julius Caesar ended centuries of conflict between the Gauls and Romans in 52 BC. Christianity was introduced in the 2nd century AD; in 508 Frankish king Clovis I united Gaul and made Paris his seat.

Conflicts

In the 12th century Scandinavian Vikings pushed towards Paris, heralding the Hundred Years' War with Norman England, which resulted in England gaining control of France in 1420. In 1429 Joan of Arc rallied French troops to defeat the English.

Revolution

The excesses of Louis XIV and his heirs triggered an uprising of Parisians on 14 July 1789, which kick-started the French Revolution. The government was consolidated in 1799 under Napoléon Bonaparte, who then conquered most of Europe before his defeat at Waterloo.

Reformation & Beyond

At the behest of Napoléon III, Baron Haussmann reshaped the cityscape. However, when Parisians heard of Napoléon III's capture in the war with Prussia in 1870, they demanded a republic. It gave rise to the glittering Belle Époque ('beautiful era').

Best Roman Legacies

Arènes de Lutèce Gladiatorial 2nd-century amphitheatre. (p160)

Musée National du Moyen Âge The site of Lutecia's Roman baths, but closed for

VICHIE81/GETTY IMAGES ©

renovations through to early 2022. (p158)

Best Medieval Buildings

Louvre Vast 12th-century fort turned palace turned museum. (p68)

Sainte-Chapelle Consecrated in 1248. (Pictured above; p144)

Notre Dame Although closed, you can still admire the magnificent Gothic façade. (p138)

Best Revolutionary Sights

Place de la Bastille Site of the former prison stormed on 14 July 1789, mobilising the Revolution. (p122)

Versailles The October 1789 March on Versailles forced the royal family to leave the château. (p198)

Place de la Concorde Louis XVI and Marie Antoinette were among thousands guillotined where the obelisk now stands. (p79)

Conciergerie Marie Antoinette was tried and imprisoned here. (p144)

Best Burial Places

Père Lachaise Famous graves fill the world's most visited cemetery. (p134)

Les Catacombes Prowl the skull- and bone-packed tunnels of Paris' ossuary. (p186)

Panthéon Mausoleum sheltering France's greatest thinkers. (p158)

Closures & Renovations

○ The Grand Palais (p60) is set to close for Olympics-related renovations from 2021 to 2024. During its closure, a temporary exhibition space will be set up on the Champ de Mars adjacent to the Eiffel Tower.

○ The Musée National du Moyen Âge (p158) is undergoing renovations until early 2022.

Parks & Gardens

Just as Paris' cafes are the city's communal lounge rooms, its parks, gardens and squares are its backyards. Larger parks are idyllic for strolling or simply soaking up the sunshine, with plenty of seating as well as kiosks and cafes. Small, secret gardens are tucked between historic buildings or even perched in the middle of the Seine.

JEAN-BERNARD CARILLET/LONELY PLANET ©

Best Traditional Gardens

Jardin du Luxembourg Paris' most popular park. (p178)

Jardin des Tuileries Part of Paris' historic axis and as classical as it gets. (p78)

Versailles Designed by André Le Nôtre, the château's gardens are fit for a king. (p199)

Best Parks

Jardin des Plantes Paris' botanic gardens include peony and rose gardens, an alpine garden, greenhouses and more. (p159)

Promenade Plantée The world's first elevated park, atop a disused railway viaduct. (p120)

Place des Vosges Paris' prettiest square, ringed by cloisters, with a park at its centre. (p120)

Best Hidden Jewels

Square du Vert-Galant Romantically situated on the tip of the Île de la Cité. (Pictured above; p145)

Square René Viviani Home to Paris' oldest tree. (p159)

Île aux Cygnes A tree-shaded walkway runs the length of the city's little-known third island. (p45)

Visiting Paris' Green Spaces

○ Opening hours vary seasonally – check closing times posted at park gates to avoid being locked in.

○ Look out for *murs végétaux* (vertical gardens), such as **L'Oasis d'Aboukir** (83 rue d'Aboukir, 2e; M Sentier).

○ Eco-minded city initiatives are seeing Paris become even greener, with many open areas being created.

Under the Radar Paris

DELPIXEL/SHUTTERSTOCK ©

Paris does not limit itself to a flurry of iconic monuments and sights. For those in search of something quirkier, lesser-known and off the beaten track, there are plenty of options.

Paris Rive Gauche

Paris' largest urban redevelopment since Haussmann's 19th-century reformation is apace in the 13e arrondissement. The renaissance of the area is known as Paris Rive Gauche. This area between Place d'Italie and Bibliothèque Nationale de France is worth a look as it is still not touristy and full of great vibes. The iconic **Tours Duo**, completed in late 2021, are the visual signature of this emerging neighbourhood. These two futuristic skyscrapers that were conceived by French architect Jean Nouvel embody a more contemporary aspect of Paris. Don't miss the floating bars and clubs nearby on the Seine.

Track updates on the area at www.parisrivegauche.com.

Petite Ceinture

Long before the tramway or even the metro, the 35km Petite Ceinture (Little Belt) steam encircled the city of Paris. Most passenger services ceased in 1934 with goods services following in 1993, and the line became an overgrown wilderness. Plans for regenerating the **Petite Ceinture** (PC 15; www.paris.fr; opposite 99 rue Olivier de Serres, 15e; admission free; ⏱9am-8.30pm Mon-Fri, from 9.30am Sat & Sun May-Aug, shorter hours rest of year; Ⓜ Balard, Porte de Versailles) railway corridor have seen the opening of three sections with walkways alongside the tracks. The most rewarding section is the Petite Ceinture du 15e, which stretches for 1.3km, with biodiverse habitats including forest, grassland and prairies – yes, prairies!

Tours

PAGE LIGHT STUDIOS/SHUTTERSTOCK ©

Parisien d'un jour – Paris Greeters (www. greeters.paris; by donation) See Paris through local eyes with these volunteer-led two- to three-hour city tours. Minimum two weeks' notice is needed.

Paris Walks (📞 01 48 09 21 40; www.paris-walks. com; 2hr tours adult/child from €15/10) Long-established and well-respected Paris Walks offers two-hour thematic walking tours (art, fashion, chocolate, the French Revolution etc).

Fat Tire Bike Tours (📞 01 82 88 80 96; www. fattiretours.com; tours adult/child from €34/32) Offers day and night bicycle tours of the city, both in central Paris and further afield.

Meeting the French (📞 01 42 51 19 80; www. meetingthefrench.com;

tours & courses from €30) Cosmetics workshops, backstage cabaret tours, fashion-designer showroom visits, market tours, baking with a Parisian and more.

Canauxrama (📞 01 42 39 15 00; www.canauxrama. com; opposite 50 bd de la Bastille, Port de l'Arsenal, 12e; adult/child €18/9; 🕒 hours vary; 🅼 Bastille) Seasonal canal cruises depart from the Bassin de la Villette near Parc de la Villette and from the Port de l'Arsenal. During the 2½-hour one-way trip, boats pass through four double locks, two swing bridges and an underground section.

Street Art Paris (📞 06 52 69 92 40; www.streetart-paris.fr; tours €20; 🕒 by reservation) Learn about the history of graffiti on fascinating tours taking in Paris' vibrant street art.

Left Bank Scooters (📞 06 78 12 04 24; www. leftbankscooters.com; 3hr tours per 1st/2nd passenger from €200/50) Runs a variety of scooter tours around Paris, both day and evening, as well as trips out to Versailles and sidecar tours. A car or motorcycle licence is required.

L'Open Tour (📞 01 42 66 56 56; www.opentourparis. com; adult/child 1-day pass €35/18, night tour €27/17) Hop-on, hop-off tours aboard open-deck buses with three different circuits and 50 stops – good for a whirlwind city tour.

Localers (📞 01 83 64 92 01; www.localers.com; tours from €49) Behind-the-scenes urban discoveries: *pétanque*, photo shoots, market tours, cooking classes and more.

Cooking & Wine-Tasting Courses

If dining in the city's restaurants whets your appetite, Paris has stacks of cookery schools with courses for all budgets and levels of ability. Where there's food in Paris, wine is never more than an arm's length away; plenty of places offer wine tastings and instruction for beginners through to connoisseurs.

KRZYSZTOF DYDYNSKI/LONELY PLANET ©

Best Culinary

Cook'n With Class
(📞01 42 57 22 84; www. cooknwithclass.com; 6 rue Baudelique, 18e; ⏰2hr classes from €109; Ⓜ Simplon, Jules Joffrin) Informal small classes.

Le Cordon Bleu (📞01 85 65 15 00; www.cordonbleu. edu/paris; 13-15 quai André Citroën, 15e; 3hr classes from €55, 2-day courses from €470; Ⓜ Javel–André Citroën, RER Javel) One of the world's foremost culinary arts schools.

La Cuisine Paris (📞01 40 51 78 18; www.lacuisineparis.com; 80 quai de l'Hôtel de Ville, 4e; 2hr cooking class/walking tour from €99; Ⓜ Pont Marie, Hôtel de Ville) Courses from bread, croissants and macarons to market classes and 'foodie walks'.

Best Wine Appreciation

Ô Château (📞01 44 73 97 80; www.o-chateau.com; 68 rue Jean-Jacques Rousseau, 1er; ⏰4pm-midnight Mon-Sat; 🛜; Ⓜ Les Halles, RER Châtelet–Les Halles) Young, fun company offering affordable wine and Champagne tastings.

Musée du Vin (📞01 45 25 63 26; www.museeduvinparis.com; 5 sq Charles Dickens, 16e; adult/child €10/free, incl glass of wine adult €13.90; ⏰10am-6pm Tue-Sun; Ⓜ Passy) In addition to its displays, Paris' wine museum offers instructive tastings.

Wine Tasting in Paris (📞06 76 93 32 88; www. wine-tasting-in-paris.com; 14 rue des Boulangers, 5e; tastings from €47; ⏰hours vary; Ⓜ Jussieu) Tastings cover methodology, wine vocabulary, interpreting wine labels and French wine-growing regions.

Booking a Class

○ Short courses are plentiful; book well ahead.

○ Many establishments run classes in English – confirm when you book.

For Kids

FERREIRO/SHUTTERSTOCK ©

Parisians adore les enfants (children) and welcome them with open arms just about everywhere. French kids are generally quiet and polite, and you'll be expected to make sure yours are, too. But kids can still burn off plenty of energy: central Paris' residential design means you'll find playground equipment in parks and squares citywide.

Amusement Parks

Just outside central Paris, amusement parks include Disneyland Resort Paris (www.disneyland-paris.com), Jardin d'Acclimatation (www.jardindacclimatation.fr) and Parc Astérix (www.parcasterix.fr).

Accommodation

Parisian buildings' limited space often means premium-priced family-size accommodation – apartments may be more economical. Check availability and costs for a *lit bébé* (cot).

Dining with Kids

Many restaurants accept little diners (confirm ahead). Children's menus aren't widespread, however, and most restaurants don't have highchairs.

Best Attractions for Kids

Le Grand Rex Kids can become movie stars on entertaining behind-the-scenes tours. (p86)

Jardin du Luxembourg Pony rides, puppet shows and more. (p178)

Vedettes de Paris Special 'Paris Mystery' Seine cruises for kids. (p23)

Galerie des Enfants Natural-history museum for six- to 12-year-olds within the Jardin des Plantes. (p160)

Getting Around with Kids

○ Children under four travel free on public transport and generally receive free admission to sights. Discounts vary for older kids.

○ Be vigilant crossing roads: Parisian drivers frequently ignore green pedestrian lights.

LGBTIQ+

Paris has less of a defined gay and lesbian 'scene' than many cities. While Le Marais – particularly around the intersection of rues Ste-Croix de la Bretonnerie and des Archives – is the mainstay of gay and lesbian nightlife, venues throughout the city attract a mixed crowd.

DESIGNIUM/SHUTTERSTOCK ©

Background

Paris was the first European capital to vote in an openly gay mayor when Bertrand Delanoë was elected in 2001. The city itself is very open – same-sex couples commonly display affection in public and checking into a hotel room is unlikely to raise eyebrows.

In 2013 France became the 13th country in the world to legalise same-sex marriage (and adoption by same-sex couples).

Typically, at least one partner needs to be a resident to get married here.

Guided Tours

For an insider's perspective on gay life in Paris, and recommendations on where to eat, drink, sightsee and party, take a tour with the **Gay Locals** (www.thegaylocals.com; 2/3hr tour €240/300). English-speaking residents lead two tours of 'the Gaybourhood' Le Marais or Montmartre, as

well as longer tours, and itinerary planning (from €40 per day) based on your interests. Its website is a good source of nightlife info.

Best LGBTIQ+ Bars

Le Tango Mingle with a cosmopolitan gay and lesbian set in a historic 1930s dance hall. (p129)

Le Open The wide terrace is prime for talent-watching. (p129)

3w Kafé Flagship cocktail bar-pub. (p129)

Quetzal Perennial favourite; cruisy at all hours. (p129)

Four Perfect Days

Day 1

Stroll through the elegant **Jardin des Tuileries** (pictured above; p78), stopping to view Monet's enormous *Water Lilies* at the **Musée de l'Orangerie** (p78). IM Pei's glass pyramid is the entrance to the labyrinthine **Louvre** (p68).

Browse the colonnaded arcades of the **Jardin du Palais Royal** (p78), and pop into the beautiful church, **Église St-Eustache** (p78). Then head to the late-opening **Centre Pompidou** (p112) for modern and contemporary art and amazing rooftop views.

There's a wealth to see in Le Marais by day – **Musée National Picasso-Paris** (p118), **Musée des Arts et Métiers** (p119)...but the neighbourhood really comes into its own at night, with a cornucopia of bars.

Day 2

Climb the mighty **Arc de Triomphe** (p54) for a pinch-yourself Parisian panorama. Promenade down the glamorous **Champs-Élysées** (p58), and give your credit card a workout at **Galeries Lafayette** (pictured above; p87) or **place de la Madeleine** (p86) before going behind the scenes of Paris' opulent opera house, the **Palais Garnier** (p79).

Check out global indigenous art at the **Musée du Quai Branly** (p44) and contemporary installations at the **Palais de Tokyo** (p61).

Sunset is the best time to ascend the **Eiffel Tower** (p38), to experience dizzying daylight views and the glittering city by night.

Day 3

Although **Notre Dame** (p138) is closed following the 2019 fire, the magnificent Gothic structure at the heart of the city still attracts crowds. For beautiful stained glass, don't miss nearby **Sainte-Chapelle** (p144). Buy a **Berthillon** (p146) ice cream before browsing Île St-Louis' enchanting boutiques.

Admire impressionist masterpieces in the magnificent **Musée d'Orsay** (p176), shop in St-Germain, sip coffee on the terrace of literary cafe **Les Deux Magots** (pictured above; p191) and laze in the lovely **Jardin du Luxembourg** (p178).

Scour the shelves of late-night bookshops including the legendary **Shakespeare & Company** (p168), then hit a jazz club such as **Café Universel** (p167).

Day 4

Montmartre's slinking streets and steep staircases lined with crooked ivy-clad buildings are enchanting places to meander. Head to hilltop **Sacré-Cœur** (p94), then brush up on the area's fabled history at the **Musée de Montmartre** (pictured above; p99).

Stroll the shaded towpaths of cafe-lined **Canal St-Martin** (p108). Sailing schedules permitting, hop on a canal cruise to Bastille.

The Bastille neighbourhood calls for a cafe crawl, especially on and around rue de la Roquette. Then salsa your socks off at the 1936 dance hall **Le Balajo** (p132) on nightlife strip rue de Lappe.

Need to Know

For detailed information, see Survival Guide (p203)

Currency
Euro (€)

Language
French

Money
ATMs widely available.
Visa and MasterCard
accepted in most
hotels, shops and
restaurants; fewer
accept American
Express.

Time
Central European Time
(GMT/UTC plus one
hour)

Tipping
Already included in
prices under French
law, though if service is
particularly good, you
might tip an extra 5%
to 10% in restaurants.
Round taxi fares up to
the nearest euro.

Visas
Not required for
citizens of the EU or
Schengen countries.
Other nationals need
ETIAS preauthorisation;
some require a
Schengen visa.

Daily Budget

Budget: Less than €100

Dorm bed: €25–50

Espresso/glass of wine/*demi* (half-pint of beer)/cocktail:
from €2/3.50/3.50/9

Metro ticket: €1.90

Baguette sandwich: €4.50–6.50

Frequent free concerts and events

Midrange: €100–250

Double room: €120–250

Two-course meal: €20–40

Admission to museums: free to around €15

Admission to clubs: free to around €20

Top end: More than €250

Double room at historic luxury hotel: from €250

Gastronomic-restaurant lunch/dinner *menu* (fixed-price
meals) from €50/80

Private two-hour city tour: from €150

Premium ticket to opera/ballet performance: from €160

Advance Planning

Two months before Book accommodation,
organise opera, ballet or cabaret tickets, check
events calendars for festivals, and make reservations for high-end/popular restaurants.

Two weeks before Sign up for a local-led tour
and start narrowing down your choices of
museums, pre-purchasing tickets online where
possible to minimise ticket queues.

Two days before Check the weather forecast
and pack your comfiest shoes to walk Paris'
streets.

Arriving in Paris

Paris is well served by air and train, including Eurostar services linking London with Gare du Nord.

✈ Charles de Gaulle Airport

Around one hour northeast of central Paris.

Trains (RER B), **buses** and **night buses** to the city centre €6 to €18.

Taxis €50 to €63.

✈ Orly Airport

Around one hour south of central Paris.

Trains (Orlyval then RER), buses and night buses to the city centre €9.50 to €12.10.

Trams T7 to Villejuif–Louis Aragon, then metro to centre (€3.80).

Taxis €30 to €40.

Getting Around

Walking is a pleasure, and Paris' efficient, inexpensive public transport system makes getting around a breeze.

Ⓜ Metro & RER

Metros and RER trains run from about 5.30am and finish around 12.35am or 1.15am (to around 2.15am on Friday and Saturday nights), depending on the line.

⚙ Bicycle & Scooters

Virtually free, pick-up, drop-off Vélib' bikes have stations citywide, while electric scooters, hired via an app, can be found all over.

🚌 Bus

Buses are convenient for parents with prams and people with limited mobility.

⛴ Boat

The handy hop-on, hop-off Batobus boat service (pictured) operates along the Seine.

🚕 Taxi

Find taxi ranks around major intersections.

Paris Neighbourhoods

Arc de Triomphe & the Champs-Élysées (p53)

This neighbourhood sees glamorous avenues flanked by flagship fashion houses, excellent museums and elegant restaurants.

Eiffel Tower & Les Invalides (p37)

Zipping up the spire is reason enough to visit, but this stately neighbourhood also has some unmissable museums.

Musée d'Orsay & St-Germain des Prés (p175)

With a literary pedigree, cafe terraces and exquisite boutiques, this gentrified neighbourhood retains a cinematic quality.

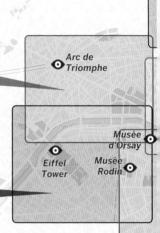

Arc de Triomphe

Musée d'Orsay

Eiffel Tower

Musée Rodin

Sacré-Cœur & Montmartre (p93)

Beneath Montmartre's basilica, painters at easels, cosy bistros and historic cabarets keep the artistic spirit of this hilly area alive.

◉ Basilique du Sacré-Coeur

Louvre, Tuileries & Opéra (p67)

Palatial museums, World Heritage–listed gardens, grand department stores and gourmet food shops are just some of the draws of this area.

◉ Centre Pompidou

◉ Musée du Louvre

◉ Père Lachaise

◉ Cathédrale Notre Dame de Paris

Centre Pompidou & Le Marais (p111)

Hip boutiques, ubercool bars, avant-garde galleries and beautiful museums all wedge within Le Marais' warren of laneways.

◉ Jardin du Luxembourg

The Latin Quarter (p153)

This lively *arrondissement* (district) is home to vast gardens, intriguing museums, a mausoleum and spirited Sorbonne university students.

Notre Dame & the Islands (p137)

Paris' Gothic cathedral dominates the Île de la Cité, while romantic little Île St-Louis has charming shops and sublime ice cream.

Explore
Paris

Worth a Trip 🔭

Paris' Walking Tours 🥾

Aerial view over Paris MATTEO COLOMBO/GETTY IMAGES ©

Explore ⊚
Eiffel Tower
& Les Invalides

Home to very well-heeled Parisians, this grande dame of a neighbourhood stretching along the Seine's Left Bank to the west is where you can get up close and personal with magnificent architecture including the city's symbolic tower, as well as some outstanding museums.

The Short List

○ **Eiffel Tower (p38)** *Ascending the icon at dusk to watch its sparkling lights blink across Paris.*

○ **Musée Rodin (p40)** *Strolling the sculpture-filled gardens of the magnificently renovated private mansion, the 1730 Hôtel Biron.*

○ **Hôtel des Invalides (p44)** *Visiting Napoléon Bonaparte's elaborate tomb within the monumental complex housing France's largest military museum.*

○ **Musée du Quai Branly – Jacques Chirac (p44)** *Finding inspiration in traditional art and craftmanship from around the world.*

Getting There & Around

Ⓜ Bir Hakeim (line 6) or Champ de Mars–Tour Eiffel (RER C).

Ⓜ From Alma Marceau (line 9), it's an easy stroll over the Pont de l'Alma bridge.

⚓ In addition to river cruises, the hop-on, hop-off Batobus starts and ends its run near the Eiffel Tower.

Neighbourhood Map on p42

Hôtel des Invalides (p44) DENNIS VAN DE WATER/SHUTTERSTOCK ©

Top Experience
Climb the Eiffel Tower

There are different ways to experience the Eiffel Tower, from a daytime trip to an evening ascent amid twinkling lights to a meal in one of its restaurants. And even though some seven million people come annually, few would dispute that each visit is unique – and something that simply has to be done when in Paris.

⊙ MAP P42, C3

www.toureiffel.paris

Champ de Mars, 5 av Anatole France, 7e

adult/child lift to top €25.90/13, lift to 2nd fl €16.60/8.30, stairs to 2nd fl €10.40/5.20

Ⓜ Bir Hakeim, RER Champ de Mars–Tour Eiffel

Tickets & Queues

Visitors must pass through security at the bullet-proof glass barriers surrounding the tower's base. The two entrances to the glass enclosure are on av Gustave Eiffel; the two exits are on quai Branly. Prepurchase lift tickets with allocated time slots online (staircase tickets must be bought at the tower) to save queuing for tickets.

1st Floor

Of the tower's three floors, the 1st (57m) has the most space but the least impressive views. The glass-enclosed Pavillon Ferrié houses an immersion film along with a small cafe and souvenir shop, while the outer walkway features a discovery circuit to help visitors learn more about the tower's ingenious design. Check out the sections of glass flooring that provide a dizzying view of the people walking on the ground far below. The 1st floor's commercial areas are powered by two sleek wind turbines within the tower.

2nd Floor

Views from this floor (115m) are the best – high, but still close enough to see the details of the city below. Telescopes and panoramic maps placed around the tower pinpoint locations in Paris and beyond. Story windows give an overview of the lifts' mechanics, and the vision allows you to gaze through glass panels to the ground. Also here are toilets, a souvenir shop and a macaron bar.

Top Floor

Views from the wind-buffeted top floor (276m) stretch up to 60km on a clear day, though at this height the panoramas are more sweeping than detailed. Celebrate your ascent with a glass of bubbly (€12 to €18) from the Champagne bar (open 10.15am to 10.15pm). Afterwards peep into Gustave Eiffel's restored top-level office where lifelike wax models of Eiffel and his daughter Claire greet Thomas Edison.

★ Top Tips

o Ascend as far as the 2nd floor (on foot or by lift), where a separate lift serves the top floor (closed during heavy winds).

o The top floor and stairs aren't accessible to people with limited mobility.

o Bring a jacket as it can be breezy at the top.

o Opening hours vary depending on season: lifts & stairs from mid-June to August run 9am to 12.45am, the rest of the year lifts run 9.30am to 11.45pm, and stairs from 9.30am to 6.30pm.

✗ Take a Break

Dine at the tower's 1st-floor at **58 Tour Eiffel** (www.restaurants-toureiffel.com; 🍴👫).

Savour cuisine at the 2nd-floor gastronomic restaurant **Le Jules Verne** (📞01 83 77 34 34; 3-course weekday lunch menus €135, 5-/7-course menus €190/230; ⏱noon-1.30pm & 6-9.30pm).

Top Experience 📷

Explore the Musée Rodin

Even if you're not an art lover, it is worth visiting this high-profile art museum to lose yourself in its romantic gardens. One of the most peaceful green oases in Paris, the formal flowerbeds and boxed-hedge arrangements framing the 18th-century mansion Hôtel Biron house original sculptures by sculptor, painter, sketcher, engraver and collector Auguste Rodin. This is where he lived and worked while in Paris.

⊙ MAP P42, G4

☎ 01 44 18 61 10

www.musee-rodin.fr

79 rue de Varenne, 7e

adult/child €12/free, garden only €4/free

🕐 10am-5.30pm Tue-Sun

Ⓜ Varenne, Invalides

Collections

In 1908 Rodin donated his entire art collection to the French state on the proviso that it dedicated his former workshop and showroom, the 18th-century mansion Hôtel Biron (1730), to displaying his works. In addition to Rodin's own paintings and sketches, don't miss his prized collection of works by artists including Van Gogh and Monet.

The 'Rodin at the Hôtel Biron' room incorporates original furniture to recreate the space as it was when he lived and worked here.

Sculptures

The first large-scale cast of Rodin's famous sculpture **The Thinker** (Le Penseur), made in 1902, resides in the garden (pictured left) – the perfect place to contemplate this heroic naked figure conceived by Rodin to represent intellect and poetry.

The Gates of Hell (La Porte de l'Enfer) was commissioned in 1880 as the entrance for a never-built museum, and Rodin worked on his sculptural masterpiece up until his death in 1917. Standing 6m high and 4m wide, its 180 figures comprise an intricate scene from Dante's Inferno.

Marble monument to love **The Kiss** (Le Baiser) was originally part of The Gates of Hell. The sculpture's entwined lovers caused controversy on completion due to Rodin's then-radical depiction of women as equal partners in ardour. The museum also features many sculptures by Camille Claudel, Rodin's protégée and muse.

★ Top Tips

o Prepurchase tickets online to avoid queuing.

o Audioguides cost €6.

o If you just want to see the outdoor sculptures, cheaper garden-only entry is available.

o A combined ticket with the Musée d'Orsay (p176) costs €21.

o Entry is free on the first Sunday of the month from October to March.

✗ Take a Break

Some of Paris' best coffee is brewed by artisan roastery Coutume Café (p49).

Enjoy classic French cooking at cosy La Laiterie Sainte Clotilde (p49).

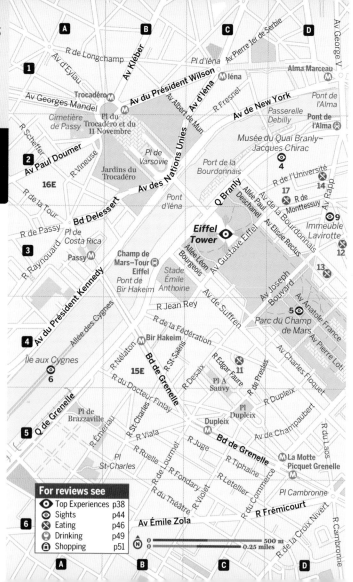

For reviews see

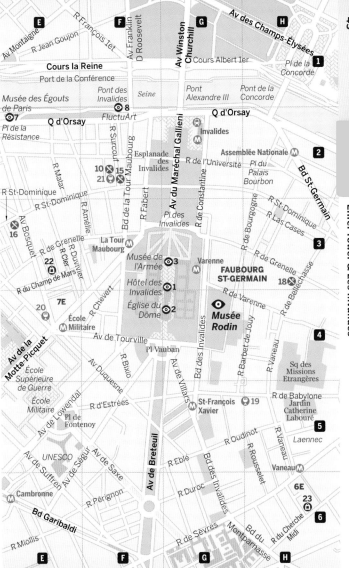

E   R François 1er   F   R Franklin D Roosevelt   Av des Champs-Élysées   H

Av Montaigne
R Jean Goujon
Av Winston Churchill
Cours Albert 1er
Pl de la Concorde   **1**

Cours la Reine
Port de la Conférence

Musée des Égouts de Paris
7
Pont des Invalides
Seine
Pont Alexandre III
Pont de la Concorde

Q d'Orsay
8
FluctuArt
Q d'Orsay

Pl de la Résistance
Invalides Ⓜ

Esplanade des Invalides
Assemblée Nationale Ⓜ   **2**

R de l'Université
Pl du Palais Bourbon
Bd St-Germain

R St-Dominique
10 **15**
21
R Surcouf
Bd de la Tour Maubourg
Av du Maréchal Gallieni
R de Constantine
R St-Dominique
R Las Cases

R St-Dominique
R Malar
R Amélie

16
Av Bosquet
R de Grenelle
R Duvivier
R Cler
La Tour Maubourg Ⓜ
Pl des Invalides
R Fabert
R de Bourgogne
R de Grenelle   **3**

22
Musée de l'Armée **3**
Varenne Ⓜ
FAUBOURG ST-GERMAIN
18
R de Bellechasse

R du Champ de Mars
Hôtel des Invalides **1**
R de Varenne

20
R Chevert
Église du Dôme **2**
Musée Rodin

7E
École Militaire Ⓜ
Bd des Invalides
R Barbet de Jouy
R de Varenne   **4**

Av de Tourville
Pl Vauban
Sq des Missions Étrangères

Av de la Motte-Picquet
École Supérieure de Guerre
R Bixio
Av de Villars
St-François Xavier Ⓜ **19**
R de Babylone
Jardin Catherine Labouré

École Militaire
R d'Estrées
R de Vaneau   **5**

Av de Lowendal
Pl de Fontenoy
Av de Breteuil
R Oudinot
R Rousselet
Laennec

UNESCO
Av de Saxe
R Éblé
Bd des Invalides
Vaneau Ⓜ   **6E**

Av de Suffren
Av de Ségur
R Pérignon
R Duroc
Bd du Montparnasse
R du Cherche Midi   **23**

Cambronne Ⓜ
Bd Garibaldi

R Miollis

E   F   G   H

Sights

Hôtel des Invalides
MONUMENT, MUSEUM

1 ◉ MAP P42, G3

Flanked by the 500m-long Esplanade des Invalides lawns, Hôtel des Invalides was built in the 1670s by Louis XIV to house 4000 *invalides* (disabled war veterans). On 14 July 1789, a mob broke into the building and seized 32,000 rifles before heading on to the prison at Bastille and the start of the French Revolution. Admission includes entry to all Hôtel des Invalides sights (temporary exhibitions cost extra). Hours for individual sites can vary – check the website for updates. (www.musee-armee.fr; 129 rue de Grenelle, 7e; adult/child €12/free; ⊙10am-6pm Apr-Oct, to 5pm Nov-Mar; Ⓜ Varenne, La Tour Maubourg)

Église du Dôme
CHURCH

2 ◉ MAP P42, G4

With its sparkling golden dome (1677–1735), the landmark church of Hôtel des Invalides is one of the finest religious edifices erected under Louis XIV and was the inspiration for the United States' Capitol building. It received the remains of Napoléon Bonaparte in 1840; the extravagant Tombeau de Napoléon 1er comprises six coffins fitting into one another like a Russian doll. (included in Hôtel des Invalides entry; ⊙10am-6pm Wed-Mon, to 9pm Tue Apr-Oct, 10am-5pm Nov-Mar; Ⓜ Varenne, La Tour Maubourg)

Musée de l'Armée
MUSEUM

3 ◉ MAP P42, G3

North of Hôtel des Invalides, in the Cour d'Honneur, is the Musée de l'Armée, which holds the nation's largest collection on French military history. (Army Museum; included in Hôtel des Invalides entry; ⊙10am-6pm Apr-Oct, to 5pm Nov-Mar; Ⓜ Varenne, La Tour Maubourg)

Musée du Quai Branly – Jacques Chirac
MUSEUM

4 ◉ MAP P42, D2

A tribute to the diversity of human culture, this museum's highly inspiring overview of indigenous and folk art spans four main sections – Oceania, Asia, Africa and the Americas. An impressive array of masks, carvings, weapons, jewellery and more make up the body of the rich collection, displayed in a refreshingly unorthodox interior without rooms or high walls. Look out for excellent temporary exhibitions and performances. (✆01 56 61 70 00; www.quaibranly.fr; 37 quai Branly, 7e; adult/child €10/free; ⊙10.30am-7pm Tue, Wed & Fri-Sun, to 10pm Thu, plus 10.30am-7pm Mon during school holidays; Ⓜ Alma Marceau, RER Pont de l'Alma)

Parc du Champ de Mars

PARK

5 ◉ MAP P42, D4

Running southeast from the Eiffel Tower, the grassy Champ de Mars – an ideal summer picnic spot – was originally used as a parade ground for the cadets of the 18th-century École Militaire, the vast French-classical building at the southeastern end of the park, which counts Napoléon Bonaparte among its graduates. The steel-and-etched-glass **Wall for Peace Memorial** (www.murpourlapaix.org), erected in 2000, is by Clara Halter. From 2021 to 2024 the park will host a temporary Grand Palais (p60) while the original undergoes Olympic renovations. (Champ de Mars, 7e; ◷24hr; Ⓜ École Militaire, RER Champ de Mars–Tour Eiffel)

Île aux Cygnes

ISLAND

6 ◉ MAP P42, A4

Paris' little-known third island, the artificially created Île aux Cygnes, was formed in 1827 to protect the river port and measures just 850m by 11m. On the western side of the Pont de Grenelle is a soaring one-quarter scale Statue of Liberty replica, inaugurated in 1889. Walk east along the Allée des Cygnes – the tree-lined walkway that runs the length of the island – for knock-out Eiffel Tower views. (Isle of Swans; btwn Pont de Grenelle & Pont de Bir Hakeim, 15e; Ⓜ Javel–André Citroën, Bir Hakeim)

Napoléon's tomb, Église du Dôme

Musée Marmottan Monet

The **Musée Marmottan Monet** (☑ 01 44 96 50 33; www.marmottan.fr; 2 rue Louis Boilly, 16e; adult/child €12/8.50; ⏰ 10am-6pm Tue, Wed & Fri-Sun, to 9pm Thu; Ⓜ La Muette) showcases the world's largest collection of works by impressionist painter Claude Monet (1840–1926) as well as paintings by Gauguin, Sisley, Pissarro, Renoir, Degas, Manet and Berthe Morisot. It also contains an important collection of French, English, Italian and Flemish illuminations from the 13th to 16th centuries.

Musée des Égouts de Paris
MUSEUM

7 Ⓞ MAP P42, E2

Raw sewage flows beneath your feet as you walk through 480m of odoriferous tunnels in this working sewer museum, which underwent important renovations between 2018 and 2020. Exhibitions cover the development of Paris' waste-water-disposal system, including its resident rats (there's an estimated one sewer rat for every Parisian above ground). Enter via a rectangular maintenance hole topped with a kiosk across the street from 93 quai d'Orsay, 7e. (☑ 01 53 68 27 81; place de la Résistance, 7e; adult/child €4.40/3.60; ⏰ 11am-5pm Mon-Wed, Sat & Sun; Ⓜ Alma Marceau, RER Pont de l'Alma)

FluctuArt
CULTURAL CENTRE

8 Ⓞ MAP P42, F2

This hip cultural centre occupying a *péniche* (barge) off pont des Invalides brings an unexpected dash of coolness to an otherwise institutional neighbourhood. It claims to be the first floating urban art centre in the world and hosts the works and creations of all kinds of emerging artists. There are exhibition spaces as well as a vibrant bar and a restaurant. (☑ 07 67 02 44 37; www.fluctuart.fr; pont des Invalides, 7e; admission free; ⏰ noon-midnight Wed-Sun winter, daily summer; Ⓜ Invalides)

Immeuble Lavirotte
NOTABLE BUILDING

9 Ⓞ MAP P42, D3

Let your eyes settle on the aesthetic minutiae of the fantastic art nouveau façade of this building, which is one of the most photogenic private edifices in the *arrondissement* (city district). It was built in 1901. (29 av Rapp, 7e; Ⓜ École Militaire)

Eating

Tomy & Co
GASTRONOMY €€

10 Ⓧ MAP P42, F2

Tomy Gousset's restaurant near the Eiffel Tower has been a sensation since day one. The French-Cambodian chef works his magic on inspired seasonal dishes using produce from his organic garden. The spectacular desserts are equally seasonal. Reservations essential. (📞01 45 51 46 93; www.tomygousset.com; 22 rue Surcouf, 7e; lunch menus €28, dinner menus €58-80, mains €33; ⏱noon-2pm & 7.30-9.30pm Mon-Fri; Ⓜ Invalides)

Le Cassenoix   MODERN FRENCH €€

11 ✗ MAP P42, C4

The Nutcracker is everything a self-respecting neighbourhood bistro should be. *'Tradition et terroir'* (tradition and provenance) dictate the menu that inspires owner-chef Pierre Olivier Lenormand to deliver feisty dishes incorporating top-quality ingredients. Vintage ceiling fans add to the wonderful retro vibe. Book ahead. (📞01 45 66 09 01; www.le-cassenoix.fr; 56 rue de la Fédération, 15e; menus €35; ⏱noon-2pm & 7-10pm Mon-Fri; Ⓜ Bir Hakeim)

Café Constant   BISTRO €€

12 ✗ MAP P42, D3

Run by Michelin-starred chef Christian Constant, this traditional neighbourhood cafe with original bar and mosaic floor cooks up some fantastic staples: poached cod with garlic mayonnaise, herb-roasted chicken or beef stew followed by vanilla rice pudding. Breakfast is served until 11am, more substantial food continuously from noon until closing time. (📞01 47 53 73 34; www.maison constant.com; 139 rue St-Dominique, 7e; menus €21-37, mains €18-29; ⏱7am-11pm Mon-Sat, 8am-11pm Sun; Ⓜ École Militaire)

Arnaud Nicolas   FRENCH €€

13 ✗ MAP P42, D3

Charcuterie maestro Arnaud Nicolas has an upmarket boutique and restaurant with a menu that changes every two weeks. A meal might start with scallop quenelles with red-squash foam, move on to foie gras and pigeon pie with green cabbage, and finish with apple sautéed in butter with fresh apple and chestnut crème. Reservations are a must. (📞01 45 55 59 59; www.arnaudnicolas.paris; 46 ave de la Bourdonnais, 7e; 2-/3-course weekday lunch menus €32/35, mains €22-35; ⏱restaurant 7-9.45pm Mon, noon-1.45pm & 7-9.45pm Tue-Sat, shop 5-9pm Mon, 10am-3pm & 5-9pm Tue-Sat; ♿; Ⓜ École Militaire)

Les Deux Abeilles   CAFE €

14 ✗ MAP P42, D2

A refuge from the Eiffel Tower crowds, delightfully old-fashioned tearoom the Two Bees has floral-patterned wallpaper, terracotta-tiled floors and white-clothed tables. It serves a variety of soups, salads, quiches, omelettes and gratins, along with homemade cakes and *citronnade* (ginger lemonade) throughout the day. In warm weather, take a seat on the pavement terrace, shaded by a dark-green awning. (📞01 45 55 64 04; 189 rue de l'Université, 7e; 3-course lunch menus €24, dishes €13-20; ⏱9am-7pm Mon-Sat; Ⓜ Alma Marceau, RER Pont d'Alma)

A Little Taste of Rue Cler

Pick up fresh bread, sandwich fillings, pastries and wine for a picnic along the typically Parisian commercial street rue Cler, 7e, which buzzes with local shoppers, especially on weekends.

Interspersed between the *boulangeries* (bakeries), *fromageries* (cheese shops), grocers, butchers, delis and other food shops (many with pavement stalls), lively cafe terraces overflow with locals.

Restaurant David Toutain

GASTRONOMY €€€

15   MAP P42, F2

Prepare to be wowed: David Toutain pushes the envelope at his eponymous Michelin-starred restaurant with some of the most creative high-end cooking in Paris. All ingredients, from chestnuts and cauliflower to salsify and porcini mushrooms, are sourced from the best purveyors around the country. A meal here is a culinary voyage. Stunning wine pairings are available. (☎01 45 50 11 10; www. davidtoutain.com; 29 rue Surcouf, 7e; menus €70-250; � 12.30-2pm & 8-10pm Mon, noon-2pm & 8-10pm Tue-Fri; M Invalides)

Le Fontaine de Mars

BISTRO €€

16   MAP P42, E3

For traditional French cooking look no further than this 1930s-styled neighbourhood bistro with signature lace curtains, checked tablecloths and – best of all – a fishmonger in front shucking oysters at his stall beneath the bistro arches. Snails, *boudin* (black pudding), *andouillette* (Lyonnais tripe sausage) and veal cutlet are among the traditional mainstays, alongside sensational seafood platters. (☎01 47 05 46 44; www. fontainedemars.com; 129 rue St-Dominique, 7e; mains €18-45; �noon-2pm & 7.30-11pm; M École Militaire)

Firmin Le Barbier

FRENCH €€

17   MAP P42, D2

A five-minute walk from the Eiffel Tower, this brick-walled bistro was opened by a retired surgeon turned gourmet whose passion is apparent in everything from the personable service to the wine list. Market-driven dishes prepared in the open kitchen are traditional French (pike soufflé, beef cheek with bone marrow). There are just eight tables, so reserve ahead. (☎01 45 51 21 55; www.firminle barbier.fr; 20 rue de Monttessuy, 7e; 3-/6-course menus €35/64, mains €25-28; �noon-2pm & 7-10.30pm Wed-Fri & Sun, 7-10.30pm Sat; ; M École Militaire, RER Pont de l'Alma)

La Laiterie Sainte Clotilde

FRENCH €

18  MAP P42, H3

Your neighbours might be diplomats or civil servants working in a ministry nearby – not a bad sign. In a very institutional area, La Laiterie is a beacon of character and cosiness, with an atmospheric decor harking back to the 1970s and French classics cooked to perfection. (📞01 45 51 74 61; www.lalaiteriesainteclotilde.fr; 64 rue de Bellechasse, 7e; mains €19-22, menus €24-28; ⏰noon-2pm & 8-10pm Mon-Fri, 8-10pm Sat; Ⓜ Solférino)

Les Ombres

FRENCH €€€

This glass-enclosed rooftop restaurant on the 5th floor of the Musée du Quai Branly – Jacques Chirac (see 4 ⓞ Map p42, D2) is named the Shadows after the patterns cast by the Eiffel Tower's webbed ironwork. Dramatic tower views are complemented by creations such as scorpion fish in bouillabaisse broth, and slow-cooked pork shoulder with apricot and foie gras stuffing. Be sure to book. (📞01 47 53 68 00; www.lesombres-restaurant.com; 27 quai Branly, 7e; 3-course menus lunch/dinner €46/74, mains €32-46; ⏰noon-2.15pm & 7-10.30pm; Ⓜ léna, RER Pont de l'Alma)

Drinking

Coutume Café

COFFEE

19 🚋 MAP P42, H5

The Parisian coffee revolution is thanks in no small part to Coutume, artisanal roaster of premium

Musée Marmottan Monet (p46)

EQROY/SHUTTERSTOCK ©

Tomy & Co (p46)

beans for scores of establishments around town. Its flagship cafe – a light-filled, post-industrial space – is ground zero for innovative preparation methods including cold extraction and siphon brews. Couple some of Paris' finest coffee with tasty, seasonal cuisine and the place is always packed out. (☑ 01 45 51 50 47; www.coutume cafe.com; 47 rue de Babylone, 7e; ⏰ 8.30am-5.30pm Mon-Fri, 9am-6pm Sat & Sun; 🛜; M St-François Xavier)

Le Gatsby LOUNGE

20 🚇 MAP P42, E4

This elegant cocktail bar has an intimate vibe upstairs with wood panels, vintage wall lamps and comfy armchairs. It's even more inviting downstairs in the vaulted cellar, where it's easy to be a little overwhelmed by the discreet charm of another era. Enjoy expertly crafted cocktails (from €12). (☑ 01 45 55 02 79; www.legatsby.fr; 64 av Bosquet, 7e; ⏰ 6.30pm-1.30am; M Ecole Militaire)

The Club COCKTAIL BAR

21 🚇 MAP P42, F2

At street level The Club has New York–warehouse brickwork and big timber cabinets, but the lounge-like basement, strewn with red and black sofas, is even cooler. Cocktails include the house-speciality Club (lime, fresh ginger and Jack Daniels honey liqueur) and seasonally changing creations (from €12). Finger food is available too. (☑ 01 45 50 31 54; www.the-club. fr; 24 rue Surcouf, 7e; ⏰ 4pm-1.30am Mon-Sat; M La Tour-Maubourg)

Café Jacques CAFE

Peacefully set in the modernist garden at the rear of the Musée du Quai Branly – Jacques Chirac (see 4 🚇 Map p42, D2), this casual spot has ringside views of the Eiffel Tower. Alongside freshly pressed juices, wine, beer, coffee, tea and hot chocolate, it serves good cafe-style food throughout the day, and Grom ice lollies for the kids. (☑ 01 47 53 68 01; www.quaibranly.fr; 27 quai Branly, 7e; ⏰ 10am-6.30pm Tue, Wed & Fri-Sun, to 9.30pm Thu; M léna, RER Pont de l'Alma)

Charles de Gaulle & WWII

The WWII battle for France began in earnest in May 1940 and by 14 June France had capitulated. Paris was occupied, and almost half the population evacuated. General Charles de Gaulle, France's undersecretary of war, fled to London. In a radio broadcast on 18 June 1940, he appealed to French patriots to continue resisting the Germans. He set up a French government-in-exile and established the Forces Françaises Libres (Free French Forces), fighting alongside the Allies. Paris was liberated on 25 August 1944 by an Allied force spearheaded by Free French units.

De Gaulle returned to Paris and set up a provisional government, but in January 1946 he resigned, wrongly believing that the move would provoke a popular outcry for his return. De Gaulle formed his own party (Rassemblement du Peuple Français) and remained in opposition until 1958, when he was brought back to power to prevent a military coup over the uprising in Algeria. He resigned as president in 1969, succeeded by Gaullist prime minister Georges Pompidou.

Shopping

Cantin
CHEESE

22 MAP P42, E3

Opened in 1950 and still run by the same family today, this exceptional shop stocks cheeses only made in limited quantities on small rural farms. They're then painstakingly ripened in Cantin's own cellars (from two weeks up to two years) before being displayed for sale. (☎01 45 50 43 94; www.cantin.fr; 12 rue du Champs de Mars, 7e; ⊗2-7.30pm Mon, 8.30am-7.30pm Tue-Sat, 8.30am-1pm Sun; MÉcole Militaire)

Chercheminippes
VINTAGE

23 🔒 MAP P42, H6

Shop for secondhand designer pieces of women's casual wear at this beautifully presented boutique. It has several other shops scattered along the same street, each specialising in a different genre: homewares at No 104, womenswear at No 109, women's accessories at No 110, men's fashion at No 111 and women's *haute couture* (high fashion) at No 114. (www.chercheminippes.fr; 102 rue du Cherche Midi, 6e; ⊗11am-7pm Mon-Sat; MVaneau)

Explore ⊛
Arc de Triomphe & the Champs-Élysées

Pomp and grandeur reign: Baron Haussmann famously reshaped the Parisian cityscape around the Arc de Triomphe, from which a dozen avenues radiate like the spokes of a wheel, including the luxury-shop-lined av des Champs-Élysées.

The Short List

○ **Arc de Triomphe (p54)** *Ascending Napoléon's triumphal arch for a 360-degree panorama.*

○ **Champs-Élysées (p58)** *Strolling the over-the-top avenue – you can't leave Paris without doing it once.*

○ **Musée Jacquemart-André (p58)** *Getting a snapshot of 19th-century Parisian high society at this this elegant art museum.*

○ **Cité de l'Architecture et du Patrimoine (p58)** *Visiting this exceptional architectural museum.*

Getting There & Around

Ⓜ Charles de Gaulle–Étoile (lines 1, 2, 6 and RER A) is adjacent to the Arc de Triomphe.

Ⓜ The Champs-Élysées' other stops are George V (line 1), Franklin D Roosevelt (lines 1 and 9) and Champs-Élysées–Clemenceau (1 and 13).

⚓ The hop-on, hop-off Batobus stops near the Champs-Élysées by Pont Alexandre III.

Neighbourhood Map on p56

Avenue des Champs-Élysées (p58) PREMIER PHOTO/SHUTTERSTOCK ©

Top Experience 📷
View Paris from the Arc de Triomphe

Napoléon's armies never did march through the Arc de Triomphe showered in honour, but the monument has nonetheless come to stand as the very symbol of French patriotism. It's not for nationalistic sentiments, however, that so many visitors huff up the narrow, spiralling staircase. Rather it's the sublime panorama from the top that makes the arch such a notable attraction.

◉ MAP P56, C2

www.paris-arc-de-triomphe.fr

place Charles de Gaulle, 8e

viewing platform adult/child €13/free, 1st Sun of month Nov-Mar free

🕑 10am-11pm Apr-Sep, to 10.30pm Oct-Mar

Ⓜ Charles de Gaulle–Étoile

Beneath the Arch

Beneath the arch at ground level lies the Tomb of the Unknown Soldier. Honouring the 1.3 million French soldiers who lost their lives in WWI, the Unknown Soldier was laid to rest in 1921, beneath an eternal flame that is rekindled daily at 6.30pm.

Bronze plaques laid into the ground mark significant moments in modern French history, such as the proclamation of the Third French Republic (4 September 1870) and the text from Charles de Gaulle's famous London broadcast on 18 June 1940, which sparked the French Resistance to life.

Sculptures

The arch is adorned with four main sculptures, six panels in relief, and a frieze running beneath the top. The most famous sculpture is the one to the right as you approach from the Champs-Élysées: *La Marseillaise* (Departure of the Volunteers of 1792). Sculpted by François Rude, it depicts soldiers of all ages gathering beneath the wings of victory, en route to drive back the invading armies of Prussia and Austria.

Viewing Platform

Climb the 284 steps to the viewing platform at the top of the 50m-high arch and you'll be suitably rewarded with magnificent panoramas over western Paris. The Arc de Triomphe is the highest point in the line of monuments known as the *axe historique* (historic axis, also called the grand axis); it offers views that swoop east down the Champs-Élysées (p58) to the gold-tipped obelisk at place de la Concorde (and beyond to the Louvre's glass pyramid), and west to the skyscraper district of La Défense, where the colossal Grande Arche (p62) marks the axis' western terminus.

★ Top Tips

○ Don't try to cross the traffic-choked roundabout above ground! Stairs on the Champs-Élysées' northeastern side lead beneath the Étoile to pedestrian tunnels that bring you out safely beneath the arch.

○ Don't risk getting skittled by traffic by taking photos while crossing the Champs-Élysées.

○ There is a lift at the arch, but it's only for visitors with limited mobility or those travelling with young children, and there are still some unavoidable steps.

✕ Take a Break

Right near the arch, **Publicis Drugstore** (☎01 44 43 75 07; www.publicisdrugstore.com; 133 av des Champs-Élysées, 8e; ⏰8am-2am Mon-Fri, 10am-2am Sat & Sun; Ⓜ Charles de Gaulle–Étoile) is handy for a meal, drink or snack.

Pair an evening visit with a traditional French dinner at Le Hide (p62).

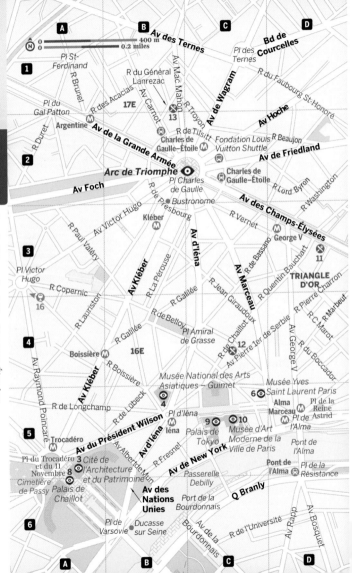

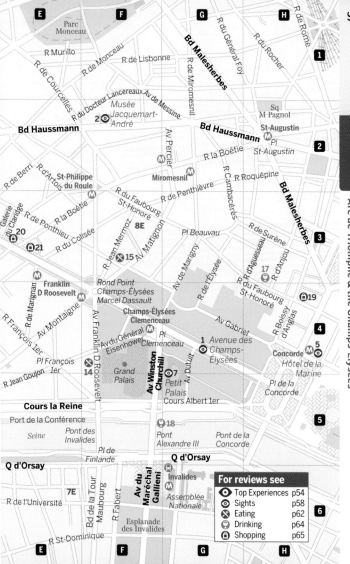

Parc
Monceau

R Murillo

R de Courcelles

R de Monceau

R de Lisbonne

R du Docteur Lancereaux

Av de Messine

Bd Malesherbes

R de Miromesnil

R du Général Foy

R du Rocher

R de Rome

Bd Haussmann

Musée
Jacquemart-
André

Sq
M Pagnol

St-Augustin

Bd Haussmann

Pl
St-Augustin

Av Percier

R la Boétie

R de Berri

R d'Artois

St-Philippe
du Roule

Miromesnil

R du Faubourg
St-Honoré

R de Penthièvre

R Roquépine

R Cambacérès

Bd Malesherbes

Galerie
du Claridge

R de La Boétie

R de Ponthieu

R du Colisée

8E

Pl Beauvau

R de Surène

20

21

R Jean Mermoz

15

Av Matignon

R d'Aguesseau

R d'Anjou

17

19

Franklin
D Roosevelt

Rond Point
Champs-Élysées
Marcel Dassault

Av de Marigny

R de l'Élysée

R du Faubourg
St-Honoré

R de Marignan

R François 1er

Av Montaigne

Av Franklin D Roosevelt

Champs-Élysées
Clemenceau

Av du Général
Eisenhower

Pl
Clemenceau

Av Gabriel

R Boissy
d'Anglas

Pl François
1er

R Jean Goujon

14

Grand
Palais

7

Petit
Palais

1 Avenue des
Champs-
Élysées

Av Dutuit

Concorde

5

Hôtel de la
Marine

Pl de la
Concorde

Av Winston Churchill

Cours Albert 1er

Cours la Reine

Port de la Conférence

Seine

Pont des
Invalides

18

Pont
Alexandre III

Pont de la
Concorde

Q d'Orsay

Pl de
Finlande

Q d'Orsay

7E

R de l'Université

Bd de la Tour Maubourg

R Fabert

Av du Maréchal Gallieni

Invalides

Assemblée
Nationale

Esplanade
des Invalides

R St-Dominique

For reviews see	
◉ Top Experiences	p54
◎ Sights	p58
✕ Eating	p62
🍷 Drinking	p64
🛍 Shopping	p65

Sights

Avenue des Champs-Élysées

STREET

1 ⦿ MAP P56, G4

No trip to Paris is complete without strolling this broad, tree-shaded avenue lined with luxury shops. Named for the Elysian Fields (heaven in Greek mythology), the Champs-Élysées was laid out in the 17th century and is part of the *axe historique*, linking place de la Concorde with the Arc de Triomphe. It's where presidents and soldiers parade on Bastille Day, where the Tour de France holds its final sprint, and where Paris turns out for organised and impromptu celebrations. (8e; M Charles de Gaulle–Étoile, George V, Franklin D Roosevelt, Champs-Élysées–Clemenceau)

Musée Jacquemart-André

MUSEUM

2 ⦿ MAP P56, F2

The home of art collectors Nélie Jacquemart and Édouard André, this opulent late-19th-century residence combines elements from different eras – seen here in the presence of Greek and Roman antiquities, Egyptian artefacts, period furnishings and portraits by Dutch masters. Its 16 rooms offer an absorbing glimpse of the lifestyle of Parisian high society: from the library, hung with canvases by Rembrandt and Van Dyck, to the marvellous Jardin d'Hiver – a glass-paned garden room backed by a magnificent double-helix staircase. (☎ 01 45 62 11 59; www.musee-jacquemart-andre.com; 158 bd Haussmann, 8e; adult/child incl audioguide €12/7.50; ⊙ 10am-6pm, to 8.30pm Mon during temporary exhibitions; M Miromesnil)

Cité de l'Architecture et du Patrimoine

MUSEUM

3 ⦿ MAP P56, A5

This mammoth 23,000-sq-metre space is an ode on three floors to French architecture. The highlight is the light-filled ground floor with a beautiful collection of plaster and wood *moulages* (casts) of cathedral portals, columns and gargoyles. Replicas of murals and stained glass originally created for the 1878 Exposition Universelle (World's Fair) are on display on the upper floors. Views of the Eiffel Tower are equally monumental. (☎ 01 58 51 52 00; www.citedelarchitecture.fr; 1 place du Trocadéro et du 11 Novembre, 16e; adult/child €8/free; ⊙ 11am-7pm Wed & Fri-Mon, to 9pm Thu, 1st Sun of month free; M Trocadéro)

Musée National des Arts Asiatiques – Guimet

GALLERY

4 ⦿ MAP P56, B5

Connoisseurs of Japanese ink paintings and Tibetan *thangkas* won't want to miss the Musée Guimet, the largest Asian art museum in France. Observe the gradual transmission of both Buddhism and artistic styles along the Silk Road, in pieces ranging from 1st-century Gandhara Buddhas from Afghanistan and

Pakistan to later Central Asian, Chinese and Japanese Buddhist sculptures and art. Audioguides are free. (📞01 56 52 54 33; www.guimet. fr; 6 place d'Iéna, 16e; adult/child €7.50/ free, 1st Sun of month free; ⏰10am–6pm Wed-Mon; Ⓜ Iéna)

Hôtel de la Marine PALACE

5 ◉ MAP P56, H4

Built to house the Garde-Meuble de la Couronne (royal furnishings) the Hôtel de la Marine is one of two grand-scale palaces (along with the Hôtel de Crillon, now a luxury hotel) commissioned by Louis XV in the late 18th century, to grace place de la Concorde. After the building was looted during the French Revolution, the French navy was headquartered here until 2015. Following renovations it will open

to the public, with guided tours providing an insight into its history. (www.hotel-de-la-marine.paris; 2 place de la Concorde, 8e; Ⓜ Concorde)

Musée Yves Saint Laurent Paris MUSEUM

6 ◉ MAP P56, C5

Housed in the legendary designer's studios (1974–2002), this museum holds retrospectives of YSL's avant-garde designs, from early sketches to finished pieces. Temporary exhibitions give an insight into the creative process of designing a *haute couture* (high fashion) collection and the history of fashion throughout the 20th century. The building can only accommodate a small number of visitors at a time, so buy tickets online or expect to

Cité de l'Architecture et du Patrimoine

Olympic Relocations

Paris' magnificent **Grand Palais** (www.grandpalais.fr; 3 av du Général Eisenhower, 8e; MChamps-Élysées–Clemenceau), first built for the 1900 Exposition Universelle (World's Fair), will be a landmark venue of the 2024 Olympic and Paralympic games, and will close for renovations from 2021 to 2024.

During this time, a temporary Grand Palais will set up on the Parc du Champ de Mars (p45), adjacent to the Eiffel Tower. This 20m-high, 10,000-sq-metre building will also have an additional temporary structure added to the main structure each year in order to expand it 8000 square metres. The space will host headlining exhibitions and events, and will also host the Olympic judo and wrestling competitions.

Also on the move is the children's science museum **Palais de la Découverte** (www.palais-decouverte.fr), which is setting up a 770-sq-metre temporary home in the **Parc André Citroën** (2 rue Cauchy, 15e; ◷8am-9.30pm Mon-Fri, from 9am Sat & Sun May-Aug, shorter hours rest of year; ♿; MJavel–André Citroën, RER Javel), from 2020 to 2024. It will open to the public by registration on weekends and during school holidays.

queue outside. (☎01 44 31 64 00; www.museeyslparis.com; 5 av Marceau, 16e; adult/child €10/7; ◷11am-6pm Tue-Thu, Sat & Sun, to 9pm Fri; MAlma Marceau)

Petit Palais

GALLERY

7 MAP P56, G4

This architectural stunner was built for the 1900 Exposition Universelle (World's Fair), and is home to the Musée des Beaux-Arts de la Ville de Paris (City of Paris Museum of Fine Arts). It specialises in medieval and Renaissance objets d'art, such as porcelain and clocks, tapestries, drawings and 19th-century French paintings and sculpture; there are also paintings by such artists as Rembrandt,

Colbert, Cézanne, Monet, Gauguin and Delacroix. An audioguide costs €5. (☎01 53 43 40 00; www.petit palais.paris.fr; av Winston Churchill, 8e; admission free; ◷10am-6pm Tue-Sun, temporary exhibitions to 9pm Fri; MChamps-Élysées–Clemenceau)

Palais de Chaillot

HISTORIC BUILDING

8 MAP P56, A6

The two curved, colonnaded wings of this building (built for the 1937 International Expo) and central terrace afford an exceptional panorama of the Jardins du Trocadéro, Seine and Eiffel Tower. The eastern wing houses the standout Cité de l'Architecture et du Patrimoine (p58), devoted to French architecture and heritage, as well as the **Théâtre National de Chaillot** (☎01 53 65 30 00; www.theatre-chaillot. fr), staging dance and theatre. The **Musée de la Marine** (Maritime Museum; www.musee-marine.fr) – closed for renovations until early 2022 – and the **Musée de l'Homme** (Museum of Humankind; ☎01 44 05 72 72; www.museedelhomme.fr; adult/child €10/free; ☯11am-7pm Wed-Mon; MPassy, Iéna) are housed in the western wing. (place du Trocadéro et du 11 Novembre, 16e; MTrocadéro)

Palais de Tokyo   GALLERY

9 ◉ MAP P56, C5

The Tokyo Palace, created for the 1937 Exposition Internationale des Arts et Techniques dans la Vie Moderne (International Exposition of Art and Technology in Modern Life), has no permanent collection. Instead, its shell-like interior of concrete and steel is a stark backdrop to interactive contemporary-art exhibitions and installations. The art- and design-focused bookshop is fabulous, and its eating, drinking and entertainment options – including sustainably themed Mediterranean restaurant Les Grands Verres, with a compacted-earth bar, and basement nightclub **Yoyo** (www.facebook.com/yoyoconcertparis; ☯hours vary) are magic. (☎01 81 97 35 88; www.palaisdetokyo.com; 13 av du Président Wilson, 16e; adult/child €12/free; ☯noon-midnight Wed-Mon; MIéna)

Musée d'Art Moderne de la Ville de Paris   GALLERY

10 ◉ MAP P56, C5

The permanent collection at Paris' modern-art museum displays works representative of just about every major artistic movement of the 20th and (nascent) 21st centuries, with works by Modigliani, Matisse, Braque and Soutine. The real jewel, though, is the room hung with canvases by Dufy and Bonnard. Look out for cutting-edge temporary exhibitions (not free). Download the free multilingual app online. (☎01 53 67 40 00; www.mam. paris.fr; 11 av du Président Wilson, 16e; admission free; ☯10am-6pm Tue, Wed & Fri-Sun, to 10pm Thu; MIéna)

Fondation Louis Vuitton

Designed by Frank Gehry, the striking glass-panelled **Fondation Louis Vuitton** (☎01 40 69 96 00; www.fondationlouisvuitton. fr; 8 av du Mahatma Gandhi, 16e; adult/child €16/5; ☯usually 10am-6pm Mon-Sat; MLes Sablons) in the Bois de Bologne hosts major temporary contemporary art exhibitions; check online for the latest show. A **shuttle** (Map p56, C2; 44 av Friedland, 8e; round trip €2; MCharles de Gaulle–Étoile) runs from the Arc de Triomphe to the museum and back during opening hours.

Grande Arche

High-rise business district La Défense's landmark edifice is the marble **Grande Arche** (📞 01 40 90 52 20; www.lagrande arche.fr; 1 Parvis de la Défense; adult/child €15/7; ⏰10am-7pm; Ⓜ La Défense Grande Arche), a cube-like arch built in the 1980s to house government and business offices. The arch marks the western end of the *axe historique* (historic axis), though Danish architect Johan-Otto von Sprekelsen deliberately placed the Grande Arche fractionally out of alignment. A lift whisks you up for spectacular views from the rooftop.

Temporary photojournalism exhibits are held in the museum (included in the rooftop visit).

Eating

Ladurée
PASTRIES €

11 ✖ MAP P56, D3

One of Paris' oldest patisseries (cake shops), Ladurée has been around since 1862 and first created the lighter-than-air, ganache-filled macaron in the 1930s. Its tearoom is the classiest spot to indulge in pastries or more formal meals on the Champs. Alternatively, pick up some pastries to go – its trademark macarons (€2.60) in particular are heavenly. (📞01 40 75 08 75; www.

laduree.fr; 75 av des Champs-Élysées, 8e; pastries €7-10.50; mains €19-33; ⏰7.30am-11pm Mon-Fri, to midnight Sat, to 10pm Sun; 📶; Ⓜ George V)

Substance
FRENCH €€€

12 ✖ MAP P56, C4

A striking contemporary dining room in shades of muted blue is the backdrop for truly original cooking by young-gun chef Matthias Marc: Normandy scallop carpaccio with smoked sea urchin roe and hay vinaigrette; foie gras and Ardennes pheasant pie with purple cauliflower, kale and quince relish; and hazelnut-crème-stuffed cabbage, with Corsican clementine and citrusy calamansi sorbet. Book ahead. (📞01 47 20 08 90; www.substance.paris; 18 rue de Chaillot, 16e; mains €24-39, 5-/7-course menus €79/95, with paired wines €124/150; ⏰noon-2pm & 7.30-10.30pm Mon-Fri; Ⓜ Iéna, Alma Marceau)

Le Hide
FRENCH €€

13 ✖ MAP P56, B1

A perpetual favourite, Le Hide is a tiny neighbourhood bistro serving scrumptious traditional French fare: lobster bisque with shaved black truffles, veal kidneys sautéed in mustard and baked shoulder of lamb. This place fills up faster than you can scamper down the steps of the nearby Arc de Triomphe – reserve well in advance. (📞01 45 74 15 81; www.lehide.fr; 10 rue du Général Lanrezac, 17e; 2-/3-course menus €34/38, mains €26-34; ⏰6-11pm

Mon-Sat, closed 2 weeks May, 3 weeks Aug; M Charles de Gaulle–Étoile)

with paired wines €260/350; ⊙7-10pm Tue-Sat; M Franklin D Roosevelt)

Lasserre

GASTRONOMY €€€

14 ⊗ MAP P56, F4

Since 1942, this exceedingly elegant Triangle d'Or (Golden Triangle) restaurant has hosted style icons, including Audrey Hepburn, and is still a superlative choice for a Michelin-starred meal to remember. A bellhop-attended lift, white-and-gold chandeliered decor, extraordinary retractable roof and flawless service set the stage for creations such as braised sea bass with caviar or crêpes Suzette flambéed tableside. Observe the dress code. (⊘01 43 59 53 43; www.restaurant-lasserre.com; 17 av Franklin D Roosevelt, 8e; mains €78-120, 4-/6-course menu €145/195,

Origines

FRENCH €€€

15 ⊗ MAP P56, F3

Chef Julien Boscus, who earned a Michelin star at Left Bank restaurant Les Climats, opened his own debonair blue-and-grey-hued Right Bank premises in 2019. Black-truffle brioche with chardonnay-poached oysters, veal sweetbreads with hazelnut and lemon butter and roast venison with burnt-pear purée are among the menu highlights. The three-course lunch is a superb deal. (⊘09 86 41 63 04; www.origines-restaurant.com; 6 rue de Ponthieu, 8e; 3-course lunch menus €44, 6-course dinner menus €85, mains €39-46; ⊙12.15-2pm & 7.30-10pm Mon-Fri; M Franklin D Roosevelt)

Moveable Feasts

🍽️

Bustronome (Map p56, B2; ⊘09 54 44 45 55; www.bustronome.com; 2 av Kléber, 16e; 4-course lunch menus €65, 6-course dinner menus €100; ⊙by reservation 1½-3hr tour 12.15pm, 12.45pm, 7.45pm & 8.45pm daily, plus 1¾hr brunch tour 11am Sun; 🚲🚻; M Kléber, Charles de Gaulle–Étoile) is a voyage into French gastronomy aboard a glass-roofed bus, with Paris' famous monuments – the Arc de Triomphe, Palais Garnier and Eiffel Tower among them – gliding by as you dine on seasonal creations prepared in the purpose-built vehicle's lower-deck galley. Children's menus for lunch/dinner cost €40/50; vegetarian, vegan and gluten-free menus are available.

Multi-Michelin-starred chef Alain Ducasse's 'floating restaurant' **Ducasse sur Seine** (Map p56, B6; ⊘01 58 00 22 08; www.ducasse-seine. com; Port Debilly, 16e; 3-course lunch menus €100, with paired wines €150, 5-course dinner menus €190, with paired wines €290; ⊙12.45-2.30pm, 4-5.30pm & 8.30-10.30pm; M Trocadéro) sails through the city, passing city icons like the Louvre, for lunch and dinner at white-clothed tables.

Drinking

St James Paris
BAR

16 🚇 MAP P56, A4

Hidden behind a stone wall, this historic mansion turned hotel opens its bar nightly to nonguests – and the setting redefines extraordinary. Winter drinks are in the wood-panelled library; summer drinks are on the impossibly romantic 300-sq-metre garden terrace with giant balloon-shaped gazebos (the first publicly displayed hot-air balloons took flight from here). It has 35 house cocktails and a premium wine list. (www.saint-james-paris.com; 43 av Bugeaud, 16e; ⏰7pm-1am; 🛜; 🚇Porte Dauphine)

Honor
COFFEE

17 🚇 MAP P56, H3

Hidden off ritzy rue du Faubourg St-Honoré in a courtyard adjoining fashion house Comme des Garçons is this opaque-plastic-sheltered black-and-white timber kiosk brewing coffee from small-scale producers around the globe. It also serves sourdough crumpets and luscious cakes (dishes €4 to €7.50), along with fresh juices, wine and beer. (www.honor-cafe. com; 54 rue du Faubourg St-Honoré, 8e; ⏰9am-6pm Mon-Fri, 10am-6pm Sat; 🚇Madeleine)

Bridge
CLUB

18 🚇 MAP P56, F5

Buried beneath Paris' most elaborate bridge, Pont Alexandre III, this

Guerlain

cavernous 1500-sq-metre space, with a capacity of 2000 clubbers, is one of the city's top nightlife destinations. Check its agenda online for DJs, video installations, parties and other events. It also opens on Sunday nights before public-holiday Mondays. (☎06 40 46 44 62; www.facebook.com/pg/bridgeparisclub; Pont Alexandre III, 8e; ⏱11pm-6am Fri & Sat; Ⓜ Champs-Élysées–Clemenceau, Invalides)

Shopping

Laulhère   HATS

19 🔒 MAP P56, H4

Founded in 1840, beret maker Laulhère still supplies the French army with the iconic headwear. Handcrafted from soft, durable and water-resistant merino wool, varieties range from plain to jewel-encrusted versions. The boutique is hidden within a courtyard off rue du Faubourg St-Honoré. (www.laulhere-store.com; 14-16 rue du Faubourg St-Honoré, 8e; ⏱11am-7pm Mon-Sat; Ⓜ Madeleine)

Guerlain   PERFUME

20 🔒 MAP P56, E3

Guerlain is Paris' most famous parfumerie (perfume maker), and its shop (dating from 1912) is one of the most beautiful in the city. With its shimmering mirror-and-marble art deco interior, it's a reminder of the former glory of the Champs-Élysées. For total indulgence, make an appointment at its sublime spa. (☎spa 01 45 62 52 57; www.guerlain.

Golden Triangle

A stroll around the legendary Triangle d'Or (Golden Triangle; bordered by avs George V, Champs-Élysées and Montaigne, 8e) constitutes the walk of fame of top French fashion. Rubbing shoulders with the world's top international designers are Paris' most influential French fashion houses, such as Chanel, Chloé, Dior, Givenchy, Hermès, Lanvin, Louis Vuitton and Saint Laurent.

com; 68 av des Champs-Élysées, 8e; ⏱9am-7pm Mon-Wed & Sat, to 8pm Thu & Fri; Ⓜ Franklin D Roosevelt)

Galeries Lafayette – Champs-Élysées   DEPARTMENT STORE

21 🔒 MAP P56, E3

The 2019-opened Galeries Lafayette on the Champs-Élysées is located in one of the avenue's grandest art deco buildings (1931), with marble columns and wrought-iron girders. Although smaller than the main Haussmann store (p87), it is undoubtedly more modern, with a layout specifically tailored to today's shoppers, a free personal stylist service (no minimum purchase) and a basement gourmet emporium. (☎01 83 65 61 00; www.galerieslafayettechampselysees.com; 60 av Champs-Élysées; ⏱10.30am-11pm Tue-Sat, to 10pm Sun & Mon; Ⓜ Franklin D Roosevelt)

Explore ⊕
Louvre, Tuileries & Opéra

Carving its way through the city, Paris' axe historique (historic axis) passes through the Tuileries before reaching IM Pei's glass pyramid at the entrance to Paris' mightiest museum, the Louvre. Gourmet shops garland Église de la Madeleine, while further north are the splendid Palais Garnier opera house and art nouveau department stores of the Grands Boulevards.

The Short List

○ **Musée du Louvre (p68)** *Exploring the Louvre's little-visited quiet corners, with timeless masterpieces at every turn.*

○ **Jardin des Tuileries (p78)** *Strolling this elegant symmetrical park.*

○ **Église St-Eustache (p78)** *Feasting on exquisite sacred art and soulful music in this landmark Gothic church.*

○ **Jardin du Palais Royal (p78)** *Strolling amid the arcaded galleries and Daniel Buren's zebra-striped columns.*

○ **Palais Garnier (p79)** *Taking in a performance or touring the mythic 19th-century opera house.*

Getting There & Around

Ⓜ The Louvre has two metro stations: Palais Royal–Musée du Louvre (lines 1 and 7), and Louvre–Rivoli (line 1).

Ⓜ Châtelet–Les Halles is Paris' main hub, with many metro and RER lines converging here.

⛴ The hop-on, hop-off Batobus stops outside the Louvre.

Neighbourhood Map on p76

Jardin des Tuileries (p78) MEANDERING TRAIL MEDIA/SHUTTERSTOCK ©

Top Experience 📷
Discover Artistic Treasures at the Louvre

Paris' pièce de résistance is one of the world's largest and most diverse museums, showcasing 35,000 works of art in palatial surrounds, including some of the best-known works ever created. It would take nine months to glance at every piece, rendering advance planning essential.

◉ MAP P76, E5

www.louvre.fr

rue de Rivoli & quai des Tuileries, 1er

adult/child €15/free,

🕐 9am-6pm Mon, Thu, Sat & Sun, to 9.45pm Wed, Fri & 1st Sat of month

Ⓜ Palais Royal–Musée du Louvre

Palais du Louvre

The Louvre today rambles over four floors and through three wings: the **Sully Wing** creates the four sides of the Cour Carrée (literally Square Courtyard) at the eastern end of the complex; the **Denon Wing** stretches 800m along the Seine to the south; and the northern **Richelieu Wing** skirts rue de Rivoli. The building started life as a fortress built by Philippe-Auguste in the 12th century – medieval remnants are still visible on the lower ground floor (Sully). In the 16th century it became a royal residence and after the Revolution, in 1793, it was turned into a national museum. Its booty was no more than 2500 paintings and objets d'art.

Over the centuries French governments amassed the paintings, sculptures and artefacts displayed today. The 'Grand Louvre' project inaugurated by the late president François Mitterrand in 1989 doubled the museum's exhibition space, and both new and renovated galleries have since opened, including the state-of-the-art Islamic art galleries (lower ground floor, Denon) in the stunningly restored Cour Visconti.

Priceless Antiquities

Whatever your plans are, don't rush by the Louvre's astonishing cache of treasures from antiquity: both Mesopotamia (ground floor, Richelieu) and Egypt (ground and 1st floors, Sully) are well represented, as seen in the *Code of Hammurabi* (Room 227, ground floor, Richelieu) and *The Seated Scribe* (Room 635, 1st floor, Sully). Room 307 (ground floor, Sully Wing) holds impressive friezes and an enormous two-headed-bull column from the Darius Palace in ancient Iran, while an enormous seated statue of Pharaoh Ramesses II highlights the temple room (Room 324, ground floor, Sully).

★ **Top Tips**

o Admission is free in the evening (6-9.45pm) on the first Saturday of the month.

o Crowds are fewest first thing in the morning and on Wednesday and Friday evenings.

o Check the Schedule of Room Closures on the website to ensure you'll be able to see what you want to see.

✗ **Take a Break**

o Tucked between the Napoléon III apartments and European decorative arts galleries on the Richelieu wing's 1st floor is a branch of renowned tearoom Angelina (www.angelina-paris.fr).

o Before or after your visit, enjoy a picnic in the Jardin des Tuileries (p78).

Also worth a look are the mosaics and figurines from the Byzantine empire (lower ground floor, Denon), and the Greek statuary collection, culminating with the world's most famous armless duo, the *Venus de Milo* (Room 346, ground floor, Sully) and the *Winged Victory of Samothrace* (Room 703, 1st floor, Denon).

Mona Lisa

Easily the Louvre's most admired work is Leonardo da Vinci's *La Joconde* (in French; *La Gioconda* in Italian), the lady with that enigmatic smile known as *Mona Lisa* (Room 711, 1st floor, Denon).

Mona (*monna* in Italian) is a contraction of *madonna,* and Gioconda is the feminine form of the surname Giocondo. Scientists used infrared technology to peer through paint layers and confirm *Mona Lisa's* identity as Lisa Gherardini (1479–1542?), wife of Florentine merchant Francesco de Giocondo. It was also confirmed her dress was covered in a transparent gauze veil typically worn in early-16th-century Italy by pregnant women or new mothers, suggesting the work was painted to commemorate the birth of her second son around 1503, when she was aged about 24.

Its immense popularity has led to controversial suggestions it should be moved to an external location, given the pressure on the Louvre's visitor numbers. You'll need to queue to see the painting; once in front of it, you'll have around two minutes before being moved on.

Mona Lisa

Accessing the Louvre

The Louvre embarked on a 30-year renovation plan in 2014, with the aim of modernising the museum to make it more accessible, including increasing the number of museum entrances. Security queues at the underground Carrousel du Louvre entrance and the **Porte des Lions** (quai François Mitterrand; ☉9am-5.30pm Wed-Mon) entrance are typically shorter than the main Grande Pyramide entrance. To guarantee entry, you'll need to prepurchase a ticket with an allocated time slot on the museum's website (€2 surcharge) or make a time slot reservation using a Paris Museum Pass. Tickets are only valid for the duration of your visit (you can no longer come and go as you please throughout the day).

French & Italian Masterpieces

The 1st floor of the Denon Wing, where the *Mona Lisa* is found, is easily the most popular part of the Louvre – and with good reason. Rooms 700 through 702 are hung with monumental French paintings, many iconic: look for the *Consecration of the Emperor Napoléon I* (David), *The Raft of the Medusa* (Géricault) and *Grande Odalisque* (Ingres).

Rooms 710, 711, 712 and 716 are also must-visits. Filled with classic works by Renaissance masters (Raphael, Titian, Uccello, Botticini), this area culminates in the crowds around the *Mona Lisa*. But you'll find plenty else to contemplate, such as the superbly detailed *Wedding Feast at Cana* (Room 711). Botticelli's frescoes grace Room 706.

Northern European Paintings

The 2nd floor of the Richelieu Wing, directly above the gilt and crystal of the Napoléon III Apartments (1st floor), allows for a quieter meander through the Louvre's inspirational collection of Flemish and Dutch paintings spearheaded by the works of Peter Paul Rubens and Pieter Bruegel the Elder. Vermeer's *The Lacemaker* can be found in Room 837, while Room 845 is devoted chiefly to works by Rembrandt.

Glass Pyramid

Almost as stunning as the masterpieces inside is the 21m-high glass pyramid designed by Chinese-American architect IM Pei (1917–2019) that crowns the main entrance to the Louvre. Beneath Pei's Grande Pyramide is the Hall Napoléon, the museum's main entrance area. To revel in another Pei pyramid of equally dramatic dimensions, head towards the **Carrousel du Louvre** (www.carrouseldulouvre.com; 99 rue de Rivoli, 1er; ☉10am-8pm Wed-Mon, 11am-7pm Tue; 🛜), a busy shopping mall that loops underground from

Louvre

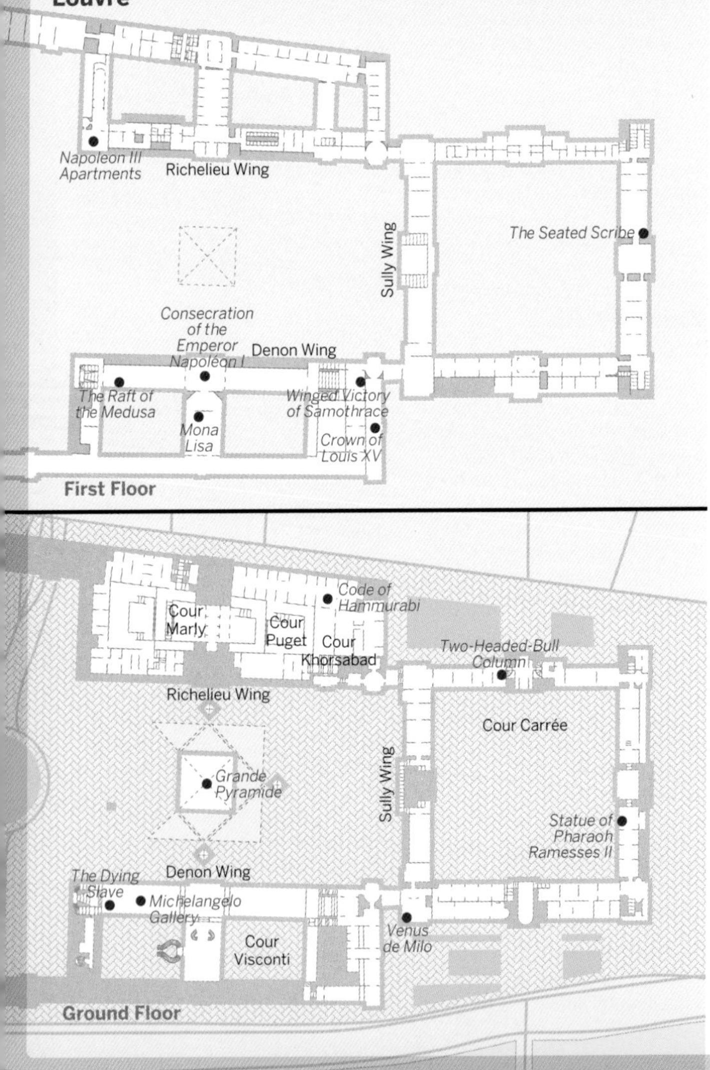

First Floor

Napoléon III Apartments

Richelieu Wing

Sully Wing

The Seated Scribe ●

Consecration of the Emperor Napoléon I

Denon Wing

● The Raft of the Medusa

● Winged Victory of Samothrace

Mona Lisa

Crown of Louis XV

Ground Floor

Cour Marly

Cour Puget

Cour Khorsabad

● Code of Hammurabi

Two-Headed-Bull Column ●

Richelieu Wing

Cour Carrée

Sully Wing

● Grande Pyramide

Denon Wing

Statue of Pharaoh Ramesses II ●

The Dying Slave ●

● Michelangelo Gallery

Cour Visconti

● Venus de Milo

the Grande Pyramide to the **Arc de Triomphe du Carrousel** (place du Carrousel, 1er) – its centrepiece is Pei's Pyramide Inversée (inverted glass pyramid).

Trails & Tours

Self-guided thematic trails range from Louvre masterpieces and the art of eating to family-friendly topics. Download trail brochures in advance from the website. Another good option is to rent a Nintendo 3DS multimedia guide (€5; ID required). More formal, English-language **guided tours** (tour excl museum entry adult/child €12/7; 11am & 2pm daily except 1st Tue & Sun of month, plus 7pm Wed) depart from the Hall Napoléon. Reserve a spot online up to 14 days in advance or sign up on arrival at the museum.

Petite Galerie

From October to June each year, the Louvre's innovative cultural education space, the Petite Galerie, mounts a major exhibition with interactive displays plus related Louvre-wide tours, alongside storytelling, readings, films and other events for all ages. Keep an eye on the website for details.

Other Louvre Museums

A trio of privately administered collections (applied arts and design, advertising and graphic design, and fashion and textiles) sit in the Rohan Wing of the vast Palais du Louvre. They are collectively known as the **Musée des Arts Décoratifs** (MAD; 01 44 55 57 50; www.madparis.fr; 107 rue de Rivoli, 1er; adult/child €14/free; 11am-6pm Tue, Wed & Fri-Sun, to 9pm Thu); admission includes entry to all three. For an extra €6, you can scoop up a combo ticket that also includes the Musée Nissim de Camondo in the 8e.

On the 1st floor is the Woodwork Fair, a recreation from the 1900 Exposition Universelle (World's Fair) designed by decorator Georges Hoentschel. The 2nd floor houses the Jewellery Gallery, with a 1200-piece chronological collection from the Middle Ages to the present day in two separate spaces linked by a glass walkway.

Spanning the Middle Ages to the art nouveau and art deco periods, the 3rd- and 4th-floor rooms display furniture, objets d'art such as ceramics and glassware, artworks, advertising posters, and textiles from silks and tapestries to prints and fashion, with creations by Christian Dior and Yves Saint Laurent, among others.

The uppermost floors are dedicated to modern and contemporary techniques, materials and designers such as Le Corbusier, Charlotte Perriand and Philippe Starck.

Walking Tour 🥾

Right Bank Covered Passages

Stepping into the passages couverts (covered shopping arcades) of the Right Bank is the best way to get a feel for what life was like in early-19th-century Paris. Around half a century later, Paris had around 150 of these decorated arcades. This walking tour is tailor-made for a rainy day, but it's best avoided on a Sunday, when some arcades are shut.

Walk Facts

Start Galerie Véro Dodat;
Ⓜ Palais Royal–Musée du Louvre

Finish Passage Verdeau;
Ⓜ Le Peletier

Length 3km; two hours

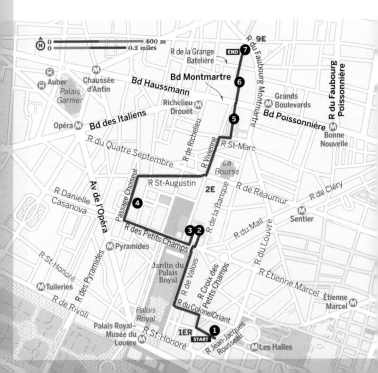

❶ Galerie Véro Dodat

At 19 rue Jean-Jacques Rousseau, **Galerie Véro Dodat** (btwn rue Jean-Jacques-Rousseau & 2 rue du Bouloi, 1er; ⏰7am-10pm Mon-Sat, shop hours vary; Ⓜ Louvre–Rivoli, Palais Royal–Musée du Louvre) retains its 19th-century skylights, ceiling murals, Corinthian columns, tiled floor, gas globe fittings (now electric) and shopfronts including furniture restorers.

❷ Galerie Vivienne

Built in 1826, Galerie Vivienne is decorated with floor mosaics and bas-reliefs on the walls. Don't miss wine shop **Legrand Filles & Fils** (📞01 42 60 07 12; www.caves-legrand. com; 1 rue de la Banque, 2e; ⏰11am-7pm Mon, 10am-7.30pm Tue-Sat; Ⓜ Bourse), Wolff et Descourtis, selling silk scarves, and Emilio Robba, one of the most beautiful flower shops in Paris.

❸ Galerie Colbert

Enter this 1826-built passage, featuring a huge glass dome and rotunda, from rue Vivienne. Exit on rue des Petits Champs (and check out the fresco above).

❹ Passage Choiseul

This 1824-built, 45m-long passage has scores of shops including many specialising in discount and vintage clothing, beads and costume jewellery as well as cheap eateries. Comedies are performed at the Théâtre des Bouffes Parisiens, which backs onto the passage's northern end.

❺ Passage des Panoramas

From 10 rue St-Marc, enter Paris' **oldest** (btwn 10 rue St-Marc, 2e & 11 bd Montmartre, 9e; Ⓜ Grands Boulevards, Richelieu Drouot) covered arcade (1800) and the first to be lit by gas (1817). It was expanded in 1834 with four interconnecting passages – Feydeau, Montmartre, St-Marc and Variétés – and is full of eateries and unusual shops, such as autograph dealer Arnaud Magistry. Exit at 11 bd Montmartre.

❻ Passage Jouffroy

Enter at 10-12 bd Montmartre into **passage Jouffroy** (Ⓜ Grands Boulevards), Paris' last major passage (1847). There's a wax museum, the Musée Grévin, and wonderful boutiques including bookshops, silversmiths and MG Segas, where Henri de Toulouse-Lautrec bought his walking sticks. Exit at 9 rue de la Grange Batelière.

❼ Passage Verdeau

Cross the road to 6 rue de la Grange Batelière to **Passage Verdeau**, (Ⓜ Le Peletier) the last of this stretch of covered arcades. There's lots to explore: vintage comic books, antiques, old postcards and more. The northern exit is at 31bis rue du Faubourg Montmartre.

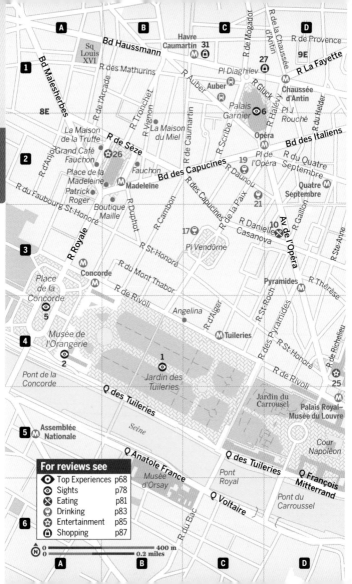

Louvre, Tuileries & Opéra

A **B** **C** **D**

Sq Louis XVI

Bd Haussmann

Havre Caumartin **31**

R de Provence

9E

R La Fayette

1

Bd Malesherbes

R des Mathurins

R de l'Arcade

R Auber

Pl Diaghilev

27

R de la Chaussée d'Antin

R de Mogador

Chaussée d'Antin

Pl J Rouché

R du Helder

8E

R Tronchet

R Vignon

La Maison du Miel

R de Caumartin

R Scribe

R Gluck

Palais Garnier **6**

R Halévy

Opéra

Bd des Italiens

La Maison de la Truffe

R de Sèze

2

Grand Café Fauchon

26

Fauchon

Pl de l'Opéra

R Daunou

19

Pl de l'Opéra

R du Quatre Septembre

Quatre Septembre

Place de la Madeleine

Madeleine

Bd des Capucines

R des Capucines

21

R Danielle Casanova

10

Av de l'Opéra

R Gaillon

R Ste-Anne

R d'Anjou

R du Faubourg St-Honoré

Patrick Roger

Boutique Maille

R Duphot

R Cambon

R de la Paix

17

R St-Honoré

Pl Vendôme

Pyramides

R Thérèse

3

R Royale

Concorde

R du Mont Thabor

R St-Roch

R de Richelieu

Place de la Concorde

5

R de Rivoli

Angelina

R d'Alger

Tuileries

R des Pyramides

R St-Honoré

25

4

Musée de l'Orangerie

2

1

Jardin des Tuileries

R de Rivoli

Pont de la Concorde

Jardin du Carrousel

Palais Royal– Musée du Louvre

Seine

Cour Napoléon

5

Assemblée Nationale

Q des Tuileries

Q Anatole France

Q des Tuileries

Q François Mitterrand

Musée d'Orsay

Pont Royal

Pont du Carrousel

For reviews see

📍	Top Experiences	p68
👁	Sights	p78
✕	Eating	p81
🍷	Drinking	p83
★	Entertainment	p85
🛍	Shopping	p87

6

R du Bac

Q Voltaire

N ↑

0 —————— 400 m
0 —————— 0.2 miles

A **B** **C** **D**

E · **F** · **G** · **H**

R du Faubourg Montmartre

R Richer

R de Trévise

R du Faubourg Poissonnière

R des Petites Écuries

1

33

R Le Peletier

R Laffitte

R Rossini

R Drouot

R de Montyon

R Ste-Cécile

R Bergère

10E

Bd Haussmann

R d'Hauteville

R d'Enghien

R de l'Échiquier

Richelieu Drouot

Grands Boulevards

Cité Bergère

Bd Poissonnière

Bonne Nouvelle

Bd de Bonne Nouvelle

11

R Favart

R de Richelieu

R St-Marc

R Feydeau

R Montmartre

34

R St-Fiacre

R du Sentier

24

R de la Lune

2

R Poissonnière

R de Cléry

Strasbourg St-Denis

R St-Augustin

La Bourse

Bourse

2E

R des Jeûneurs

R de Réaumur

R d'Aboukir

R St-Denis

R Vivienne

R de la Banque

R du Mail

R d'Aboukir

R du Nil

R du Caire

R de Réaumur

3

Sentier

12

Réaumur Sébastopol

R des Petits Champs

14

Pl des Victoires

R d'Argout

R Léopold Bellan

R Montorgueil

R St-Sauveur

20

Au Rocher de Cancale

29

4

Jardin du Palais Royal

R Coquillière

R du Louvre

R Montmartre

22

23

R Mandar

Stohrer

R Tiquetonne

R St-Denis

Palais Royal

R de Valois

R Croix des Petits Champs

32

R Étienne Marcel

Étienne Marcel

R de Turbigo

4

R du Colonel Driant

16

R du Jour

3 Église St-Eustache

1ER

Collection Pinault— Paris

7

Les Halles

Forum des Halles

R Rambuteau

R aux Ours

R St-Denis

Bd de Sébastopol

R St-Martin

Pl du Palais Royal

R St-Honoré

8

Châtelet- Les Halles

Rambuteau

5

15

Pl M Quentin

28

Musée du Louvre

Louvre- Rivoli

R Bailleul

13

R des Prouvaires

Pl M de Navarre

R Berger

Châtelet

Centre Pompidou

R du Renard

Cour Carrée

Pont Neuf

30

R de l'Arbre Sec

R de la Monnaie

R du Pont Neuf

R de Rivoli

Sunset & Sunside

Le Baiser Salé

Châtelet

R des Lombards

6

Pont des Arts

9

Pont Neuf

Q du Louvre

Q de la Mégisserie

18

Duc des Lombards

E · **F** · **G** · **H**

Sights

Jardin des Tuileries PARK

1 ⊙ MAP P76, B4

Filled with fountains, ponds and sculptures, the formal 28-hectare Tuileries Garden, which begins just west of the Jardin du Carrousel, was laid out in its present form in 1664 by André Le Nôtre, architect of the gardens at Versailles. The Tuileries soon became the most fashionable spot in Paris for parading about in one's finery. It now forms part of the Banks of the Seine Unesco World Heritage Site. (rue de Rivoli, 1er; ⏰7am-11pm Jun-Aug, 7am-9pm Apr, May & Sep, 7.30am-7.30pm Oct-Mar; Ⓜ Tuileries, Concorde)

Musée de l'Orangerie MUSEUM

2 ⊙ MAP P76, A4

Monet's extraordinary cycle of eight enormous *Decorations des Nymphéas* (Water Lilies) occupies two huge oval rooms purpose-built in 1927 on the artist's instructions. The lower level houses more of Monet's impressionist works and many by Sisley, Renoir, Cézanne, Gauguin, Picasso, Matisse and Modigliani, as well as Derain's *Arlequin et Pierrot*. The orangery and photography gallery **Jeu de Paume** (☎01 47 03 12 50; www. jeudepaume.org; adult/child €10/free; ⏰11am-9pm Tue, to 7pm Wed-Sun) are all that remains of the former Palais des Tuileries, which was razed during the Paris Commune

in 1871. Audioguides cost €5. (☎01 44 77 80 07; www.musee-orangerie. fr; place de la Concorde, 1er; adult/ child €9/free; ⏰9am-6pm Wed-Mon; Ⓜ Concorde)

Église St-Eustache CHURCH

3 ⊙ MAP P76, G4

Just north of the gardens adjoining the city's old marketplace, now the Forum des Halles (p80), is one of the most beautiful churches in Paris. Majestic, architecturally magnificent and musically outstanding, St-Eustache was constructed between 1532 and 1632 and is primarily Gothic. Artistic highlights include a work by Rubens, Raymond Mason's colourful bas-relief of market vendors (1969) and Keith Haring's bronze triptych (1990) in the side chapels. (☎01 42 36 31 05; www.saint-eustache.org; 146 rue Rambuteau, 1er; ⏰9.30am-7pm Mon-Fri, 10am-7.15pm Sat, 9am-7.15pm Sun; Ⓜ Les Halles, RER Châtelet–Les Halles)

Jardin du Palais Royal GARDENS

4 ⊙ MAP P76, E4

The Jardin du Palais Royal is a perfect spot to sit, contemplate and picnic between boxed hedges, or to shop in the trio of beautiful arcades that frame the garden: the Galerie de Valois (east), Galerie de Montpensier (west) and Galerie Beaujolais (north). However, it's the southern end of the complex, polka-dotted with sculptor Daniel Buren's 260 black-and-white striped columns, that has become the garden's signature feature.

(www.domaine-palais-royal.fr; 2 place Colette, 1er; ⏲8am-10.30pm Apr-Sep, to 8.30pm Oct-Mar; MPalais Royal–Musée du Louvre)

Place de la Concorde SQUARE

5 ◉ MAP P76, A4

Paris spreads around you, with views of the Eiffel Tower, the Seine and along the Champs-Élysées, when you stand in the city's largest square. Its 3300-year-old pink granite obelisk was a gift from Egypt in 1831. The square was first laid out in 1755 and originally named after King Louis XV, but its royal associations meant that it took centre stage during the Revolution – Louis XVI was the first to be guillotined here in 1793. (8e; MConcorde)

Palais Garnier HISTORIC BUILDING

6 ◉ MAP P76, C1

The fabled 'phantom of the opera' lurked in this opulent opera house, designed in 1860 by Charles Garnier (then an unknown 35-year-old architect). Reserve a spot on a 90-minute English-language guided tour, or visit on your own (audioguides available; €5). Don't miss the Grand Staircase and gilded auditorium with red velvet seats, a massive chandelier and Marc Chagall's ceiling fresco. Also worth a peek is the museum, with posters, costumes, backdrops, original scores and other memorabilia. (☎08 92 89 90 90; www. operadeparis.fr; cnr rues Scribe & Auber, 9e; adult/child self-guided tours €14/10, guided tours €17/9.50;

Palais Garnier

Snacking on Rue Montorgueil

Rue Montorgueil was the oyster market of the erstwhile Les Halles. Immortalised by Balzac in *La Comédie humaine*, this vibrant strip is still lined with food shops.

Highlights include patisserie (cake shop) **Stohrer** (Map p76, G4; www.stohrer.fr; 51 rue Montorgueil, 2e; pastries €2.50-6; ⏱7.30am-8.30pm; MÉtienne Marcel, Sentier), which opened in 1730, with the pastel murals added in 1864 by Paul-Jacques-Aimé Baudry, who also decorated the Palais Garnier's Grand Foyer, and oyster restaurant **Au Rocher de Cancale** (Map p76, G4; ☏01 42 33 50 29; 78 rue Montorgueil, 2e; dozen oysters €20, seafood platter €30; ⏱8am-2am; MSentier, Les Halles, RER Châtelet–Les Halles).

⏱self-guided tours 10am-6pm mid-Jul–early Sep, to 4pm early Sep–mid-Jul, English-language guided tours 11am & 2.30pm; MOpéra)

Collection Pinault – Paris   MUSEUM

7 ⊙ MAP P76, F5

This much-anticipated art museum opened in 2021. It occupies the Bourse de Commerce, an 18th-century rotunda that once held the city's grain market and stock exchange. Japanese architect Tadao Ando designed the ambitious interior, where three floors of galleries will display contemporary works collected by François Pinault, who previously teamed up with Ando to open Venice's Palazzo Grassi and Punta della Dogana. Exhibitions will span varying scales and media, from painting, sculpture, photography and video to installations. (www.collectionpinaultparis.com; 2 rue de Viarmes, 1er; MLes Halles, RER Châtelet–Les Halles)

Forum des Halles   NOTABLE BUILDING

8 ⊙ MAP P76, G5

Paris' main wholesale food market stood here for nearly 800 years before being replaced by this underground shopping mall in 1971. Long considered an eyesore by many Parisians, the mall's exterior was finally demolished in 2011 to make way for its golden-hued translucent canopy, unveiled in 2016. Below, four floors of stores (125 in total), 23 restaurants, cafes and fast-food outlets, and entertainment venues including cinemas and a swimming pool, extend down to the city's busiest metro/RER hub. (www.forumdeshalles.com; 1 rue Pierre Lescot, 1er; ⏱shops 10am-8.30pm Mon-Sat, 11am-7pm Sun; MLes Halles, RER Châtelet–Les Halles)

Eating

Maison Maison   MEDITERRANEAN €€

9 MAP P76, F6

Halfway down the stairs by Pont Neuf is this wonderfully secret space beneath the *bouquinistes* (used-book sellers; p186), where you can watch the *bateaux-mouches* (river-cruise boats) float by as you dine on creations such as butternut squash and blue cheese *millefeuille* or smoked black mullet with radish dressing. In nice weather, don't miss a cocktail on the glorious riverside terrace. (☑09 67 82 07 32; www.facebook.com/maisonmaisonresto; 63 Parc Rives de Seine, 1er; 2-/3-course lunch menus €20/25, small plates €7-16; ☺kitchen noon-11.30pm Tue-Sat, to 6pm Sun, bar to 2am; Ⓜ Pont Neuf)

Cédric Grolet Opéra   PASTRIES €

10 ✖ MAP P76, D3

Executive pastry chef, wunderkind Cédric Grolet, opened his own *boulangerie-pâtisserie* (bakery-cake shop) in 2019. *Viennoiseries* (sweet baked goods) including *pains au chocolat* are sold from 8.30am to 11.30am, and filled still-warm baguettes (one vegetarian, one meat) from noon to 2pm. From 2.30pm to 6.30pm, order signature pastries, such as caramel-and-Tahitian-vanilla St-Honoré, to take away or dine upstairs in the herringbone-floored tearoom. (35 av de l'Opéra, 2e; pastries €4-17; ☺8.30am-7pm Mon-Sat; Ⓜ Opéra, Pyramides)

Richer   BISTRO €€

11 ✖ MAP P76, G1

Richer's pared-back, exposed-brick decor is a smart setting for genius creations including wild plaice cerviche with fennel purée and confit tomato jelly or lacquered pork with chorizo curry. It doesn't take reservations, but it serves snacks and Chinese tea, and has a full bar (open until midnight). It's run by the same team as **L'Office** (☑01 47 70 67 31; www.office-resto.com; 3 rue Richer, 9e; mains €22-30; ☺noon-2pm & 7-10.15pm Mon-Fri) across the street. (www.lericher.com; 2 rue Richer, 9e; mains €17-28; ☺noon-2.30pm & 7.30-10.30pm; Ⓜ Poissonnière, Bonne Nouvelle)

Frenchie   BISTRO €€€

12 ✖ MAP P76, G3

Tucked down an inconspicuous alley, this tiny bistro with wooden tables and old stone walls is always packed and for good reason: Gregory Marchand's modern, market-driven, unpretentious dishes, which have earned him a Michelin star. Only five-course *menus* (fixed-price meals) are available at dinner. Reserve well in advance. Alternatively, head to **Frenchie Bar à Vins** (www.frenchie-bav.com; 6 rue du Nil, 2e; small plates €11-34; ☺6.30-11pm) opposite. (☑01 40 39 96 19; www.frenchie-ruedunil.com; 5 rue du Nil, 2e; 3-/5-course menus €50/88; ☺6-10pm Mon-Wed, noon-2pm & 6-10pm Thu & Fri; Ⓜ Sentier)

Paris' Best Hot Chocolate

Dating from 1903, beautifully frescoed tearoom **Angelina** (Map p76, C4; 01 42 60 82 00; www.angelina-paris.fr; 226 rue de Rivoli, 1er; 7.30am-7pm Mon-Thu, to 7.30pm Fri, 8.30am-7.30pm Sat & Sun; Tuileries) serves decadent pastries, but it's the super-thick 'African' hot chocolate, which comes with a pot of whipped cream, that prompts the constant queue for a table.

Chez La Vieille FRENCH €€

13 MAP P76, F5

In salvaging this history-steeped spot within a 16th-century building, star chef Daniel Rose pays homage to the former wholesale markets, erstwhile legendary owner Adrienne Biasin (many of her timeless dishes have been updated, from terrines and rillettes to veal blanquette), and the soul of Parisian bistro cooking itself. Dine at the street-level bar or upstairs in the peacock-blue dining room. (01 42 60 15 78; www.chezlavieille. fr; 1 rue Bailleul, 1er; mains €26-39; noon-2pm & 6-10.30pm Tue-Sat, closed Aug; Louvre–Rivoli)

Le Grand Véfour GASTRONOMY €€€

14 MAP P76, E3

Holding two Michelin stars, this 18th-century jewel on the northern edge of the Jardin du Palais Royal has been a dining favourite since 1784; the names ascribed to each table span Napoléon and Victor Hugo to Colette (who lived next door). Expect a voyage of discovery from chef Guy Martin in one of the most beautiful restaurants in the world. (01 42 96 56 27; www. grand-vefour.com; 17 rue de Beaujolais, 1er; lunch/dinner menus €115/315, mains €99-128; noon-2.30pm & 7.30-10.30pm Mon-Fri; Pyramides)

La Tour de Montlhéry – Chez Denise FRENCH €€

15 MAP P76, F5

The most traditional eatery near the former Les Halles marketplace, this boisterous old half-timbered bistro with red-chequered tablecloths stays open until dawn and has been run by the same family since 1966. If you're ready to feast on all the French classics including snails in garlic sauce, veal liver, steak tartare, braised beef cheeks and house-made pâté. Reservations are in order. (01 42 36 21 82; 5 rue des Prouvaires, 1er; mains €23-28; noon-2.30pm & 7.30pm-5am Mon-Fri mid-Aug–mid-Jun; Les Halles, RER Châtelet–Les Halles)

Au Pied de Cochon BRASSERIE €€

16 MAP P76, F4

Enduring brasserie Au Pied de Cochon, with huge mirrors, crimson banquettes and frosted-glass lamps, opens around the clock, just as it did when workers at the former Les Halles wholesale markets started and ended their day here. Specialities include sensational crouton-filled onion soup topped with melted emmental cheese, pigs' trotters, tails, ears and snouts, and spectacular shellfish platters. (☎01 40 13 77 00; www.pieddecochon.com; 6 rue Coquillière, 1er; mains €19-41, seafood platters per person €30-80; ⏱24hr; 🛜; M Les Halles, RER Châtelet–Les Halles)

Drinking

Bar Hemingway   COCKTAIL BAR

17 🔵 MAP P76, C3

Black-and-white photos and memorabilia (hunting trophies, old typewriters and framed handwritten letters by the great writer) fill this snug bar inside the Ritz. Head bartender Colin Peter Field mixes monumental cocktails, including three different Bloody Marys made with juice from freshly squeezed seasonal tomatoes. Legend has it that Hemingway himself, wielding a machine gun, helped liberate the bar during WWII. (www.ritzparis.com; Hôtel Ritz Paris, 15 place Vendôme, 1er; ⏱6pm-2am; 🛜; M Opéra)

Scilicet   BAR

18 🔵 MAP P76, G6

An elongated stone archway houses this hidden riverside bar, with digital light displays projected on the ceiling, and DJs spinning from 8pm nightly in summer and regularly through the rest of the year. Its greatest asset, though, is its sprawling Seine-side terrace, with front-row views of quintessential Parisian landmarks like the turreted Conciergerie and Eiffel

Rue Montorgueil (p80)

Louvre, Tuileries & Opéra Drinking

Tower, spectacularly illuminated at night. (www.scilicet.fr; 134 voie Georges Pompidou, 1er; ⊗noon-2am daily Jun-Aug, 6pm-2am Wed-Fri, 4pm-2am Sat Sep-May; 🛜; 🅜Châtelet, RER Châtelet–Les Halles)

Baby Doll COCKTAIL BAR

19 🅟 MAP P76, C2

Paying homage to legendary Parisian musician Serge Gainsbourg (1928–91), this seductive bar has foliage-print carpets replicated from his 7e mansion, ruby-and-emerald velvet banquettes, pleated leather armchairs and a smooth soundtrack. Gainsbourg-inspired cocktails include Couleur Café (chocolate-infused tequila, mezcal and coriander) and Bloody & G, a reinvented Bloody Mary with caper- and horseradish-infused gin. (www.babydollparis.com; 16 rue de Daunou, 2e; ⊗6pm-2am Tue-Thu & Sun, to 5am Fri & Sat; 🛜; 🅜Opéra)

Experimental Cocktail Club COCKTAIL BAR

20 🅟 MAP P76, G4

Behind black curtains, this retro-chic speakeasy is a sophisticated flashback to those années folles (crazy years) of Prohibition New York. Cocktails are individual and fabulous, and DJs keep the party going until dawn at weekends. It's not a large space, however, and fills to capacity quickly. (ECC; www.experimentalcocktailclub.fr; 37 rue St-Sauveur, 2e; ⊗7pm-2am Mon-Thu, to 4am Fri & Sat, 8pm-2am Sun; 🅜Réaumur Sébastopol)

Harry's New York Bar COCKTAIL BAR

21 🅟 MAP P76, C2

One of the most popular American-style bars in the pre-war years, Harry's once welcomed writers including F Scott Fitzgerald and Ernest Hemingway, who no doubt sampled the bar's unique cocktail creation: the Bloody Mary. The Cuban mahogany interior dates from the mid-19th century and was brought over from a Manhattan bar in 1911. (📞01 42 61 71 14; www.facebook.com/harrysnewyorkbarparis; 5 rue Daunou, 2e; ⊗noon-2am Mon-Sat, 4pm-1am Sun; 🅜Opéra)

Matamata COFFEE

22 🅟 MAP P76, F4

Beans from France's best micro-roasteries are expertly brewed at this small, two-level space with tables and light fittings made from recycled timber and repurposed metal, and subtropical fern wall-paper. In summer, cool down with a cold-drip coffee over ice. (📞01 71 39 44 58; www.matamatacoffee.com; 58 rue d'Argout, 2e; ⊗8am-5pm Mon-Fri, from 9am Sat & Sun; 🛜; 🅜Sentier)

Le Tambour BAR

23 🅟 MAP P76, F4

Insomniacs head to local landmark 'the Drummer' for its rowdy, good-natured atmosphere and filling, inexpensive French fare (including legendary desserts such as its tarte Tatin – traditional

Rue des Lombards
Jazz Clubs

Rue des Lombards is the street to swing by for live jazz. **Le Baiser Salé** (Map p76, G6; 01 42 33 37 71; www.lebaisersale.com; 58 rue des Lombards, 1er; hours vary; Châtelet, RER Châtelet–Les Halles), meaning the Salty Kiss, is known for its Afro and Latin jazz, and jazz fusion concerts. You'll find two venues in one at well-respected **Sunset & Sunside** (Map p76, G6; 01 40 26 46 60; www.sunset-sunside.com; 60 rue des Lombards, 1er; hours vary; Châtelet, RER Châtelet–Les Halles): electric jazz, fusion and occasional salsa downstairs at Sunset; acoustics and concerts on the ground floor at Sunside. Founded in 1984, intimate, sophisticated jazz club **Duc des Lombards** (Map p76, G6; 01 42 33 22 88; www.ducdeslombards.com; 42 rue des Lombards, 1er; 7-11.30pm Mon-Thu, to 3.30am Fri & Sat; Châtelet, RER Châtelet–Les Halles) typically hosts two concerts per night and regular free jam sessions (you'll need to buy a drink).

upside-down caramelised-apple tart) served until 3am. But what makes this place truly magical is its salvaged decor, such as an old Stalingrad metro map and Parisian street furniture. (01 42 33 06 90; 41 rue Montmartre, 2e; 8.30am-5.30am; Étienne Marcel, Sentier)

Le Rex Club
CLUB

Attached to the art deco Grand Rex cinema (see 24 Map p76, G2), with a capacity 850 clubbers, this is Paris' premier house and techno venue where some of the world's hottest DJs strut their stuff on a 70-speaker, multidiffusion sound system. (01 42 36 10 96; www.rexclub.com; 5 bd Poissonnière, 2e; midnight-7am Thu-Sat; Bonne Nouvelle)

Entertainment

Palais Garnier
OPERA, BALLET

The city's original opera house (see 6 Map p76, C1) is smaller than its Bastille counterpart, but has perfect acoustics. Due to its odd shape, some seats have limited or no visibility – book carefully. Ticket prices and conditions (including last-minute discounts) are available from the **box office** (international calls 01 71 25 24 23, within France 08 92 89 90 90; www.operadeparis.fr; cnr rues Scribe & Auber; 10am-6.30pm Mon-Sat; Opéra). Online flash sales (*les rendez-vous du mercredi*) are held from noon on Wednesdays. (www.operadeparis.fr; place de l'Opéra, 9e; Opéra)

Place de la Madeleine

Ultragourmet food shops garland **place de la Madeleine** (Map p76, B2; place de la Madeleine, 8e; M Madeleine); many have in-house dining options. Notable names include truffle dealers **La Maison de la Truffe** (Map p76, A2; 01 42 65 53 22; www.maison-de-la-truffe.com; 19 place de la Madeleine; 10am-10.30pm Mon-Sat, closed mid-late Aug); mustard specialist **Boutique Maille** (Map p76, B2; www.maille.com; 6 place de la Madeleine; 10am-7pm Mon-Sat, 11am-6pm Sun); Paris' most famous caterer, **Fauchon** (Map p76, B2; 01 70 39 38 00; www.fauchon. com; 24 & 30 place de la Madeleine; 10am-8.30pm Mon-Sat), with mouth-watering delicacies from foie gras to jams, chocolates and pastries, plus a **grand cafe** (Map p76, A2; 01 87 86 28 23; www.grand-cafefauchon.fr; 11 place de la Madeleine; 2-/3-course lunch menus €45/55, 4-/5-course dinner menus €48/78; 7am-midnight;); and extravagant chocolate sculptures at **Patrick Roger** (Map p76, A2; 09 67 08 24 47; www.patrickroger.com; 3 place de la Madeleine; 10.30am-7.30pm). Nearby is **La Maison du Miel** (Map p76, B2; 01 47 42 26 70; www. maisondumiel.fr; 24 rue Vignon, 9e; 9.30am-7pm Mon-Sat; M Madeleine), in the honey business since 1898.

Le Grand Rex
CINEMA

24 ⭐ MAP P76, G2

Blockbuster screenings and concerts aside, this 1932 art deco cinematic icon runs 50-minute behind-the-scenes tours (English soundtracks available) during which visitors – tracked by a sensor slung around their neck – are whisked up (via a lift) behind the giant screen, tour a soundstage and experiment in a recording studio. Whiz-bang special effects along the way will stun adults and kids alike. (01 45 08 93 58; www. legrandrex.com; 1 bd Poissonnière, 2e; adult/child tours €11/9, cinema tickets €15/12; tours 10am-6pm Wed, Sat & Sun, extended hours during school holidays; M Bonne Nouvelle)

Forum des Images
CINEMA

A five-screen cinema showing films set in Paris is the centrepiece of the city's film archive. Created in 1988 to establish an audiovisual archive of the city, the complex (see 8 ◎ Map p76, G5) has a library and research centre with newsreels, documentaries and advertising. Its online program lists thematic series, festivals and events. (01 44 76 63 00; www.forumdesimages. fr; Forum des Halles, 2 rue du Cinéma, Porte St-Eustache, 1er; cinema tickets adult/child €6.50/4.50; 5-9pm Tue & Thu, from 1pm Wed, from 4pm Fri, from 10.30am Sat & Sun; Ⓜ Les Halles, RER Châtelet–Les Halles)

Comédie Française

THEATRE

25 ⭐ MAP P76, D4

Founded in 1680 under Louis XIV, this state-run theatre bases its repertoire on the works of classic French playwrights. The theatre has its roots in an earlier company directed by Molière at the Palais Royal. (www.comedie-francaise.fr; 1 place Colette, 1er; Ⓜ Palais Royal–Musée du Louvre)

Kiosque Théâtre Madeleine

BOOKING SERVICE

26 ⭐ MAP P76, B2

Pick up half-price tickets for same-day performances of ballet, opera and music at this freestanding kiosk. (www.kiosqueculture.com; opposite 15 place de la Madeleine, 8e; ⏱ 12.30-2.30pm & 3-7.30pm Tue-Sat, 12.30-3.45pm Sun; Ⓜ Madeleine)

Shopping

Galeries Lafayette

DEPARTMENT STORE

27 🅰 MAP P76, C1

Grande-dame department store Galeries Lafayette is spread across the main store (its magnificent neo-Byzantine stained-glass dome dates from 1912), its **men's store** (48 bd Haussmann), and **homewares store** (35 bd Haussmann) with **gourmet emporium** (35 bd Haussmann).

Catch modern art in the 1st-floor **gallery** (📞 01 42 82 87 98;

Place de la Madeleine

www.galeriedesgaleries.com; 40 bd Haussmann; admission free; ⏰11am-7pm Wed-Mon), take in a **fashion show** (40 bd Haussmann; adult/child €14/9; ⏰3pm Fri mid-Feb–mid-Dec by online reservation), ascend to a free, windswept rooftop panorama or take a break at one of its many restaurants and cafes. (☏01 42 82 34 56; http://haussmann.galeries lafayette.com; 40 bd Haussmann, 9e; ⏰9.30am-8.30pm Mon-Sat, 11am-8pm Sun; 🛜; Ⓜ Chaussée d'Antin, RER Auber)

L'Exception   DESIGN

28 🔒 MAP P76, G5

More than 400 different French designers come together under one roof at this light-filled concept store, which showcases rotating collections of men's and women's fashion along with accessories including lingerie and swimwear, shoes, eyewear, gloves, hats, scarves, belts, bags, watches and jewellery. It also sells design books, cosmetics, candles, vases and other gorgeous homewares, and has a small in-house coffee bar. (☏01 40 39 92 34; www.lexception. com; 24 rue Berger, 1er; ⏰11am-7pm Sun-Fri, to 8pm Sat; Ⓜ Les Halles, RER Châtelet–Les Halles)

Didier Ludot   VINTAGE

29 🔒 MAP P76, E4

In the rag trade since 1975, collector Didier Ludot sells the city's finest couture creations of yes-teryear, hosts exhibitions and has published a book portraying the evolution of the little black dress. (☏01 42 96 06 56; www.didierludot. fr; 20 & 24 Galerie de Montpensier, 1er; ⏰10.30am-7pm Mon-Sat; Ⓜ Palais Royal–Musée du Louvre)

La Samaritaine   DEPARTMENT STORE

30 🔒 MAP P76, F6

One of Paris' four big department stores, the 10-storey La Samaritaine has finally emerged from its much-contested and drawn-out 15-year, €700-million overhaul. Pritzker Prize–winning Japanese firm Sanaa has preserved much of the building's gorgeous art nouveau and art deco features, including the glass ceiling topping the central Hall Jourdain. (www.la samaritaine.com; 19 rue de la Monnaie, 1er; Ⓜ Pont Neuf)

Le Printemps   DEPARTMENT STORE

31 🔒 MAP P76, C1

Famous department store Le Printemps encompasses Le Printemps de la Mode, for women's fashion; Le Printemps de la Beauté et Maison, for beauty and home-wares, with a staggering display of perfume, cosmetics and accessories; Le Printemps de l'Homme, for men's fashion; and the gourmet emporium Le Printemps du Goût, with two floors dedicated to artisan French produce. (☏01 42 82 50 00; www.printempsfrance.com; 64 bd Haussmann, 9e; ⏰9.35am-8pm

Mon-Wed, Fri & Sat, 9.35am-8.45pm Thu, 11am-8pm Sun; 🛜; Ⓜ Havre Caumartin)

E Dehillerin
HOMEWARES

32 🔵 MAP P76, F4

Founded in 1820, this extraordinary two-level store – more like an old-fashioned warehouse than a shiny, chic boutique – carries an incredible selection of professional-quality *matériel de cuisine* (kitchenware). Poultry scissors, turbot poacher, professional copper cookware or an Eiffel Tower–shaped cake tin – it's all here. (📞 01 42 36 53 13; www.edehillerin.fr; 18-20 rue Coquillière, 1er; ⊙ 9am-12.30pm & 2-6pm Mon, 9am-7pm Tue-Fri, 9am-6pm Sat; Ⓜ Les Halles, RER Châtelet–Les Halles)

À la Mère de Famille
FOOD & DRINKS

33 🔵 MAP P76, F1

Founded in 1761, this is the original location of Paris' oldest *chocolatier* (chocolate maker). Its beautiful Belle Époque (beautiful era) façade (a listed historic monument) is as enchanting as the rainbow of sweets, caramels and chocolates inside. (📞 01 47 70 83 69; www.lameredefamille.com; 35 rue du Faubourg Montmartre, 9e; ⊙ 9.30am-8pm Mon-Sat, 10am-7.30pm Sun; Ⓜ Le Peletier)

Sézane
FASHION & ACCESSORIES

34 🔵 MAP P76, G2

Affordable French fashion label Sézane, founded by Parisian entrepreneur-designer Morgane Sézalory, has cult status in Paris. Its chic women's tops, trousers, skirts, dresses, knitwear, outerwear, handbags, shoes and homewares such as bed linen are all sustainably sourced, with many proceeds donated to Demain, its own children's charity. There's also an adjoining charity shop selling past collections. (www.sezane.com; 1 rue St-Fiacre, 2e; ⊙ 11am-8pm Tue-Sat, to 7pm Sun; Ⓜ Grands Boulevards)

Walking Tour 🥾

Seine-Side Romantic Meander

The world's most romantic city has no shortage of beguiling spots, but the Seine and its surrounds are Paris at its most seductive. On this walk you'll pass graceful gardens, palaces, intimate parks, a flower market and an enchanting bookshop. Descend the steps along the quays wherever possible to stroll along the water's edge.

Getting There

Tracing the course of Paris' lifeline river in several neighbourhoods including the Champs-Élysées area, Louvre and Les Halles, the Islands and the Latin Quarter.

Ⓜ Concorde/Quai de la Rapée

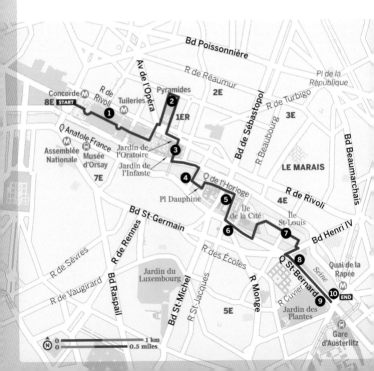

❶ Jardin des Tuileries

After taking in the panorama from place de la Concorde (p79), stroll through the **Jardin des Tuileries** (p78).

❷ Jardin du Palais Royal

Browse the arcades flanking the **Jardin du Palais Royal** (p78), adjoining the 17th-century palace where Louis XIV once lived.

❸ Cour Carrée

Walk through the Jardin de l'Oratoire to the Cour Carrée courtyard of the **Louvre** (p68) and exit at the Jardin de l'Infante (Garden of the Princess).

❹ Square du Vert-Galant

From **Pont Neuf** (p144), take the steps to the park at Île de la Cité's tip, Square du Vert-Galant, before ascending to place du Pont Neuf to cross place Dauphine.

❺ Marché aux Fleurs Reine Elizabeth II

For centuries Parisians have been buying bouquets at the **Marché aux Fleurs Reine Elizabeth II** (p149), renamed in 2014 in honour of Britain's Queen Elizabeth II. Choose carefully: tradition has it that chrysanthemums are only for cemeteries, carnations bring bad luck and yellow roses imply adultery.

❻ Shakespeare & Company

Amid handpainted quotations, make a wish in the wishing well, leave a message on the 'mirror of love' or curl up with a volume of poetry in the magical bookshop **Shakespeare & Company** (p168). Afterwards, break for a coffee or organic chai tea at the bookshop's adjacent cafe.

❼ Berthillon

Cross Pont de l'Archevêché to Île de la Cité, then take Pont St-Louis to Île St-Louis and share an ice cream from *glacier* (ice-cream maker) **Berthillon** (p146).

❽ Musée de la Sculpture en Plein Air

Along quai St-Bernard, wander among more than 50 late-20th-century unfenced sculptures by artists such as César and Brancusi at the **open-air sculpture museum** (p160).

❾ Jardin des Plantes

Prolong your romantic meander amid rose gardens, blossoming peonies and beautiful, vintage glass-and-steel greenhouses in the tranquil **Jardin des Plantes** (p159), founded in 1626 as a medicinal herb garden for Louis XIII.

❿ Romance Afloat

For the ultimate denouement, cruise back along the Seine by **Batobus** (p209) from quai St-Bernard.

Explore ⊗

Sacré-Cœur & Montmartre

Montmartre's steep, narrow lanes and ivy-clad buildings retain a fairy-tale charm despite its popularity. Crowned by the Sacré-Cœur basilica, Montmartre's lofty views, wine-producing vines and vibrant cafe life have lured artists since the 19th century. Heading downhill, Pigalle is a (tame) red-light district known for its inventive food and cocktail culture.

The Short List

○ **Basilique du Sacré-Cœur (p94)** *Hiking up high for panoramic city views.*

○ **Moulin Rouge (p104)** *Rousing the spirits with a night out at a traditional Parisian cabaret.*

○ **Marché aux Puces de St-Ouen (p106)** *Uncovering unexpected curiosities at Paris' biggest flea market.*

○ **Musée de Montmartre (p99)** *Time-travelling to Montmartre's bohemian past at this engaging museum.*

○ **Le Mur des je t'aime (p97)** *Learning how to say 'I love you' in numerous languages in a bijou park.*

Getting There & Around

Ⓜ Anvers (line 2) is the most convenient for Sacré-Cœur and its funicular.

Ⓜ Abbesses and Lamarck–Caulaincourt (line 12) are in Montmartre's heart.

Ⓜ Blanche and Pigalle (line 2) are best for Pigalle's restaurants and nightlife.

Neighbourhood Map on p98

Moulin Rouge (p104) MAXOZEROV/GETTY IMAGES ©

Top Experience 📷

Wonder at the Sacré-Cœur

More than just a place of worship, the distinctive dove-white domed Basilique du Sacré-Cœur (Sacred Heart Basilica) is a veritable experience. Reached by 270 steps, the parvis (forecourt) in front of the basilica provides a postcard-perfect city panorama. Buskers and street artists perform on the steps, while picnickers spread out on the hillside park.

◎ MAP P98, D2

www.sacre-coeur-montmartre.com

Parvis du Sacré-Cœur, 18e

basilica free, dome adult/child €7/4

🕐 basilica 6am-10.30pm, dome 8.30am-8pm May-Sep, 9am-5pm Oct-Apr

Ⓜ Anvers, Abbesses

History

Initiated in 1873 to atone for the bloodshed and controversy during the Franco-Prussian War (1870–71) and begun in 1875, the Roman-Byzantine basilica designed by architect Paul Abadie was funded largely by private, often small, donations. It was completed in 1914 but wasn't consecrated until after WWI in 1919.

In 1944, 13 Allied bombs were dropped on Montmartre. Although Sacré-Cœur's stained-glass windows were shattered, miraculously no one died and the basilica sustained no other damage.

Blessed Sacrament

In a sense, atonement here has never stopped: a prayer 'cycle' that began in 1835 continues around the clock, with perpetual adoration of the Blessed Sacrament that's on display above the high altar. Pilgrims can stay overnight in the basilica's guesthouse.

The Dome

Outside, west of the main entrance, 300 spiralling steps lead you to the basilica's dome and one of Paris' most spectacular panoramas; it's said you can see for 30km on a clear day.

France's Largest Bell

La Savoyarde, in the basilica's huge square bell tower, is the largest bell in France, weighing in at 19 tonnes. It can be heard ringing out across the neighbourhood and beyond.

The Christ in Majesty Mosaic

The magnificent apse mosaic *Christ in Majesty*, designed by Luc-Olivier Merson in 1922, is one of the largest of its kind in the world. Its golden hues lighten Sacré-Cœur's otherwise dark interior.

★ Top Tips

o Skip most of the climb up to the basilica with the short but useful **Funicular de Montmartre** (www.ratp.fr; place St-Pierre, 18e; 6am-12.45am; M Anvers or Abbesses); use a metro ticket.

o For the best views, pick a blue-sky day to visit; avoid the dome climb in bad weather.

o Download a free audioguide online.

✗ Take a Break

On fine days head to **L'Été en Pente Douce** (01 42 64 02 67; http://lete-en-pente-douce.business.site; 8 rue Paul Albert, 18e; mains €10.70-18.50; noon-midnight; M Château Rouge) for French fare on a terrace with pretty green-lawn view.

Enjoy expertly brewed coffee or brunch at **Hardware Société** (01 42 51 69 03; 10 rue Lamarck, 18e; 9.30am-3.30pm Thu, Fri & Mon, to 4pm Sat & Sun; M Château Rouge).

Walking Tour 🚶

Art in Montmartre

For centuries Montmartre was a bucolic country village filled with moulins (mills) that supplied Paris with flour. Incorporated into the capital in 1860, its picturesque – and affordable – charm attracted painters Manet, Degas, Renoir, Van Gogh, Toulouse-Lautrec, Dufy, Picasso, Utrillo, Modigliani and Dalí in its late 19th- and early 20th-century heyday. Much frequented by tourists today, its local village atmosphere endures.

Walk Facts

Start Café des Deux Moulins; Ⓜ Blanche

Finish Sq Jehan Rictus; Ⓜ Abbesses

Length 1.65km; 1.5 hours

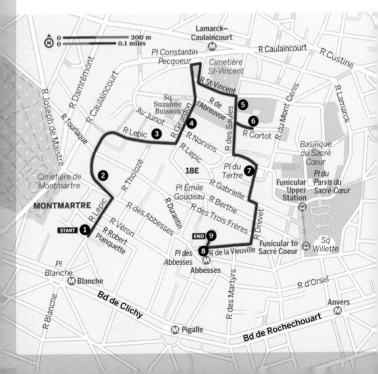

❶ Amélie's Cafe

Start with a coffee at **Café des Deux Moulins** (www.cafedesdeux moulins.fr; 15 rue Lepic; ⏱7.30am–2am Mon-Fri, from 8am Sat & Sun; 📶; Ⓜ Blanche), the cafe where Amélie worked as a waitress in the film of the same name.

❷ Van Gogh's House

Vincent Van Gogh stayed at his brother Théo's house at **54 rue Lepic** for two years from 1886.

❸ Renoir's Dance Hall

Montmartre's surviving windmills are the **Moulin Radet** (83 rue Lepic; Ⓜ Abbesses), now a restaurant, and the **Moulin Blute Fin** (rue Lepic; Ⓜ Abbesses) which, in the 19th century, hosted the open-air dance hall Le Moulin de la Galette. In 1876 Renoir immortalised it in his painting *Le Bal du Moulin de la Galette*, now at the Musée d'Orsay.

❹ Aymé's Wall Walker

Crossing place Marcel Aymé, spot a man emerging from a stone wall. The **Passe-Muraille statue** (place Marcel Aymé; Ⓜ Abbesses) portrays Dutilleul, the hero of Marcel Aymé's short story *Le Passe-Muraille* (The Walker Through Walls). Rub the statue's left hand to ensure good luck.

❺ Montmartre's Vineyard

Paris' most celebrated vineyard **Clos Montmartre** (18 rue des Saules; Ⓜ Lamarck–Caulaincourt),

from 1933, produces an average 800 bottles of wine each October, celebrated by the five-day Fête des Vendanges de Montmartre.

❻ History in Art

Local history comes to life through art at the **Musée de Montmartre** (p99), a 17th-century garden-set manor where Renoir, Utrillo and Dufy once lived, and Suzanne Valadon had her studio.

❼ Artists at Work

Portraitists, buskers and crowds create an unmissable carnival-like atmosphere on **place du Tertre** (Ⓜ Abbesses), the main square of the original village. Local artists paint and sell their work here.

❽ The Art of Travel

With its original glass canopy, wrought-iron lamps and green-on-yellow 'Metropolitain' sign still intact, **Abbesses** (places des Abbesses) is the finest remaining art nouveau metro entrance by Hector Guimard.

❾ Je t'aime!

On the same square, duck into the tiny gated park to admire the **'I Love You' wall** (www.lesjetaime.com; Sq Jehan Rictus, place des Abbesses; ⏱8am-9.30pm Mon-Fri, from 9am Sat & Sun mid-May–Aug, shorter hours Sep–mid-May; Ⓜ Abbesses) mural by artists Frédéric Baron and Claire Kito. Its 511 blue enamel tiles feature the phrase 'I love you' 311 times in 250 languages.

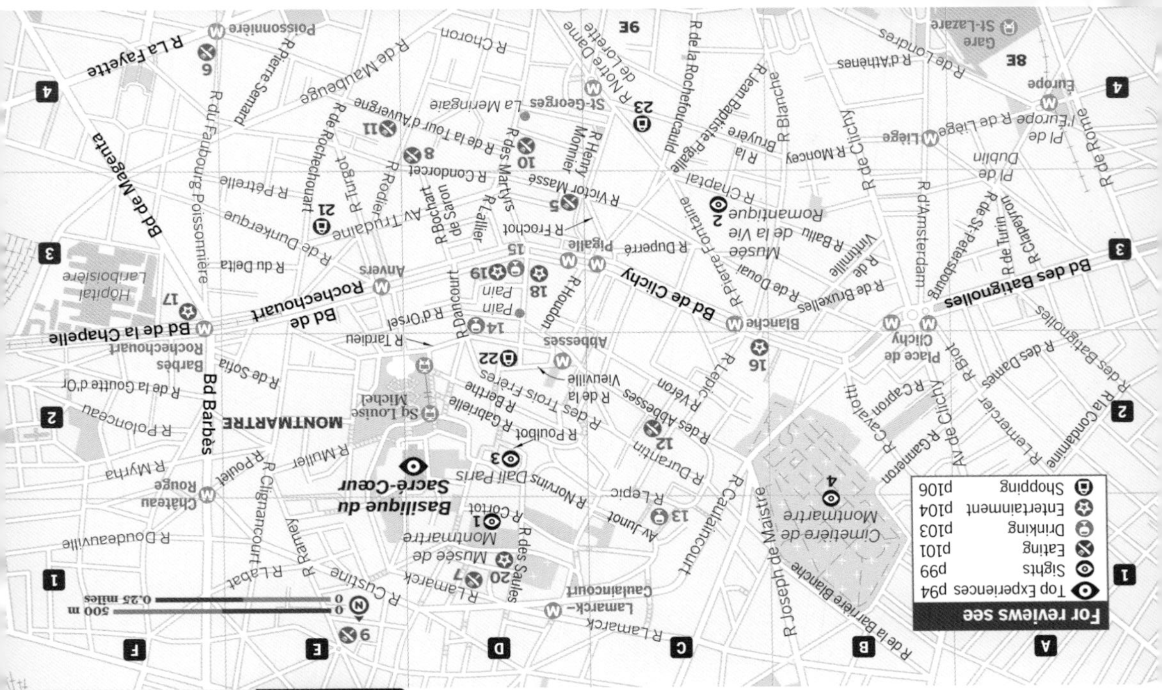
For reviews see
Top Experiences p94
Sights p99
Eating p101
Drinking p103
Entertainment p104
Shopping p106
Basilique du Sacré-Cœur
MONTMARTRE
Musée de Montmartre
Cimetière de Montmartre
Musée de la Vie Romantique
Sq Louise Michel
Hôpital Lariboisière
Gare St-Lazare
Place de Clichy
Bd de Clichy
Bd de Rochechouart
Bd de la Chapelle
Bd de Magenta
Bd des Batignolles
Bd Barbès
R La Fayette
R du Faubourg Poissonnière
R Lamarck
R Custine
R Ramey
R Labat
R Doudeauville
R Myrha
R Polonceau
R de la Goutte d'Or
R Clignancourt
R Poulet
R Muller
R de Sofia
R Caulaincourt
R Joseph de Maistre
R de la Barrière Blanche
R des Saules
R Cortot
R Norvins
Dalí Paris
R Poulbot
R Gabrielle
R Berthe
R des Trois Frères
R de la Vieuville
R des Abbesses
R Véron
R Lepic
R Durantin
Av Junot
R Tardieu
R d'Orsel
R Dancourt
R Houdon
R Frochot
R Victor Massé
R Henry Monnier
R des Martyrs
R Lallier
R Bochart de Saron
R Condorcet
R de la Tour d'Auvergne
La Meringaie
R Rodier
Av Trudaine
R Turgot
R de Rochechouart
R de Dunkerque
R du Delta
R Pétrelle
R Pierre Semard
R de Maubeuge
R Choron
R Notre Dame de Lorette
R de la Rochefoucauld
R Jean Baptiste Pigalle
R Chaptal
R Pierre Fontaine
R Duperré
R de Douai
R de Bruxelles
R de Vintimille
R Ballu
R la Bruyère
R Blanche
R Moncey
R de Clichy
R d'Amsterdam
R de St-Pétersbourg
R de Turin
R Clapeyron
Pl de Dublin
Pl de l'Europe
R de Liège
R de Rome
R d'Athènes
R de Londres
R des Batignolles
R des Dames
R la Condamine
R Lemercier
R Biot
Av de Clichy
R Ganneron
R Capron
R Cavalotti
Pain Pain
Lamarck–Caulaincourt
Château Rouge
Barbès Rochechouart
Anvers
Abbesses
Pigalle
Blanche
St-Georges
Poissonnière
Liège
Europe
9E
8E
500 m
0.25 miles
A
B
C
D
E
F
1
2
3
4

Sights

Musée de Montmartre   MUSEUM

1 〇 MAP P98, D1

This delightful 'village' museum showcases paintings, lithographs and documents illustrating Montmartre's bohemian, artistic and hedonistic past – one room is dedicated entirely to the French cancan. It's housed in a 17th-century manor where several artists, including Renoir and Raoul Dufy, had their studios in the 19th century. You can also visit the studio of painter Suzanne Valadon, who lived and worked here with her son Maurice Utrillo and partner André Utter between 1912 and 1926. (📞 01 49 25 89 39; www.museedemontmartre.fr; 12 rue Cortot, 18e; adult/child €12/6, garden only €5; 🕑 10am-7pm Fri-Wed, to 10pm Thu Jul & Aug, 10am-7pm Apr-Sep, to 6pm Oct-Mar; M Lamarck–Caulaincourt)

Musée de la Vie Romantique   MUSEUM

2 〇 MAP P98, C3

Framed by green shutters, this mansion where painter Ary Scheffer once lived sits in a cobbled courtyard at the end of a tree-shaded alley. The objects exhibited create a wonderful flashback to Romantic-era Paris, when George Sand (Amantine Lucile Aurore Dupin), Chopin (Sand's lover), Delacroix et al attended salons here. Temporary exhibitions command an admission fee (adult/reduced €9/7). End with tea and cake in the

Sacré-Cœur & Montmartre Sights

Musée de Montmartre grounds

museum cafe's enchanting summer garden. (📞01 55 31 95 67; www.vie-romantique.paris.fr; 16 rue Chaptal, 9e; admission free; ⏱10am-6pm Tue-Sun; Ⓜ Blanche, St-Georges)

Dalí Paris
GALLERY

3 ◉ MAP P98, D2

More than 300 works by Salvador Dalí (1904–89), the flamboyant Catalan surrealist printmaker, painter and sculptor, are on display at this basement museum located west of place du Tertre. The private collection includes Dalí's strange sculptures, lithographs, many illustrations and furniture, including the famous *Mae West Lips Sofa*. (📞01 42 64 40 10; www.daliparis.com; 11 rue Poulbot, 18e; adult/child €12/9; ⏱10am-8.30pm Jul & Aug, to 6.30pm Sep-Jun; Ⓜ Abbesses)

Cimetière de Montmartre
CEMETERY

4 ◉ MAP P98, B1

This 11-hectare cemetery opened in 1825. It contains the graves of writers Émile Zola (whose ashes are now in the Panthéon), Alexandre Dumas *fils* and Stendhal; composers Jacques Offenbach and Hector Berlioz; artists Edgar Degas and Gustave Moreau; film director François Truffaut and dancer Vaslav Nijinsky, among others. (www.paris.fr/equipements/cimetiere-de-montmartre-5061; 20 av Rachel, 18e; admission free; ⏱8am-6pm Mon-Fri, to 6.30pm Sat, 9am-6pm Sun mid-Mar–Oct, 8am-5.30pm Mon-Sat, 9am-5.30pm Sun Nov–mid-Mar; Ⓜ Place de Clichy)

Belle Époque Paris

The Belle Époque (beautiful era) saw creativity flourish from the advent of France's Third Republic in 1870. This 'beautiful era' launched art nouveau architecture, a whole field of artistic 'isms' from impressionism onwards, and advances in science and engineering, including the first metro line (1900). World Exhibitions were held in the capital in 1889 (showcased by the Eiffel Tower) and again in 1900 (as demonstrated by the Grand Palais and Petit Palais).

The Paris of nightclubs and artistic cafes first made its appearance around this time, and Montmartre became a magnet for artists, writers, pimps and prostitutes, with artists such as Henri de Toulouse-Lautrec creating cabaret posters of the Moulin Rouge's cancan dancers. Other glamorous hot spots still operating include the restaurant Maxim's and the Ritz Paris. The Musée d'Orsay contains a wealth of artistic expression from this era.

This inspired time lasted until the onset of WWI in 1914 – it was named in retrospect, recalling a peaceful 'golden age'.

Along the Rue des Martyrs

Stretching 960m from the 18e (Ⓜ Abbesses) to the 9e (Ⓜ Notre Dame de Lorette), sloping rue des Martyrs is a foodie's fantasyland, lined with gourmet shops (cheese, tea, wine, jam and more), award-winning *boulangeries* (bakeries), such as **Pain Pain** (Map p98, D3; ☏ 01 42 23 62 81; www.pain-pain.fr; 88 rue des Martyrs, 18e; sandwiches & pastries €1.20-4.90; ⏱ 7am-8pm Tue-Sat, 7.30am-7.30pm Sun; Ⓜ Abbesses), and patisseries (cake shops), including specialists such as **La Meringaie** (Map p98, D4; ☏ 01 42 45 62 87; www.lameringaie.com; 35 rue des Martyrs, 9e; ⏱ 10am-8pm Mon-Fri, 9am-7pm Sat), solely devoted to lighter-than-air meringues smothered in seasonal fresh fruit and lashings of exquisitely piped flavoured cream (almond, pistachio, chestnut or hibiscus, perhaps).

Interspersed between them are a mix of traditional Parisian cafes and bistros, and eateries cooking up fare from other parts of the globe. Down the southern end, grocers, fishmongers and butchers set up pavement stalls.

Eating

Django FRENCH €€

5 ⊗ MAP P98, D3

What was a corner shop selling guitars in trendy Pigalle has morphed into a stylish *bar à manger* (dining bar) where fashionistas hobnob until the wee hours over craft cocktails, natural wines and inventive shared plates by chef Khelil Morin. Offerings might include leeks in fig vinaigrette with tangy 12-month-aged Comté, shrimp ravioli or roast cauliflower with piquillo pepper and caraway 'ketchup'. (☏ 01 74 64 64 84; www.django-pigalle.fr; 24, rue Victor Massé, 9e; 2-/3-course lunch menus €16/19, shared plates €6-9; ⏱ noon-2pm & 7pm-2am Tue-Fri, 7pm-2am Sat; Ⓜ Pigalle)

Abri BISTRO €€

6 ⊗ MAP P98, F4

It's no bigger than a shoebox and the decor is borderline nonexistent, but that's all part of the charm. Katsuaki Okiyama is a seriously talented chef with an artistic flair, and his surprise tasting menus (three courses at lunch, six at dinner) are exceptional. On Saturdays, a giant gourmet sandwich (€14) is all that's served for lunch. Reserve months in advance. (☏ 01 83 97 00 00; 92 rue du Faubourg Poissonnière, 9e; lunch/dinner menus €30/60; ⏱ 12.30-2pm Mon, 12.30-2pm & 7.30-10pm Tue-Fri, 12.30-3pm & 7.30-10pm Sat; Ⓜ Poissonnière)

Alix et Mika

FRENCH €

7 ⊗ MAP P98, D1

'French cut lovers' is the strapline of this corner bistro specialising in hand-cut tartare, served with fantastic duck-fat-cooked fries and boutique French cheeses to follow. The tartare menu is pick-and-mix style, offering a tantalising choice of organic meats (beef, veal) and fish (salmon, tuna, white fish) prepared a dozen different ways: French, Italian, Mexican etc. (☎01 73 71 19 90; www.alixetmika.com; 37 rue Lamarck, 18e; tartares €6-10, sides €4-5; ⏰7-10.30pm Wed-Fri, noon-3pm & 7-10.30pm Sat & Sun; Ⓜ Lamarck-Caulaincourt)

Mamiche

BAKERY €

8 ⊗ MAP P98, D4

Take one bite into a cinnamon roll, apricot crostata or signature *babka* (orange-blossom and chocolate brioche) at this new-generation *boulangerie* (bakery) and you'll be hooked. Young entrepreneurs Cécile Khayat and Victoria Effantin quit their day jobs to open this neighbourhood bakery and their artisan *pains* (breads) and pastries are now the hottest thing here since sliced bread. (☎01 53 21 03 68; www.mamiche.fr; 45 rue Condorcet, 9e; pastries €2-5; ⏰8am-8pm Tue-Fri, to 7pm Sat; Ⓜ Anvers)

Abattoir Végétal

VEGAN €

9 ⊗ MAP P98, E1

Mint-green wrought-iron chairs and tables line the pavement out-side the 'plant slaughterhouse' (it occupies a former butcher shop), while the light, bright interior has bare-bulb downlights, distempered walls and greenery-filled hang-ing baskets. Cold-pressed juices, 'wellness lattes', a delicious ginger pear cider and other artisan drinks accompany creative vegan dishes, and a 100% *végétalien* brunch (€27) is served at weekends. (www.abattoirvegetal.fr; 61 rue Ramey, 18e; 2-/3-course lunch menus €17/20, mains €15.50-17; ⏰6-10.30pm Tue-Fri, 11am-10.30pm Sat, 11am-3.30pm Sun; 🛜 🐾; Ⓜ Jules Joffrin)

Belle Maison

SEAFOOD €€

10 ⊗ MAP P98, D4

With hip blue-and-white-tiled decor in happening SoPi (south Pigalle), Belle Maison is always busy. It's named after a small beach on Île d'Yeu, off France's Atlantic coast, where the owners holiday. Here, the kitchen cooks up scallops, oysters, cockles and other shellfish aplenty. Sophisticated mains include Earl Grey–marinated mullet and grilled mackerel with crispy wasabi root and miso caramel. (☎01 42 81 11 00; 4 rue de Navarin, 9e; mains €22-23; ⏰12.30-2pm & 7.30-10pm Tue-Sat; Ⓜ St-Georges)

Aspic

BISTRO €€€

11 ⊗ MAP P98, E4

Chef Quentin Giroud ditched the high-flying world of finance for the stoves, and this small, vintage-style space with semi-open kitchen is testament to his conviction. No-choice tasting menus that change weekly feature inspired creations like peppercorn pancetta with kaffir-lime butter, warm octopus with cashew purée, skin-on plaice with popcorn capers, and celeriac with mustard shoots and grated raw cauliflower. (📞09 82 49 30 98; www.aspic-restaurant. fr; 24 rue de la Tour d'Auvergne, 9e; 7-course tasting menus €69, with wine €100; ⏱7.30-10.30pm Tue-Sat; 🛜; Ⓜ Anvers)

La Mascotte
SEAFOOD €€

12 ❌ MAP P98, C2

Founded in 1889, this neighbourhood bar with romantic sage-green-and-white-striped awnings is an enchanting spot on Montmartre's main street for gorging on seafood with locals. Grab a seat at the bar or on the buzzing pavement terrace and indulge in a glass of wine, freshly shucked Breton oysters (€15.60 to €24.50 per half-dozen) and flaming crêpe Suzette doused in Grand Marnier. (📞01 46 06 28 15; www.la-mascotte-montmartre.com; 52 rue des Abbesses, 18e; mains €25-45; ⏱noon-11.30pm; Ⓜ Abbesses)

Drinking

Le Très Particulier
COCKTAIL BAR

13 🍸 MAP P98, C1

The clandestine cocktail bar of boutique Hôtel Particulier Montmartre is an entrancing spot for a summertime alfresco cocktail.

Abbesses metro station entrance (p97)

Each cocktail (€10 to €16) is inspired by a film and comes with tasting notes. Ring the buzzer at the unmarked black gated entrance and make a beeline for the 1871 mansion's flowery walled garden, or, if it's raining, to the lavish conservatory-style interior. (📞01 53 41 81 40; www.hotel-particulier-montmartre.com; 23 av Junot, 18e; ⏰6pm-2am Tue-Sat; Ⓜ Lamarck–Caulaincourt)

Le Progrès
BAR

14 🍴 MAP P98, D3

A real live *café du quartier* (neighbourhood cafe) perched in the heart of Abbesses, the Progress occupies a corner site with huge windows that attracts a relaxed mix of local artists, writers and more. It's great for convivial evenings, but it's also a good place to come for Auvergne specialities or coffee. (7 rue des Trois Frères, 18e; ⏰9am-2am; Ⓜ Abbesses)

La Fourmi
BAR

15 🍴 MAP P98, D3

A Pigalle institution, sociable La Fourmi hits the mark with its high ceilings, long zinc bar, timber-panelled walls and unpretentious vibe. It's a great place to find out about live music and club nights or grab a drink before heading out to a show. Bonus: table football. (📞01 42 64 70 35; 74 rue des Martyrs, 18e; ⏰8am-2am Mon-Thu, to 4am Fri 9am-4am Sat, 10am-2am Sun; Ⓜ Pigalle)

La Machine du Moulin Rouge
CLUB

Part of the original Moulin Rouge (well, the boiler room, anyway; see 16 ⭐ Map p98, C2), this club packs 'em in on weekends with a dance floor, concert hall, the Bar à Bulles (aka Champagne bar) serving weekend brunch (€24), an outdoor terrace and rooftop. Admission is €9 to €16. (📞01 53 41 88 89; www.lamachinedumoulinrouge.com; 90 bd de Clichy, 18e; ⏰club midnight-6am Fri & Sat, bar 6pm-midnight Wed & Thu, 6pm-2am Fri, noon-2am Sat, noon-4pm Sun; Ⓜ Blanche)

Entertainment

Moulin Rouge
CABARET

16 ⭐ MAP P98, C2

Immortalised in Toulouse-Lautrec's posters and later in Baz Luhrmann's film, Paris' legendary cabaret twinkles beneath a 1925 replica of its original red windmill. Yes, it's packed with bus-tour crowds, but from the opening bars of music to the last high cancan kick, it's a whirl of fantastical costumes, sets, choreography and Champagne. Book in advance and dress smartly – no trainers/sneakers. (📞01 53 09 82 82; www.moulinrouge.fr; 82 bd de Clichy, 18e; show only from €88, dinner & show from €190; ⏰show only 9pm & 11pm, dinner & show 7pm; Ⓜ Blanche)

Le Louxor
CINEMA

17 ⭐ MAP P98, F3

Built in neo-Egyptian art deco style in 1921 and saved from demolition

SoPi Cocktails

There is no finer street in the whole of Paris to kick off a cocktail-bar crawl than rue Frochot in south Pigalle (SoPi) where a line-up of dolled-up former girlie bars seduce cocktail lovers: **Lipstick** (www. facebook.com/lipstickbar; 5 rue Frochot, 9e; ⏰6pm-5am Tue-Sat; Ⓜ Pigalle) with its bordello-style decor; Prohibition-era New Orleans–styled **Lulu White** (www.luluwhite.bar; 12 rue Frochot, 9e; ⏰7pm-2am Mon, Wed, Thu & Sun, to 4am Fri & Sat; Ⓜ Pigalle); and tiki bar **Dirty Dick** (☎01 48 78 74 58; www.facebook.com/dirtydickparis; 10 rue Frochot, 9e; ⏰6pm-2am; Ⓜ Pigalle). For a change from the cocktail norm or quick bite Berliner-style, duck into **Berliner Pigalle** (www.berliner.paris; 14 rue Frochot, 9e; ⏰6pm-2am Mon-Sat; Ⓜ Pigalle), a German beer bar with a feisty *currywurst* (hot dog with curry sauce) alongside other lavishly-topped dogs. If craft cocktails and paired shared plates in a sophisticated *bar à manger* (dining bar) is more your cup of tea, book a table at nearby Django (p101).

by a neighbourhood association seven decades later, this historical monument is a palatial place to catch new releases, classics, piano-accompanied 'ciné-concerts', short-film festivals, special workshops (such as singalongs) or live-music performances. Don't miss a drink at its bar, which opens onto an elevated terrace overlooking Sacré-Cœur. (☎01 44 63 96 98; www. cinemalouxor.fr; 170 bd de Magenta, 10e; tickets adult/child €9.90/5; Ⓜ Barbès Rochechouart)

Le Divan du Monde & Chez Madame Arthur LIVE MUSIC

18 ⭐ MAP P98, D3

Very much an iconic, crosscultural address at the foot of Montmartre, this hybrid cabaret-club has played host to cabaret troupe Madame Arthur since 1946. The first show is at 8pm, and the dance floor thrives with clubbers from midnight. Soirées are themed around a music genre, band or artist: 100% *musique française*, Britney Spears, 1980s French pop group Les Rita Mitsouko, Françoise Hardy etc. (☎01 40 05 08 10; www.divandumonde.com; 75 rue des Martyrs, 18e; cabaret before 10pm €20, club from midnight Fri & Sat/Wed & Thu €15/free; ⏰8pm-6am Wed-Sat; Ⓜ Pigalle)

La Cigale LIVE MUSIC

19 ⭐ MAP P98, D3

Now classed as a historical monument, this music hall dates from 1887 but was redecorated a century later by Philippe Starck. Artists who have performed here include Ryan Adams, Ibrahim Maalouf and the Dandy Warhols. (☎01 49 25 89

Flea Markets of Paris

Spanning 9 hectares, the vast flea market **Marché aux Puces de St-Ouen** ([phone] guided tours 01 55 87 67 50; www.marcheauxpuces-saintouen.com; rue des Rosiers, St-Ouen; individual hours vary; [hours] Sat-Mon; [M] Porte de Clignancourt) was founded in 1870 and is said to be Europe's largest. Over 2000 stalls are grouped into 15 *marchés* (markets) selling everything from 17th-century furniture to 21st-century clothing. Each market has different opening hours – check the website for details. There are miles upon miles of 'freelance' stalls; come prepared to spend some time. Dining options here include the legendary **Chez Louisette** ([phone] 01 40 12 10 14; Marché Vernaison, allée 10, 136 av Michelet, St-Ouen, Marché aux Puces de St-Ouen; mains €14.50-20; [hours] 11am-6pm Sat-Mon; [M] Porte de Clignancourt), where singers perform rousing *chansons* (French songs).

Nearby, an abandoned station of the Petite Ceinture (the steam-train line that once encircled Paris) has been repurposed as **La REcyclerie** ([phone] 01 42 57 58 49; www.larecyclerie.com; 83 bd Ornano, 18e; [hours] 8am-midnight Mon-Thu, to 2am Fri & Sat, to 10pm Sun early Jan–mid-Dec; [M] Porte de Clignancourt), an eco-hub with an urban farm along the old railway line, featuring community vegetable and herb gardens and chickens, a mostly vegetarian cafe-canteen, workshops and events, including its own flea markets.

99; www.lacigale.fr; 120 bd de Roche-chouart, 18e; [M] Pigalle)

Au Lapin Agile
CABARET

20 ⭐ MAP P98, D1

Named after *Le Lapin à Gill*, a mural of a rabbit jumping out of a cooking pot by caricaturist André Gill, which can still be seen on the western exterior wall, this rustic cabaret venue was favoured by artists and intellectuals in the early 20th century and traditional *chansons* (French songs) are still performed here. The evening-long show includes singing and poetry. ([phone] 01 46 06 85 87; www.au-lapin-agile.

com; 22 rue des Saules, 18e; adult €28, student except Sat €20; [hours] 9pm-1am Tue-Sun; [M] Lamarck–Caulaincourt)

Shopping

Balades Sonores
MUSIC

21 🔒 MAP P98, E3

One of Paris' best vinyl shops, Balades Sonores sprawls over two adjacent buildings. The ground floor of 1 av Trudaine stocks contemporary pop, rock, metal, garage and French music (all genres). Its basement holds secondhand blues, country, new wave and punk from the '60s to '90s. Next door,

No 3 has soul, jazz, funk, hip hop, electronica and world music. (📞01 83 87 94 87; www.baladessonores.com; 1-3 av Trudaine, 9e; 🕐noon-8pm Mon-Sat; M Anvers)

Spree
FASHION & ACCESSORIES

22 🔒 MAP P98, D2

Allow plenty of time to browse this super-stylish boutique-gallery, with a carefully selected collection of designer fashion put together by stylist Roberta Oprandi and artist Bruni Hadjadj. What makes shopping here fun is that all the furniture – vintage 1950s to 1980s pieces by Eames and other midcentury designers – is also for sale, as is the contemporary artwork on the walls. (www.spree.fr; 16 rue de la Vieuville, 18e; 🕐11am-7.30pm Tue-Sat, 3-7pm Sun; M Abbesses)

La Seinographe et Atelier Mouti
CONCEPT STORE

23 🔒 MAP P98, C4

Bringing together the carefully curated 'Made in France' homewares of lifestyle-blog-turned-boutique La Seinographe and the exquisite paper creations of Atelier Mouti, this stylish boutique is a wonderful spot for gift shopping, with fanciful paper products and textiles, jewellery and other homewares, all crafted in Paris or France. (www.shop.la-seinographe.fr; 41 Rue Notre Dame de Lorette, 9e; 🕐11am-7.30pm Tue-Sat; M St-Georges)

Walking Tour 🚶

Exploring Canal St-Martin & the 10e

Bordered by shaded towpaths and crossed with vintage iron footbridges, the Canal St-Martin legs it from the Seine to Paris' northeastern suburbs. Mooch the on-trend cafes, artsy boutiques and hip bars here, in the edgy 10e, to understand why Parisian creatives and bobos (bourgeois bohemians) love this reinvented 'hood so much.

Getting There

The tranquil, 4.5km-long Canal St-Martin is about 4km north of Notre Dame.

Ⓜ République (lines 3, 5, 8, 9, 11) is centrally located. Château d'Eau, Jacques Bonsergent & Gare de l'Est are also useful stations.

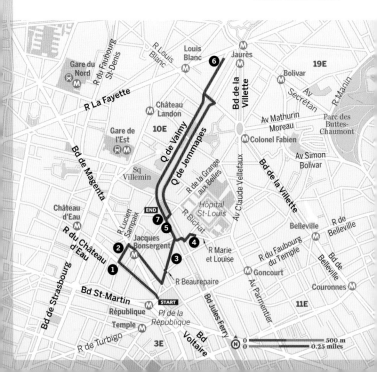

❶ Too Cool for Skool

Get in the right mindset with a chill strut along rue du Château d'Eau, abuzz these days with trendy pop-up design stores, sustainable ecoconscious bistros and edgy concept stores such as white-on-white concept store **O/HP/E** (📞 01 42 41 58 16; www.facebook.com/ohpeparis10; 27 rue du Château d'Eau, 10e; ⏰ 2-7pm Tue, 8.30am-7pm Wed & Thu, to 7.30pm Fri, 9.30am-7.30pm Sat, 9.30am-5.30pm Sun; Ⓜ Jacques Bonsergent) selling chic homewares, cosmetics, stationery, gifts and gourmet delicacies.

❷ Coffee, Eggs & Pancakes

Outstandingly friendly vibes, sassy breakfast 'n lunch dishes and specialist coffee is the USP of **Holybelly** (www.holybellycafe.com; 5 & 19 rue Lucien Sampaix, 10e; dishes €3.50-13.50; ⏰ 9am-5pm; 📶 🍴; Ⓜ Jacques Bonsergent), an overwhelmingly popular twinset of coffee shops doors apart on the same street.

❸ Vintage Fashion

Flip through colour-coded racks of vintage cast-offs at **Frivoli** (www.facebook.com/frivolidepot; 26 rue Beaurepaire, 10e; ⏰ 1-7pm Mon, 11am-7pm Tue-Fri, 2-7pm Sat & Sun; Ⓜ République, Jacques Bonsergent), on boutique-lined rue Beaurepaire.

❹ New-Gen Bakery

Observe artisan bakers at work and grab an out-of-this-world *chausson aux pommes* (apple turnover) to go at **Sain Boulangerie** (📞 07 61 23 49 44; www.sain-boulangerie.com; 15 rue Marie et Louise, 10e; pastries from €1.50; ⏰ 7.30am-2.30pm & 4.15-8pm Tue-Sat, 8am-1pm Sun; Ⓜ Goncourt, Jacques Bonsergent) the gourmet kitchen-bakery of chef Anthony Courteille.

❺ Designer Books & Looks

Watch the canal's vintage road bridge swing open in front of leading design bookshop **Artazart** (www.artazart.com; 83 quai de Valmy, 10e; ⏰ 10.30am-7.30pm Mon-Fri, from 11am Sat, from 1pm Sun; Ⓜ Jacques Bonsergent); the shop also sells quirky collector's items and re-cycled messenger bags.

❻ Rooftop Cool

Come dusk, the underground crowd gravitates to buzzy concert venue-club **Point Éphémère** (📞 01 40 34 02 48; www.pointephemere.org; 200 quai de Valmy, 10e; ⏰ noon-2am Mon-Sat, to 11pm Sun; 📶; Ⓜ Jaurès, Louis Blanc) for sundown drinks on its rooftop bar. The former fire station and squat later morphs into a throbbing club and concert venue.

❼ The Stolen Glass

No wine bar–restaurant is as mythical or loved as **Le Verre Volé** (📞 01 48 03 17 34; www.leverrevole.fr; 67 rue de Lancry, 10e; mains €12-25; ⏰ 12.30-2.30pm & 7.30pm-1am; 📶; Ⓜ Jacques Bonsergent), with shabby chic façade a stone's skim from the water's edge. Last orders for dinner: 10.30pm.

Centre Pompidou & Le Marais

Fashionable bars and restaurants, designers' bou-tiques and thriving gay and Jewish communities all squeeze into the vibrant neighbourhood of Le Marais and its equally fashionable, eastern neighbour, Bas-tille, on Paris' right bank. Beyond rises one of the city's most eye-catching cultural hubs, Centre Pompidou.

The Short List

○ **Centre Pompidou (p112)** *Contemplating Europe's largest collection of modern art and admiring the city atop of one of Paris' most whimsical buildings.*

○ **Musée National Picasso (p118)** *Immersing yourself in the life and art of one of the world's most eccentric modern artists, Pablo Picasso.*

○ **Mémorial de la Shoah (p118)** *Gaining a poignant insight into German-occupied Paris and Holocaust horrors.*

○ **Place des Vosges (p120)** *Lapping up the grace and architectural beauty of Paris' most elegant square.*

○ **Atelier des Lumières (p118)** *Discover dazzling digital art in a 19th-century foundry.*

Getting There & Around

Ⓜ Rambuteau (line 11) is the most convenient for the Centre Pompidou.

Ⓜ Other central metro stations include Hôtel de Ville (lines 1 and 11), St-Paul (line 1) and Bastille (lines 1, 5 and 8).

⛴ The hop-on, hop-off Batobus stops outside Hôtel de Ville.

Neighbourhood Map on p116

Centre Pompidou (p112) PICS FACTORY/SHUTTERSTOCK ©
BUILDING: PIANO & ROGERS

Top Experience 📷
Delight at the Centre Pompidou

The Centre Pompidou has amazed and delighted visitors ever since it opened in 1977, for its outstanding collection of modern art and for its radical architectural statement. The dynamic and vibrant arts centre enthrals with its galleries and exhibitions, hands-on workshops, dance performances, bookshop, design boutique, cinemas, research library and entertainment venues.

◎ MAP P116, A2

www.centrepompidou.fr

pl Georges Pompidou, 4e

museum, exhibitions & panorama adult/child €14/free, panorama only €5/free

🕙 11am-9pm Wed-Mon, temporary exhibits to 11pm Thu

Ⓜ Rambuteau

The Architecture

Former French president Georges Pompidou wanted an ultracontemporary artistic hub and he got it: competition-winning architects Renzo Piano and Richard Rogers designed the building inside out, with utilitarian features like plumbing, pipes, air vents and electrical cables forming part of the external façade, freeing up the interior space for exhibitions and events.

The then-controversial, now much-loved centre opened in 1977. Viewed from a distance its primary-coloured, box-like form amid a sea of muted-grey Parisian rooftops makes it look like a child's Meccano set abandoned on someone's elegant living-room rug.

Musée National d'Art Moderne

Europe's largest collection of modern art fills the airy, well-lit galleries of the National Museum of Modern Art. On a par with the permanent collection are the two temporary exhibition halls (on the ground floor/basement and the top floor) which host memorable blockbuster exhibits. There's a wonderful children's gallery on the 1st floor.

The permanent collection changes every two years, but incorporates artists such as Picasso, Matisse, Chagall, Kandinsky, Kahlo, Warhol, Pollock and many more. The 5th floor showcases artists active between 1905 and 1970 (give or take a decade) and the 4th floor focuses on more contemporary creations, roughly from the 1990s onward.

The Rooftop

The Centre Pompidou is just six storeys high, but Paris' low-rise cityscape means sweeping panoramic views extend from its rooftop, reached by external escalators enclosed in tubes.

★ Top Tips

o The Centre Pompidou opens late every night (except Tuesday, when it's closed), so head here around 5pm to avoid the daytime crowds.

o You'll still have to queue to get through security, but the entry process will go faster if you buy museum and events tickets online.

o Rooftop entry is included in museum and exhibition admission; alternatively, buy a panorama ticket (€5) just for the roof.

✕ Take a Break

Georges' outdoor terrace on the 6th floor is fabulous for drinks with view.

For a meal or a casual drink, head to nearby **Café La Fusée** (📞01 42 76 93 99; 168 rue St-Martin, 3e; 🕙9am-2am Mon-Sat, from 10am Sun; Ⓜ Rambuteau, Étienne Marcel), a laid-back indie hang-out with a lively awning-shaded terrace.

Walking Tour 🥾

The Fashionable Haut Marais

For a more intimate look at the movers and shakers – emerging and established – quietly making their mark on Paris' dynamic fashion and design scene, lose yourself in the Haut Marais (upper, ie northern Marais). Its warren of narrow streets is a hub for fashion designers, art galleries, and specialist vintage, accessories and homewares boutiques. Watch for new openings and pop-ups.

Walk Facts

Start Merci;
Ⓜ St-Sébastien Froissart

Finish Le Mary Céleste;
Ⓜ Filles du Calvaire

Length 2km; 1.5 hours

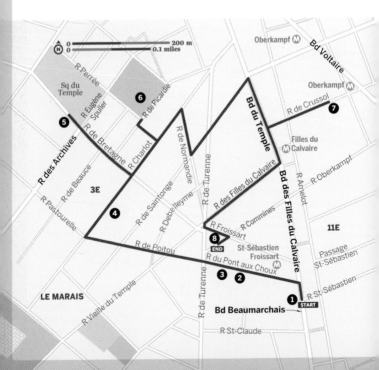

❶ Charitable Fashion

Fronted by a Fiat Cinquecento, unique concept store **Merci** (p132) donates all profits from its cutting-edge fashions, homewares, gifts, cafe and canteen to a children's charity in Madagascar.

❷ Coffee Fix

Reboot with a Parisian-roasted coffee at **Boot Café** (19 rue du Pont aux Choux, 3e; ⏱10am-6pm; 📶; Ⓜ St-Sébastien Froissart). Set inside an old cobbler's shop, which has a beautifully preserved original washed-blue façade and 'Cordon-nerie' lettering.

❸ A Moveable Feast

Every few weeks the bright white interior of chameleon concept store **Heureux les Curieux** (www.heureuxlescurieux.com; 23 rue du Pont aux Choux, 3e; ⏱11am-7pm Tue-Sat, noon-6pm Sun; Ⓜ St-Sébastien Froissart) showcases a different brand or designer. 'Made in France' is a common theme, but anything goes.

❹ Ethical Upcycling

At his workshop-boutique, French designer **Samy Chalon** (📞01 44 59 39 16; 24 rue Charlot, 3e; ⏱11.30am-7.30pm Tue-Sat; Ⓜ St-Sébastien Froissart) transforms secondhand Hermès scarves, Chanel dresses and other *haute couture* (high fashion) pieces into whimsical tops, flowing skirts and downright cool frocks oozing femininity and sass.

❺ Cake Art

Break for buttery *sablés* (short-bread), a punchy *tarte au citron* (lemon tart) and other exquisite treats at jewel-box-like patisserie (cake shop) **Bontemps** (📞01 42 74 10 68; www.facebook.com/bontemps patisserie; 57 rue de Bretagne, 3e; tea or coffee & cake €20; ⏱11am-7.30pm Wed-Fri, from 10am Sat, 10am-6pm Sun; Ⓜ Temple), with tearoom and peppermint-green tables in a romantic courtyard.

❻ Culture Hub

Admire the *quartier's* former covered market with magnificent art nouveau ironwork at **Le Carreau du Temple** (📞01 83 81 93 30; www.carreaudutemple.eu; 2 rue Perrée, 3e; ⏱10am-10pm Mon-Fri, from 9am Sat, box office 10am-6pm Mon-Sat; Ⓜ Temple), a contemporary host to exhibitions, concerts, sports classes and a bar.

❼ Crafting Paris

Parisian creatives mingle with other like-minded souls over artsy *ateliers* (workshops) in knitting, macramé, embroidery, scrapbooking, flower arranging, paper crafting, jewellery-making etc at **Seize** (📞01 48 06 86 19; www.seizeparis.com; 16 rue de Crussol, 11e; ⏱2-7pm Tue-Fri, from 11am Sat; Ⓜ Oberkampf).

❽ Cocktail Hour

Snag a stool at the central circular bar of ubercool **Le Mary Céleste** (p127) for creative cocktails and tapas-style 'small plates'.

1

Bd de Sébastopol

Musée des
Arts et
Métiers ⊙ **5**

R de Turbigo

R Réaumur

R du Temple

R Dupetit Thouars

R Béranger

Bd du Temple

Bd Voltaire

R au Maire
Le Tango ⊙
R des Gravilliers

R Martin

R St-Martin

R Beaubourg

R Chapon

3E

Sq du
Temple

R de Bretagne **38**

30

26

R de Saintonge

12

R de Turenne

Filles du
Calvaire

R aux Ours

2

R Michel
le Comte

R du Temple

Marché des
Enfants
Rouges •

R Pastourelle

R Charlot

25

R des Filles
du Calvaire

R Commines

R Amelot

Musée d'Art et
d'Histoire du
Judaïsme

R Rambuteau

Rambuteau Ⓜ

R des Archives

R de Poitou

39

St-Sébastien
Froissart Ⓜ

24

Bd Beaumarchais

⊙
**Centre
Pompidou**

R des Quatre-Fils

16

14

R des
Coutures
St-Gervais

1

R St-Claude

36

3

Lafayette
Anticipations

R du Renard

R Ste-Croix de la

7

42

Le
Open

R des Blancs
Manteaux

LE MARAIS

R Vieille du Temple

R de Thorigny

Musée
National
Picasso-
Paris

R du Parc Royal

R de Turenne

37

41

Hôtel de
Ville Ⓜ

R de la Verrerie

R de Moussy

Quetzal

R des Francs Bourgeois

23

R des Rosiers

Musée
Cognacq-Jay

10

R Elzévir

4

Musée
Carnavalet

R St-Gilles

R de Béarn

21

Chemin
Vert Ⓜ

4

Hôtel de
Ville ⊙ **9**

Le Perchoir
Marais

R de Rivoli

R François Miron

Mémorial de
la Shoah

R du Roi de Sicile

3w Kafé

Art Nouveau
Synagogue

R Pavée

R Malher

R de Sévigné

Place des
Vosges

R du Pas
de la Mule

R des Tournelles

Seine

Q de l'Hôtel de Ville

R Geoffroy
l'Asnier

2

31

St-Paul Ⓜ

R François
Miron

Maison
de Victor
Hugo

20

Pont Louis-
Philippe

Île de la
Cité

6

Parc Rives de
Seine

Pont
Marie

R des Nonnains
d'Hyères

R Charlemagne

R St-Antoine

R de la
Bastille

R St-Paul

R Charles V

R du Petit Musc

Bastille Ⓜ

Pont
St-Louis

Île St-Louis

Pont
Marie
Q d'Anjou

Q des Célestins

4E

Sully–
Morland Ⓜ

Bd Henri IV

R St-Louis en l'île

Pont de
Sully

Bd Morland

R Mornay

R de la Bastille

Bd Bourdon

5

6

N ⊙ 0 ———— 400 m
0 ———— 0.2 miles

A   **B**   **C**   **D**

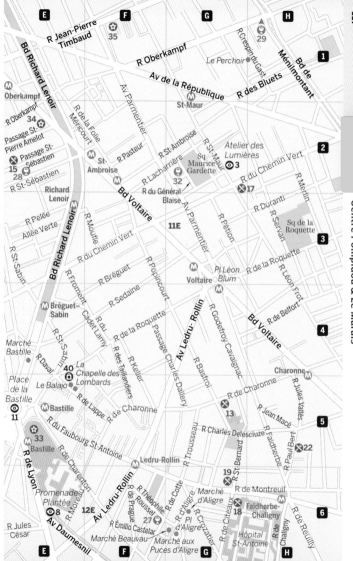

Centre Pompidou & Le Marais

E F G H

1
Bd Richard Lenoir
R Jean-Pierre Timbaud
R Oberkampf
35
R des Bluets
R Crespin du Gast
29
Le Perchoir
Av de la République
Bd de Ménilmontant

Oberkampf
R Oberkampf 34
Passage St-Pierre Amelot
15 28 Passage St-Sébastien
R St-Sébastien
R de la Folie Méricourt
R Pasteur
St-Ambroise
R St-Ambroise
R Lacharrière
R du Général Blaise
32
St-Maur
R St-Maur
Sq Maurice Gardette
Atelier des Lumières
3
17
R du Chemin Vert

2

Richard Lenoir
R Pelée
Allée Verte
R St-Sabin
Bd Voltaire
R Mouffe
R du Chemin Vert
R Froment
R Bréguet
R Sedaine
R Popincourt
Av Parmentier
R Pétion
R Duranti
R Servan
Sq de la Roquette
11E

3

Bréguet-Sabin
R St-Sabin
R du Cadet Larmy
R de la Roquette
Passage Charles Dallery
Voltaire
Pl Léon Blum
R de la Roquette
R Léon Frot
R de Belfort
Bd Voltaire

4

Marché Bastille
R Daval
40
La Chapelle des Lombards
Le Balajo
R de Lappe
R des Taillandiers
R Keller
Av Ledru-Rollin
R Godefroy Cavaignac
R Basfroi
Charonne

Place de la Bastille
11
Bastille
33
Bastille
R de Charonne
R du Faubourg St-Antoine
Ledru-Rollin
R Trousseau
13
R de Charonne
R Jean Macé
R Charles Delescluze
R Faidherbe
R Jules Vallès
R Paul Bert
22

5

R de Lyon
Promenade Plantée
8
12E
Av Ledru-Rollin
R de Charenton
Av Daumesnil
R Théophile Roussel
27
R de Cotte
R de Prague
R Émilio Castelar
Marché Beauvau
Marché d'Aligre
Pl d'Aligre
Marché aux Puces d'Aligre
R d'Aligre
R Crozatier
19
R St-Bernard
R de Montreuil
Faidherbe-Chaligny
18
R de Reuilly
R de Citeaux
Hôpital St-Antoine
R de Chaligny

6

R Jules César

Sights

Musée National Picasso-Paris
MUSEUM

1 📍 MAP P116, C3

One of Paris' most treasured art collections is showcased inside the mid-17th-century Hôtel Salé, an exquisite private mansion owned by the city since 1964. The Musée National Picasso is a staggering art museum devoted to Spanish artist Pablo Picasso (1881–1973), who spent much of his life living and working in Paris. The collection includes more than 5000 drawings, engravings, paintings, ceramic works and sculptures by the *grand maître* (great master), although they're not all displayed at the same time. (📞 01 85 56 00 36; www.museepicassoparis.fr; 5 rue de Thorigny, 3e; adult/child €14/free; ⏰ 10.30am-6pm Tue-Fri, from 9.30am Sat & Sun; Ⓜ Chemin Vert, St-Paul)

Mémorial de la Shoah
MUSEUM

2 📍 MAP P116, B4

Established in 1956, the Memorial to the Unknown Jewish Martyr has metamorphosed into the Memorial of the Shoah – 'Shoah' is a Hebrew word meaning 'catastrophe' and it's synonymous in France with the Holocaust. Museum exhibitions relate to the Holocaust and German occupation of parts of France and Paris during WWII. The actual memorial to the victims stands at the entrance. The wall is inscribed with the names of 76,000 men, women and children deported from France to Nazi extermination camps. (📞 01 42 77 44 72; www.memorialdelashoah.org; 17 rue Geoffroy l'Asnier, 4e; admission free; ⏰ 10am-6pm Sun-Wed & Fri, to 10pm Thu; Ⓜ Pont Marie, St-Paul)

Atelier des Lumières
MUSEUM

3 📍 MAP P116, G2

A former foundry dating from 1835 that supplied iron for the French navy and railroads now houses Paris' first digital-art museum. The 1500-sq-metre La Halle mounts dazzling light projections that take over the bare walls. Long programs lasting around 30 minutes are based on historic artists' works; there's also a shorter contemporary program. Screenings are continuous. In the separate Le Studio space, you can discover emerging and established digital artists.

Children under 13 must be accompanied by an adult. (📞 01 80 98 46 00; www.atelier-lumieres.com; 38-40 rue St-Maur, 11e; adult/child/family €14.50/9.50/42; ⏰ 10am-6pm Mon-Thu, to 10pm Fri & Sat, to 7pm Sun; Ⓜ Voltaire)

Musée Carnavalet
MUSEUM

4 📍 MAP P116, C4

Paris' history museum, spanning Gallo-Roman times onwards, rambles over a pair of remarkable *hôtels particuliers* (private mansions), the 1560-built Hôtel Carnavalet and 1688-built Hôtel Le Peletier de St-Fargeau. The museum reopened in 2021 after a multi-year renovation. Check the website for details. (📞01 44 59 58 58; www.carnavalet.paris.fr; 23 rue de Sévigné, 3e; admission free; Ⓜ St-Paul, Chemin Vert)

Musée des Arts et Métiers

MUSEUM

5 ◎ MAP P116, B1

The Arts and Crafts Museum, dating to 1794 and Europe's oldest science and technology museum, is a must for families – or anyone with an interest in how things tick or work. Housed inside the sublime 18th-century priory of St-Martin des Champs, some 2400 instruments, machines and working models from the 18th to 20th centuries are displayed across three floors. In the priory's

attached church is Foucault's original pendulum, introduced to the world at the Universal Exhibition in Paris in 1855. (📞01 53 01 82 75; www.arts-et-metiers.net; 60 rue de Réaumur, 3e; adult/child €8/free, 6-9.30pm Fri & 1st Sun of month free; ⊙10am-6pm Tue-Thu, Sat & Sun, to 9.30pm Fri; Ⓜ Arts et Métiers)

Parc Rives de Seine

PARK

6 ◎ MAP P116, B5

Following the success of the former expressway turned park on the Left Bank (p185), this 4.5km stretch of Unesco-listed Right Bank is also now a car-free Parisian playground. The park has cycling and walking paths, *pétanque* (similar to lawn bowls) and other sporting facilities, along with kids play areas, climbing walls, huge chalkboards to write

Musée National Picasso-Paris

TAKASHI IMAGES/SHUTTERSTOCK ©

Place des Vosges

Inaugurated in 1612 as place Royale and thus Paris' oldest square, **place des Vosges** (Map p116, D4; 4e; Ⓜ Bastille, Chemin Vert) is a strikingly elegant ensemble of 36 symmetrical houses with ground-floor arcades, steep slate roofs and large dormer windows arranged around a leafy square with four symmetrical fountains and an 1829 copy of a mounted statue of Louis XIII. The square received its present name in 1800 to honour the Vosges *département* (administrative division) for being the first in France to pay its taxes.

Between 1832 and 1848 the celebrated novelist and poet Victor Hugo lived in an apartment in Hôtel de Rohan-Guéménée, a townhouse straddling the northeastern corner of the square. The beautifully renovated **house-museum** (Map p116, D4; 📞 01 42 72 10 16; www.maisonsvictorhugo.paris.fr; 6 place des Vosges, 4e; Ⓜ Bastille) exhibits the writer's personal letters and musings, drawings and portraits, and has a lovely cafe.

or draw on to your heart's content, plus year-round bars, and hammocks, sunloungers and umbrella-shaded tables in summer. (btwn Port de l'Arsenal, 4e & quai des Tuileries, 1er; admission free; Ⓜ Quai de la Rapée, Pont Marie, Pont Neuf)

Lafayette Anticipations

ARTS CENTRE

 7 MAP P116, A3

In 2018 the corporate foundation of French retailer Galeries Lafayette opened this unique multi-disciplinary space for producing, experimenting with and exhibiting new works of contemporary art, design and fashion. Transformed by architect Rem Koolhaas, the 1891 building now has 2500 sq metres of exhibition space and a striking 18m-high glass tower. Three to four free exhibitions take place annually, alongside ticketed performances and workshops. (Fondation d'entreprise Galeries Lafayette; 📞 01 57 40 64 17; www.lafayette-anticipations.com; 9 rue du Plâtre, 4e; admission free; ⏱ during exhibitions 11am-7pm Mon, Wed, Sat & Sun, to 9pm Thu & Fri, other times 11am-7.30pm Wed-Mon; Ⓜ Rambuteau)

Promenade Plantée

PARK

 8 MAP P116, E6

The disued 19th-century Vincennes railway viaduct was reborn in 1993 as the world's first elevated park, planted with a fragrant profusion of cherry trees, maples, rose trellises, bamboo corridors and lavender. Three storeys above ground, it provides a unique aerial vantage point on the city. Along the first, northwestern section, above av Daumesnil, art-gallery workshops beneath the arches form the **Viaduc des Arts** (www.le viaducdesarts.com; 1-129 av Daumesnil, 12e; ⊙hours vary; M Bastille, Gare de Lyon). Staircases provide access (lifts here invariably don't work). (Coulée Verte René-Dumont; cnr rue de Lyon & av Daumesnil, 12e; ⊙8am-9.30pm Mon-Fri, from 9am Sat & Sun Mar-Oct, 8am-5.30pm Mon-Fri, from 9am Sat & Sun Nov-Feb; M Bastille, Gare de Lyon, Daumesnil)

Hôtel de Ville ARCHITECTURE

9 ◉ MAP P116, A4

Paris' beautiful town hall was gutted during the Paris Commune of 1871 and rebuilt in luxurious neo-Renaissance style between 1874 and 1882. The ornate façade is decorated with 108 statues of illustrious Parisians, and the

outstanding temporary exhibitions (admission free; enter at 29 rue de Rivoli) have a Parisian theme. (www.paris.fr; place de l'Hôtel de Ville, 4e; admission free; M Hôtel de Ville)

Musée Cognacq-Jay MUSEUM

10 ◉ MAP P116, C3

This museum inside the Hôtel de Donon displays oil paintings, pastels, sculpture, objets d'art, jewellery, porcelain and furniture from the 18th century, assembled by Ernest Cognacq (1839–1928), founder of La Samaritaine department store, and his wife Louise Jay. Although Cognacq appreciated little of his collection, boasting that he had never visited the Louvre and was only acquiring collections for the status, the artwork and objets d'art give a good idea of

Lafayette Anticipations

CHRISTOPHE SIMON/GETTY IMAGES ©

Pre-Revolutionary Architecture

Le Marias largely escaped Baron Haussmann's large-scale renovations, and today it's one of the few neighbourhoods of Paris that still has much of its pre-revolutionary architecture intact. This includes the house at 3 rue Volta, 3e, parts of which date to 1292; Paris' oldest building still standing (now a restaurant) at 51 rue de Montmorency, 3e, built in 1407 and once the residence of celebrated alchemist and writer Flamel (1330–1417); and the half-timbered 16th-century building at 11 & 13 rue François Miron, 4e.

upper-class tastes during the Age of Enlightenment. (☏ 01 40 27 07 21; www.museecognacqjay.paris.fr; 8 rue Elzévir, 3e; admission free; ⊙ 10am-6pm Tue-Sun; Ⓜ St-Paul, Chemin Vert)

Place de la Bastille   SQUARE

11 ◉ MAP P116, E5

A 14th-century fortress built to protect the city gates, the Bastille became a prison under Cardinal Richelieu, which was mobbed on 14 July 1789, igniting the French Revolution. At the centre of the square is the 52m-high **Colonne de Juillet** (www.colonne-de-juillet.fr), a green-bronze column topped by a gilded, winged Liberty. Revolutionaries from the uprising of 1830 are buried beneath; the crypt will

open to the public following major redevelopments in 2020 linking the square to Bassin de l'Arsenal. (12e; Ⓜ Bastille)

Eating

Jacques Genin   PASTRIES €

12 🍴 MAP P116, D1

Wildly creative *chocolatier* (chocolate maker) Jacques Genin is famed for his flavoured caramels, *pâtes de fruits* (fruit jellies) and exquisitely embossed *bonbons de chocolat* (chocolate sweets). But what completely steals the show at his elegant chocolate showroom is the *salon de dégustation* (aka tearoom), where you can order a pot of outrageously thick hot chocolate and legendary Genin *millefeuille*, assembled to order. (☏ 01 45 77 29 01; www.jacquesgenin.fr; 133 rue de Turenne, 3e; pastries €9-12; ⊙ 11am-7pm Tue-Fri & Sun, to 7.30pm Sat; Ⓜ Oberkampf, Filles du Calvaire)

Septime   GASTRONOMY €€€

13 🍴 MAP P116, G5

The alchemists in Bertrand Grébaut's Michelin-starred kitchen produce truly beautiful creations, served by blue-aproned waitstaff. The menu reads like an obscure shopping list: each dish is a mere listing of three ingredients, while the mystery *carte blanche* dinner *menu* (fixed-price meals) puts you in the hands of the innovative chef. Reservations require planning and perseverance – book at least three weeks in advance.

Its nearby wine bar **Septime La Cave** (3 rue Basfroi, 11e; ◷4-11pm; Ⓜ Charonne) is ideal for a pre- or post-meal drink. For stunning small seafood plates, its sister restaurant **Clamato** (www.clamato-charonne.fr; 80 rue de Charonne, 11e; small plates €7-15, half-dozen oysters €23; ◷ noon-2.30pm & 7-11pm Mon-Fri, noon-11pm Sat & Sun) is right next door. (☎ 01 43 67 38 29; www.septime-charonne.fr; 80 rue de Charonne, 11e; with/without wine 5-course lunch menus €105/60, 7-course dinner menus €155/95; ◷ 7.30-10pm Mon, 12.15-2pm & 7.30-10pm Tue-Fri; Ⓜ Charonne)

Au Top   MEDITERRANEAN €€

14 ⊗ MAP P116, C3

Impressively unfindable unless you're in the know, this clandestine rooftop lounge bar and restaurant – roofless and star-topped on summer nights – brazenly enjoys a 360-degree skyline view. Inventive Mediterranean cuisine, served as shared plates with drinks or a full meal, is equally compelling: oysters, spicy sea bass tartare in yuzu cream, oven-roasted Breton artichoke, various steaks grilled on a charcoal fire.

Waiting staff in white boiler suits, seating around the open kitchen or at green marble-topped tables, and an eclectic playlist by Nova rounds off the trendy, party-loving ambience. To find Au Top step through the red door at No 93, search out the lift at the far right back of the courtyard and ride it to the 5th floor. (☎ 01 43 56 50 50; www.au-top.paris; 93 rue Vieille du Temple, 3e; dishes €8-30; ◷ 6pm-2am Mon-Fri, from 9am Sat & Sun; ☎; Ⓜ Rambuteau)

Au Passage   BISTRO €€

15 ⊗ MAP P116, E2

Rising-star chefs continue to make their name at this *petit bar de quartier* (little neighbourhood bar). Choose from a good-value, uncomplicated selection *of petites assiettes* (small tapas-style plates) of cold meats, raw or cooked fish, vegetables and more, and larger meat dishes such as slow-roasted lamb shoulder or *côte de bœuf* (rib-eye steak) to share. Reservations are essential. (☎ 01 43 55 07 52; www.restaurant-aupassage.fr; 1bis passage St-Sébastien, 11e; small plates €5-12, meats to share €28-75; ◷ 7-11pm Tue-Sat, bar to 1.30am Tue-Sat; Ⓜ St-Sébastien–Froissart)

Breizh Café   CRÊPES €

16 ⊗ MAP P116, C2

Everything at the Breizh ('Breton' in Breton) is 100% authentic, including its organic-flour crêpes and *galettes* (savoury buckwheat crêpes) that top many Parisians' lists for the best in the city. Other specialities include Cancale oysters (€18.50 for half a dozen) and 20 types of cider. Tables are limited and there's often a wait; book ahead or try its deli, **L'Épicerie** (☎ 01 42 71 39 44; 111 rue Vieille du Temple, 3e; crêpes & galettes €4.50-14.50; ◷ 11.30am-10pm), next door. (☎ 01 42 72 13 77; www.breizhcafe.com;

109 rue Vieille du Temple, 3e; crêpes & galettes €6.50-14.50; ⏱10am-11pm; Ⓜ St-Sébastien–Froissart)

Le Servan BISTRO €€

17 Ⓧ MAP P116, G2

Ornate cream-coloured ceilings with moulded cornices and pastel murals, huge windows and wooden floors give this neighbourhood neobistro near Père Lachaise a light, airy feel on even the greyest Parisian day. Seared mackerel with yuzu and miso dressing, and duck and coriander dumplings are among the inventive creations on the daily changing menu. Reserve to avoid missing out. (📞01 55 28 51 82; www.leservan.fr; 32 rue St-Maur, 11e; 3-course lunch menus €28, mains €25-38; ⏱8.30am-10am, noon-2pm & 7.30-10pm; Ⓜ Voltaire, Rue St-Maur, Père Lachaise)

Madito LEBANESE €

18 Ⓧ MAP P116, G6

Teensy Madito prepares startlingly good Lebanese cuisine daily from scratch (there's no microwave or freezer on the premises). With just 20 seats, you'll need to book ahead to feast on starters such as makdous (aubergine stuffed with red peppers and walnuts) or warak enab (vine-leaf-wrapped rice and spiced beef), followed by mains like tawouk (lemon- and yoghurt-marinated chicken). (📞01 45 35 89 72; www.madito.fr; 38 rue de Citeaux, 12e; mains €11-15, tasting menu €28; ⏱noon-3pm & 7-11pm Tue-Sat; 📷; Ⓜ Faidherbe-Chaligny)

Mokonuts CAFE €

19 Ⓧ MAP P116, G6

Much-loved hole-in-the-wall Mokonuts, with a beautiful mosaic-tiled floor, makes a cosy refuge for snacks like flourless chocolate layer cake, clementine almond cake and white-chocolate and roasted-almond cookies. Sea bream with chickpeas and capers, and lamb shoulder with hummus are among the all-organic lunch-time mains (book well ahead). Natural wines and craft beers feature on the drinks list. Bookings are recommended.

Alternatively, head around the corner to its offspring **Mokoloco** (74 rue de Charonne, 11e; sandwiches €9-10; ⏱11.30am-5pm Tue-Sat; Ⓜ Charonne) for gourmet sandwiches, salads and famous cookies – look for the same mint-green façade. (📞09 80 81 82 85; www. mokonuts.com; 5 rue St-Bernard, 11e; pastries €2.50-7, mains €12-25; ⏱9am-2.30pm Mon-Fri, closed Aug; 📶; Ⓜ Faidherbe-Chaligny)

Brasserie Bofinger BRASSERIE €€

20 Ⓧ MAP P116, D5

Founded in 1864, Bofinger is reputedly Paris' oldest brasserie, though its polished art nouveau brass, glass and mirrors indicate redecoration a few decades later. Alsatian-inspired specialities include six kinds of choucroute (sauerkraut), along with oysters (€16.80 to €28.20 per half-dozen) and magnificent seafood platters (€30 to €90). Ask for a seat

Pletzl's Jewish Community

Cacher (kosher) grocery shops, butchers, restaurants, delis and takeaway felafel joints cram the narrow streets of Pletzl (from the Yiddish for 'little square'), home to Le Marais' long-established Jewish community. It starts in rue des Rosiers and continues along rue Ste-Croix de la Bretonnerie to rue du Temple. Don't miss the **art nouveau synagogue** (Agoudas Hakehilos Synagogue; Map p116, C4; 10 rue Pavée, 4e; M St-Paul) designed in 1913 by Hector Guimard, who was also responsible for the city's famous metro entrances.

For an in-depth look at Jewish history, visit the **Musée d'Art et d'Histoire du Judaïsme** (Map p116, B2; ☎ 01 53 01 86 60; www.mahj.org; 71 rue du Temple, 3e; adult/child €10/free; ⊙ 11am-6pm Tue-Fri, from 10am Sat & Sun; M Rambuteau), housed in Pletzl's sumptuous Hôtel de St-Aignan, dating from 1650. Highlights include documents relating to the Dreyfus Affair, and artworks by Chagall, Modigliani and Soutine. The museum also runs guided walking tours of the 'hood (including museum entrance €23/17; English available).

downstairs beneath the *coupole* (stained-glass dome). (☎ 01 42 72 87 82; www.bofingerparis.com; 5-7 rue de la Bastille, 4e; 2-/3-course menus €19.90/33, mains €18.50-37; ⊙ noon-3pm & 6.30pm-midnight Mon-Fri, noon-3.30pm & 6.30pm-midnight Sat, noon-11pm Sun; 🛜 🚹; M Bastille)

For the Love of Food
INTERNATIONAL €

21 ⊗ MAP P116, D3

This groundbreaking place, opened in late 2019, is all about sustainability and innovation. Dubbed Paris' first chef-incubator restaurant for 'curious gastronomes', it invites a different trio of chefs each month to create its menu. Produce must be seasonal and responsibly sourced, and meals are ordered in advance

online to ensure zero waste. Dining is in an attractive, minimalist space around shared wooden tables. (www.fortheloveoffood.paris; 80 rue des Tournelles, 3e; 2-/3-course lunch €20/24, 4-course dinner menus €38; ⊙ 12.15-2.30pm & 7-11pm Fri-Sun; M Chemin Vert)

Le Bistrot Paul Bert
BISTRO €€

22 ⊗ MAP P116, H5

When food writers list Paris' best bistros, Paul Bert's name consistently pops up. The timeless decor and classic dishes, such as *steak-frites* (steak and chips) and hazelnut-cream Paris-Brest pastry, reward booking ahead. Siblings in the same street: **L'Écailler du Bistrot** (☎ 01 43 72 76 77; 22 rue Paul Bert, 11e; oysters per half-dozen €10-24, mains €36-52, seafood platters

Market Talk

If you only get to one open-air street market in Paris, make it **Marché Bastille** (Map p116, E4; bd Richard Lenoir, 11e; ⏰7am-2.30pm Thu, to 3pm Sun; Ⓜ️Bastille, Bréguet–Sabin), stretching between Bastille and Richard Lenoir metro stations. Its 150-plus stalls are piled high with fruit and veg, meats, fish, shellfish, cheeses and seasonal specialities such as truffles, alongside clothing, leather goods and a smattering of antiques and knick-knacks.

Another street favourite with chefs and locals is the **Marché d'Aligre** (Map p116, G6; rue d'Aligre, 12e; ⏰7.30am-1.30pm Tue-Fri, to 2.30pm Sat & Sun; Ⓜ️Ledru-Rollin), with stalls fronting specialist shops stocking cheeses, coffee, chocolates, meat, seafood and wine; and covered market hall **Marché Beauvau** (Map p116, G6; place d'Aligre, 12e; ⏰9am-1pm & 4-7.30pm Tue-Fri, 9am-1pm & 3.30-7.30pm Sat, 9am-1.30pm Sun; Ⓜ️Ledru-Rollin) next door. The small but bargain-filled flea market **Marché aux Puces d'Aligre** (Map p116, G6; place d'Aligre, 12e; ⏰7.30am-1.30pm Tue-Fri, to 2.30pm Sat & Sun; Ⓜ️Ledru-Rollin) takes place on the square.

For dining market-style, hit Paris' oldest covered market, **Marché des Enfants Rouge** (Map p116, C2; 39 rue de Bretagne & 33bis rue Charlot, 3e; ⏰8.30am-1pm & 4-7.30pm Tue-Sat, 8.30am-2pm Sun, individual stall hours vary; Ⓜ️Filles du Calvaire), around since 1615. Its glorious maze of food stalls sell ready-to-eat dishes from around the globe, with shared tables and bar stools to eat around.

per person from €44; ⏰noon-2.30pm & 7.30-11pm Tue-Sat) for seafood; **La Cave Paul Bert** (📞01 58 53 50 92; 16 rue Paul Bert, 11e; ⏰noon-midnight, kitchen noon-2pm & 7.30-11.30pm), a wine bar with small plates; and **Le 6 Paul Bert** (📞01 43 79 14 32; www.le6paulbert.com; 6 rue Paul Bert, 12e; mains €27-32; ⏰noon-2pm & 7.30-11pm Tue-Fri, 7.30-11pm Sat) for modern cuisine. (📞01 43 72 24 01; 18 rue Paul Bert, 11e; 3-course menus €41, mains €29; ⏰noon-2pm & 7.30-11pm Tue-Thu, 7.30-11pm Fri, noon-2.30pm Sat, closed Aug; Ⓜ️Faidherbe-Chaligny)

L'As du Fallafel

FELAFEL €

23 ❌ MAP P116, B3

The lunchtime queue stretching halfway down the street from this place says it all. This Parisian favourite, 100% worth the inevitable wait, is the address for kosher, perfectly deep-fried falafel (chickpea balls) and turkey or lamb shawarma sandwiches. Do as every Parisian does and get them to take away. (📞08 99 34 43 64; www.l-as-du-fallafel.zenchef.com; 34 rue des Rosiers, 4e; takeaway €6.50-9.50, mains €12-18; ⏰noon-

11pm Sun-Thu, to 4pm Fri, 6.30-11pm Sat; ; MSt-Paul)

Drinking

Le Mary Céleste   COCKTAIL BAR

24 🚇 MAP P116, D2

Snag a stool at the central circular bar at this eternally fashionable, brick-and-timber-floored cocktail bar or reserve one of a handful of tables online. Innovative cocktails mix weird and wonderful ingredients (curry leaves, green cardamom, dried Iranian lemon, turmeric syrup), often seasonal, and there are lovely natural wines too – all perfect partners to tapas-style 'small plates' (grilled duck hearts, devilled eggs) to share. (www.quixotic-projects.com/venue/mary-celeste; 1 rue Commines, 3e;

⏲bar 6pm-2am, kitchen 7-11.30pm Mon-Fri, noon-2am Sat & Sun; MFilles du Calvaire)

Candelaria   COCKTAIL BAR

25 🚇 MAP P116, D2

A lime-green *taqueria* serving homemade tacos, quesadillas and tostadas conceals one of Paris' coolest cocktail bars through an unmarked internal door. Phenomenal cocktails made from agave spirits, including mezcal, are inspired by Central and South America, such as a Guatemalan El Sombrerón (tequila, vermouth, bitters, hibiscus syrup, pink-pepper-infused tonic and lime). Weekend evenings kick off with DJ sets. (www.quixotic-projects.com/candelaria; 52 rue de Saintonge, 3e; ⏲bar 6pm-2am, taqueria noon-10.30pm

Jacques Genin (p123)

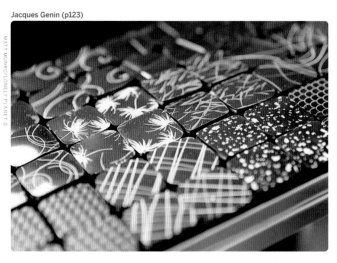

Sun-Wed, to 11.30pm Thu-Sat; M Filles du Calvaire)

Grand Café Tortoni

CAFE

26 MAP P116, C2

A favourite address with hobnob-bing socialites in the 19th century, this historic Italian cafe is sud-denly the trendiest spot in Haut Marais to linger over coffee or an egg-and-pastry breakfast at the red marble-topped bar, or to shop for exquisite Officine Universelle Buly fragrances and candles in the polished, old-world setting.

Wood panelling and shelves lined with glass jars of unusual dried ingredients that go into the natural body butters, perfumes and so on evoke a centuries-old apothecary, and a calligrapher scribes a beautiful dedication

on the packaging of each item purchased. Oh, and florist Miyoko works her magic in the hidden courtyard out back. (☑01 42 72 28 92; www.facebook.com/grandcafe tortoni; 45 rue de Saintonge, 3e; ☀9am-7pm Tue-Sat, 11am-6pm Sun; M Filles du Calvaire)

Le Baron Rouge

WINE BAR

27 MAP P116, F6

Just about the ultimate Paris-ian wine-bar experience, this wonderfully unpretentious local meeting place, where everyone is welcome, has barrels stacked against the bottle-lined walls and serves cheese, charcuterie, and oysters on weekends in season. It's especially busy on Sunday after the Marché d'Aligre wraps up. For a small deposit, you can fill up 1L

An LGBTIQ+ favourite; rue des Archives

Gay & Lesbian Marais

Guys' favourite venues in Le Marais include sociable **Le Open** (Map p116, A3; www.facebook.com/opencafeparis; 17 rue des Archives, 4e; ⏰11am-2am Sun-Thu, to 3am Fri & Sat; Ⓜ Hôtel de Ville) and cruisy **Quetzal** (Map p116, B4; 10 rue de la Verrerie, 4e; ⏰5pm-4am; Ⓜ Hôtel de Ville).

Girls will want to head to **3w Kafé** (Map p116, B4; www.facebook.com/3wkafe; 8 rue des Écouffes, 4e; ⏰7pm-3am Wed & Sun, to 4am Thu, to 6.30am Fri & Sat; Ⓜ St-Paul), which stands for 'women with women'.

A mixed gay and lesbian crowd loves **Le Tango** (Map p116, B1; 📞01 48 87 25 71; www.boite-a-frissons.fr; 13 rue au Maire, 3e; admission Fri & Sat €10, Sun €6; ⏰10pm-5am Fri & Sat, 6-11pm Sun; Ⓜ Arts et Métiers), especially during Sunday's legendary gay tea dance.

bottles straight from the barrel. (www.lebaronrouge.net; 1 rue Théophile Roussel, 12e; ⏰5-10pm Mon, 10am-2pm & 5-10pm Tue-Fri, 10am-10pm Sat, 10am-4pm Sun; Ⓜ Ledru-Rollin)

Bambino   WINE BAR

28 Ⓜ MAP P116, E2

A cool headquarters for devotees of both *vin* (wine) and vinyls, Bambino mixes music with an outstanding wine list packed with natural wines. Linger by the polished concrete bar and watch the DJ at work, spinning old-fashioned vinyl on the turntable. Delicious tapas to share – parsley-laced duck hearts, artichokes, creamy polenta and so on – provides the icing on the cake. (📞01 43 55 68 20; www.facebook.com/bambino restaurantparis; 25 rue St-Sébastien, 11e; ⏰6pm-2am Thu-Tue; Ⓜ St-Sébastien–Froissart)

La Commune   COCKTAIL BAR

29 Ⓜ MAP P116, H1

An atrium-style covered timber deck strewn with plants and comfy sofas marks the entrance to La Commune. Like its 10e sibling **Le Syndicat** (51 rue du Faubourg St-Denis, 10e; ⏰6pm-2am; Ⓜ Château d'Eau), cocktails made from French spirits are its raison d'être. Here, the speciality is punch bowls containing five to eight glasses, such as Bisso Na Bissap (Corsican cedar brandy, apricot liqueur, French whisky, bissap juice and fresh citrus). (www.syndicatcocktail club.com/la-commune; 80 bd de Belleville, 20e; ⏰6pm-2am Tue-Sat; 🛜; Ⓜ Couronnes)

Little Red Door   COCKTAIL BAR

30 Ⓜ MAP P116, C2

Behind an inconspicuous timber façade, a tiny crimson doorway is the illusionary portal to this low-lit,

Rooftop Cocktails

An inconspicuous courtyard leads to the lift that will zip you up to 7th-floor **Le Perchoir** (Map p116, H1; ☎01 48 06 18 48; www.leperchoir.tv; 14 rue Crespin du Gast, 11e; ☺6pm-2am Tue-Sat; 🛜; MMénilmontant) looking out over the Parisian rooftops. Department store BHV also has a **rooftop bar** (Map p116, A3; ☎01 48 06 18 48; www.facebook.com/LePerchoirMarais; 37 rue de la Verrerie, 4e, BHV; ☺8.15pm-1.30am Mon-Sat, from 8.45am Sun; MHôtel de Ville).

bare-brick drinking den filled with flickering candles. Ranked among the World's 50 Best Bars, it's a must for serious mixology fans. Its annual collection of 11 cocktails, in themes from 'art' to 'architecture', are intricately crafted from ingredients such as glacier ice and paper syrup. (☎01 42 71 19 32; www.lrdparis.com; 60 rue Charlot, 3e; ☺6pm-2am Sun-Thu, to 3am Fri & Sat; MFilles du Calvaire)

La Caféothèque COFFEE

31 MAP P116, B4

From the industrial grinder to elaborate tasting notes, this coffee house and roastery is serious. Grab a seat, and pick your bean, filtration method (Aeropress, V60 filter, piston or drip) and preparation style. The in-house coffee school has tastings and

various courses including two-hour Saturday-morning tasting initiations (five *terroirs*, five extraction methods) for €60 (English available). (☎01 53 01 83 84; www.lacafeotheque.com; 52 rue de l'Hôtel de Ville, 4e; ☺8.30am-7.30pm Mon-Fri, to 9.30pm Sat, 10am-7.30pm Sun; 🛜; MPont Marie, St-Paul)

Beans on Fire COFFEE

32 MAP P116, G2

Outstanding coffee is guaranteed at this innovative space. Not only a welcoming local cafe, it's also a collaborative roastery, where movers and shakers on Paris' reignited coffee scene come to roast their beans (ask about two-hour roasting workshops, available in English, if you're keen to roast your own). Overlooking a park, the terrace is a neighbourhood hotspot on sunny days. Cash only. (www.thebeansonfire.com; 7 rue du Général Blaise, 11e; ☺8am-6pm Mon-Fri, from 10am Sat & Sun; 🛜; MSt-Ambroise)

Entertainment

Opéra Bastille OPERA

33 ✪ MAP P116, E5

Paris' premier opera hall, Opéra Bastille's 2745-seat main auditorium also stages ballet and classical concerts. Online tickets go on sale up to three weeks before telephone or box-office sales (from noon on Wednesdays; online flash sales offer significant discounts). Limited standing-only tickets (*places débouts*; €5) are available 90 minutes before performances. French-language 90-minute **guided tours** (tours adult/child €17/12; ☺tours Sep–mid-Jul) take you backstage. (☎01 71 25 24 23; www.operadeparis.fr; 2-6 place de la Bastille, 12e; ☺box office noon-6.30pm Mon-Sat, 1hr prior to performances Sun; ⓂBastille)

Le Bataclan
LIVE MUSIC

34 ⭐ MAP P116, E2

Built in 1864, intimate concert, theatre and dance hall Le Bataclan was Maurice Chevalier's debut venue in 1910. The 1497-capacity venue reopened with a concert by Sting on 12 November 2016, almost a year to the day following the tragic 13 November 2015 terrorist attacks that took place here, and it once again hosts

French and international rock and pop legends. (☎01 43 14 00 30; www.bataclan.fr; 50 bd Voltaire, 11e; ⓂOberkampf, Filles du Calvaire)

L'Alimentation Générale
LIVE MUSIC

35 ⭐ MAP P116, F1

This true hybrid, known as the Grocery Store to Anglophones, is a massive space, fronted at street level by its in-house Italianate canteen-bar with big glass windows and retro 1960s Belgian furniture. But music is the big deal here, with an impressive line-up of live gigs and DJs spinning pop, rock, electro, soul and funk to a packed dance floor. (☎09 81 86 42 50; www.alimentation-generale.net; 64 rue Jean-Pierre Timbaud, 11e; admission

Beans on Fire

RIVER THOMPSON/ACQUA ©

Rue de Lappe

Quiet during the day, little rue de Lappe comes alive at night when its string of bars are in full swing. Catch music at the 1936-opened dance hall **Le Balajo** (Map p116, E5; 📞01 47 00 07 87; www.balajo.fr; 9 rue de Lappe, 11e; ⏰hours vary; Ⓜ Bastille), with everything from salsa to R&B, plus old-time tea dancing during *musettes* (accordion gigs) from 2pm to 7pm on Sundays and Mondays. Or try **La Chapelle des Lombards** (Map p116, E5; 📞01 43 57 24 24; www.la-chapelle-des-lombards.com; 19 rue de Lappe, 11e; ⏰11pm-2am Tue & Wed, to 5.30pm Thu-Sat, 6.30pm-1.30am Sun; Ⓜ Bastille), which has regular live concerts.

Wed, Thu & Sun free, Fri & Sat €10; ⏰7pm-2am Wed, Thu & Sun, to 5am Fri & Sat; Ⓜ Parmentier)

Shopping

Merci

CONCEPT STORE

36 🔒 MAP P116, D3

A Fiat Cinquecento marks the entrance to this unique concept store, which donates all its profits to a children's charity in Madagascar. Shop for fashion, accessories, linens, lamps and nifty designs for the home. Complete the experience with a coffee in its hybrid used-bookshop-cafe, a juice at its **Cinéma Café** (⏰10am-6.30pm Mon-Sat) or its stylish **La Cantine de Merci** (mains €14-20; ⏰noon-6pm Mon-Sat) for lunch. (📞01 42 77 00 33; www.merci-merci.com; 111 bd Beaumarchais, 3e; ⏰10am-7.30pm Mon-Sat, noon-7pm Sun; Ⓜ St-Sébastien–Froissart)

Kerzon

HOMEWARES, COSMETICS

37 🔒 MAP P116, D3

Candles made from natural, biodegradable wax in Parisian scents such as Jardin du Luxembourg (with lilac and honey), Place des Vosges (rose and jasmine) and Parc des Buttes-Chaumont (cedar and sandalwood) make aromatic souvenirs of the city. The pretty white and sage-green boutique also stocks room fragrances, scented laundry liquids, and perfumes, soaps, bath oils and other toiletries. (www.kerzon.paris; 68 rue de Turenne, 3e; ⏰11.30am-8pm Tue-Sat; Ⓜ St-Sébastien–Froissart)

Empreintes

DESIGN

38 🔒 MAP P116, C2

Spanning four floors, this design emporium is a concept store for unique, handcrafted pieces by emerging and established French artists and designers. Exquisite jewellery, fashion and art are displayed alongside striking homewares (ceramics, cushions, furniture, lighting, books and more). (www.empreintes-paris.com; 5 rue de Picardie, 3e; ⏰11am-7pm Tue-Sat; Ⓜ Temple)

Veja
FASHION & ACCESSORIES

39 🔒 MAP P116, C2

Living proof that Parisian fashionistas are increasingly green: every Saturday and Sunday huge queues snake outside this 2019-opened store, much-loved for its ecofriendly, unisex trainers (sneakers) and plastic-free running shoes. All the shoes are made in Brazil and crafted from organic raw materials (cotton, rubber, recycled polyester fabrics etc), hence their sustainable '100% vegan' unique selling point. (www.veja-store.com/fr_fr/; 15 rue de Poitou, 3e; ⏰11am-8pm Mon-Sat, 2-7pm Sun; Ⓜ Filles du Calvaire)

La Manufacture de Chocolat
CHOCOLATE

40 🔒 MAP P116, E5

If you dine at superstar chef Alain Ducasse's restaurants, the chocolate will have been made here at Ducasse's own chocolate factory (the first in Paris to produce 'bean-to-bar' chocolate), which he set up with his former executive pastry chef Nicolas Berger. Deliberate over ganaches, pralines and truffles and no fewer than 47 flavours of chocolate bar. (📞01 48 05 82 86; www.lechocolat-alainducasse.com; 40 rue de la Roquette, 11e; ⏰10.30am-7pm Mon-Sat; Ⓜ Bastille)

Maison Plisson
FOOD

41 🔒 MAP P116, D3

Framed by glass-canopied wrought-iron girders, this gourmet emporium incorporates a covered-market-style, terrazzo-floored food hall filled with exquisite, mostly French produce: meat, vegetables, cheese, wine, chocolate, jams, freshly baked breads and much more. If your appetite's whetted, its cafe, opening to twin terraces, serves charcuterie, foie gras and cheese platters, bountiful salads and delicacies such as olive-oil-marinated, Noilly Prat–flambéed sardines. (📞01 71 18 19 09; www.lamaisonplisson.com; 93 bd Beaumarchais, 3e; ⏰9.30am-9pm Mon, 8.30am-9pm Tue-Sat, 9am-8pm Sun; Ⓜ St-Sébastien–Froissart)

Eataly
FOOD & DRINKS

42 🔒 MAP P116, A3

Lovers of Italian food will have a field day in this culinary paradise combining several eateries with market counters selling meat, breads, cheese, fresh pasta, pizza slices, buxom fruit and veg, deli goods and so on. There's an extensive Italian wine cellar, plus a cooking school offering various themed two-hour classes (from €35) for adults and children. (📞01 83 65 81 00; www.eataly.net/fr_fr/magasins/paris-marais; 37 rue Ste-Croix de la Bretonnerie, 4e; ⏰10am-10pm, restaurant hours vary; Ⓜ Hôtel de Ville)

Top Experience 📷
Stroll Through the Père Lachaise

The world's most visited cemetery opened in 1804. Its 44 hectares hold more than 70,000 ornate tombs and a stroll here is akin to exploring a verdant sculpture garden. Père Lachaise was intended as a response to local neighbourhood graveyards being full – at the time, it was ground-breaking for Parisians to be buried outside the quartier *in which they'd lived.*

📞 01 55 25 82 10

www.pere-lachaise.com

8 bd de Ménilmontant & 16 rue du Repos, 20e

admission free

🕐 8am–6pm Mon–Fri, from 8.30am Sat, from 9am Sun mid-Mar–Oct, to 5.30pm daily Nov–mid-Mar

Ⓜ Père Lachaise, Gambetta

A Perfect City Stroll

Ironically Père Lachaise is one of central Paris'
biggest green spaces, with 5300 trees and
shrubs, and a trove of magnificent 19th-century
sculptures by artists such as David d'Angers,
Hector Guimard, Visconti and Chapu. Follow
the walking tour detailed in *Meet Me at Père
Lachaise* by Anna Erikssön and Mason Bende-
wald; or simply begin with the neoclassical
chapel and portal at the main entrance and get
lost at leisure.

Famous Occupants

Paris residency was the only criterion needed
to be buried in Père Lachaise. Among its
800,000-odd occupants are composer Chopin;
playwright Molière; poet Apollinaire; writers
Balzac, Proust, Gertrude Stein and Colette;
actors Simone Signoret, Sarah Bernhardt and
Yves Montand; painters Pissarro, Seurat, Modigliani and Delacroix; *chanteuse* (singer) Édith
Piaf alongside her two-year-old daughter; and
dancer Isadora Duncan.

The grave of Irish playwright and humorist
Oscar Wilde (1854–1900), division 89, is among
the most visited (hence the glass barrier
erected around his sculpted tomb to prevent
fans impregnating the stone with red lipstick
imprints). The other big hitter is 1960s rock
star Jim Morrison (1943–71), division 6.

War Memorial

Approaching the cemetery along bd de Ménilmontant, reflect upon the Monument aux Morts
Parisiens de la Première Guerre Mondiale,
unveiled on the cemetery's outside western
wall on 11 November 2018, the centenary of
the armistice marking the end of WWI. The
280m-long, black metal panel, engraved with
the names of the 94,415 known Parisians killed
in combat and another 8000 missing, runs the
entire length of the street.

★ **Top Tips**

○ Take a photo of the
cemetery map inside
the main bd de Mé-
nilmontant entrance,
or grab a paper copy
from the Conserva-
tion Office (16 rue du
Repos, 20e).

○ Père Lachaise is
photography bliss;
sunny autumn morn-
ings after rain are
best.

✕ **Take a Break**

Reserve a table at
neobistro Le Servan
(p124).

For on-trend Franco-
Asian cuisine, try
Double Dragon
(52 rue St-Maur, 11e;
3-course lunch menus
€18, mains €15.50-
28; ◷noon-2.30pm
Wed, noon-2.30pm &
7.30-10.30pm Thu-Sun;
Ⓜ Rue St-Maur).

ⓘ **Getting There**

Ⓜ Take line 3 or
3bis to Gambetta;
line 2 or 3 to Père
Lachaise; or line 2 to
Philippe Auguste or
Alexandre Dumas.

Explore ✦

Notre Dame & the Islands

Paris' geographic and spiritual heart is here. The larger of the two inner-city islands, Île de la Cité is dominated by the landmark cathedral Notre Dame, currently being rebuilt after the devastating 2019 fire. To its east, serene Île St-Louis is graced with elegant residences, boutique hotels and charming restaurants.

The Short List

○ *Cathédrale Notre Dame de Paris (p138)* Revelling in glorious medieval Gothic architecture, and thanking the heavens that it survived the flames.

○ *Sainte-Chapelle (p144)* Reading richly coloured biblical tales told through stained-glass imagery.

○ *Conciergerie (p144)* Learning how Marie-Antoinette and thousands of others spent their final days at this 14th-century palace turned prison.

○ *Berthillon (p146)* Savouring the sweetness of this famous Parisian ice cream on a riverbank stroll.

○ *Marché aux Fleurs Reine Elizabeth II (p149)* Shopping for romantic blooms at Paris' oldest flower market.

Getting There & Around

Ⓜ Cité (line 4) on the Île de la Cité is the islands' only metro station, and the most convenient for Notre Dame.

Ⓜ Pont Marie (line 7), on the Right Bank, is the Île St-Louis' closest station.

🚤 The hop-on, hop-off Batobus stops opposite Notre Dame on the Left Bank.

Neighbourhood Map on p142

Sainte-Chapelle (p144) MAZIARZ/SHUTTERSTOCK ©

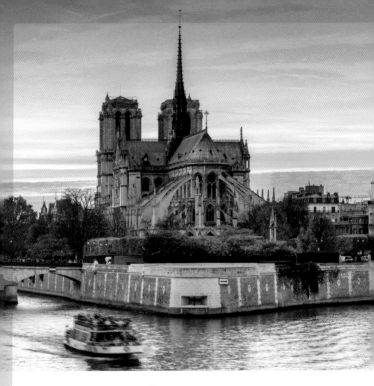

Top Experience 📷
Admire Notre Dame

Majestic and monumental, Paris' iconic French Gothic cathedral was the capital's most visited unticketed site until 2019, when fire blazed through it, leaving the vast cathedral interior inaccessible for years to come. The 14 million annual visitors who once crossed its threshold can now only eyeball its grotesque gargoyle-fringed bell towers and admire its darkened, scaffolding-draped exterior from afar.

◉ **MAP P142, E4**

www.notredamedeparis.fr

6 Parvis Notre Dame – place Jean-Paul-II, 4e

⊙ closed indefinitely

Ⓜ Cité

Architecture

Built on a site occupied by earlier churches and, a millennium prior, a Gallo-Roman temple, Notre Dame was begun in 1163 and largely completed by the early 14th century. The cathedral was badly damaged during the Revolution, prompting architect Eugène Emmanuel Viollet-le-Duc to oversee extensive renovations between 1845 and 1864. There are good views of the magnificent forest of ornate **flying buttresses** encircling the cathedral chancel and supporting its walls from the riverside (eastern) end of rue du Cloître Notre Dame and quai de l'Archevêché.

Notre Dame is sublimely balanced, but look closely to spot minor asymmetrical elements introduced to avoid monotony. These include the slightly different shapes of the three main **portals**, whose statues were once brightly coloured to make them more effective as a *Biblia pauperum* – a 'Bible of the poor' – to help the illiterate faithful understand Old Testament stories, the Passion of the Christ and the lives of the saints.

Fire of April 2019

On the evening of 15 April 2019 a blaze broke out under the cathedral's roof. Firefighters controlled the fire and saved the church, including its two bell towers, spectacular rose windows and western façade. But the damage remained devastating: both the roof and iconic spire – a 19th-century addition – were destroyed and the interior was severely damaged. Several statues and artefacts had already been removed from the cathedral as part of a restoration programme underway prior to the fire. While flames engulfed the cathedral, Paris firefighters and the fire brigade's chaplain formed a human chain to save many of the remaining cathedral treasures.

Rebuilding Notre Dame

After the fire, French President Emmanuel Macron said he'd like the cathedral to be rebuilt by 2024, in time for the Olympic Games. Ac-

★ Top Tips

○ The best views of the cathedral are from rue de la Cité, rue du Cloître Notre Dame, Pont St-Louis & Pont de l'Archevêché.

○ Catch Notre Dame's soul-soaring Gregorian and polyphonic Sunday Masses (10am and 6.30pm respectively) at Église St-Germain l'Auxerrois (p141) near the Louvre instead.

✕ Take a Break

Pop across to adjacent Île St-Louis for a drink, snack or meal at Café Saint Régis (p146).

Buy a creatively stuffed baguette and a juicy fruit tart from Huré (p147) and have a picnic with flying-buttress views on the left bank of the Seine.

cording to experts, it's doubtful that all the works will be completed by then. Within days of the fire, private donors had pledged some €600 million to assist with this and by early 2020 the fund had hit €830 million. Restoration work started in late 2021 after the construction site had been secured and deemed safe. There were delays due to the coronavirus lockdown.

Immediately after the fire, debate raged over the future look of Notre Dame: should it be restored to its original design, complete with wooden roof; to the 19th-century update or something contemporary? A flurry of designs that circulated in the aftermath of the fire included a state-of-the-art glass roof, a new spire in dazzling crystal or stained glass, even a 3D-print of the original cathedral using a 3D-printable pow-der made from ash, dust and rubble salvaged from the site. After months of heated discussions, it was decided to rebuild the roof and the spire to be identical – to the disappointment of those who had supported a futuristic version of Notre Dame. By late 2021, more than 1000 oak trees had been cut and prepared for the reconstruction of the spire.

Salvaged Treasures

Notre Dame's sacred relics – displayed in the cathedral treasury until 2019 – and priceless artworks survived the fire remarkably intact and were transferred to vaults in the Louvre for safekeeping and/or restoration work. Among them were several **Mays** – huge 3m-tall paintings commemorating one of the Acts of the Apostles, accompanied by a poem or literary explana-

The western façade survived the 2019 fire

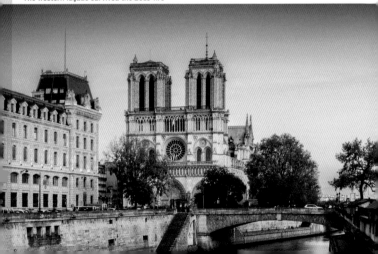

Notre Dame Timeline

1160 The Bishop of Paris, Maurice de Sully, orders the demolition of the original 4th-century cathedral St Étienne (St Stephen).

1163 Construction begins on Notre Dame.

1182 The apse and choir are completed.

1225 The western façade is completed.

1250 Work is finished on the western towers and north rose window.

Mid-1200s To 'modernise' the cathedral, the transepts are remodelled in the Rayonnant style.

1345 The cathedral reaches completion.

1548 Huguenots storm the cathedral following the Council of Trent.

1793 Damage during the most radical phase of the French Revolution sees many of Notre Dame's treasures plundered or destroyed.

1845–64 Following petitions to save the by-then-derelict cathedral from demolition, architect Eugène Viollet-le-Duc carries out extensive repairs and architectural additions.

1991 A lengthy maintenance and restoration programme is initiated.

2013 Notre Dame celebrates 850 years since construction began.

2019 Fire topples the cathedral spire, destroys most of the roof and damages the interior,

tion – offered to Notre Dame by city goldsmiths. By the early 18th century, when the brotherhood of goldsmiths was dissolved, the cathedral had received 76 such monumental paintings; 13 were on display at the time of the fire.

Pilgrims flocked to **Église St-Germain l'Auxerrois** (www.saintgermainauxerrois.cef.fr; 2 place du Louvre, 1er; ⏰9am-7pm; Ⓜ Louvre Rivoli, Pont Neuf), the former parish church of the Louvre, in September 2019 for an exceptional veneration of Notre Dame's **Ste-Couronne** (Holy Crown), purportedly the crown of thorns placed on Jesus' head before he was crucified. Originally preserved in the cathedral treasury and exhibited at the cathedral on the first Friday of each month, every Friday during Lent, and on Good Friday, the relic now remains in a safe at the Louvre and will only be shown during Lent at the St-Germain l'Auxerrois church.

There are plans to set up an exhibition in the Louvre in late 2023, which would display most relics salvaged from the fire.

In late 2021 restoration work also began on the Great Organ (the largest in France, which emerged from the fire with minor damage) and the Choir Organ (which needs to be entirely rebuilt).

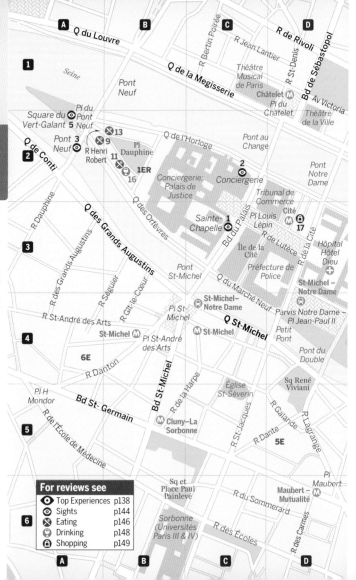

Notre Dame & the Islands

Q du Louvre

R de Rivoli

R Bertin Poirée

R Jean Lantier

R St-Denis

Bd de Sébastopol

Théâtre Musical de Paris

Châtelet Ⓜ

Pl du Châtelet

Av Victoria

Théâtre de la Ville

Seine

Q de la Megisserie

Pont Neuf

Q de l'Horloge

Pont au Change

Pont Notre Dame

Square du Vert-Galant **5**

Pl du Pont Neuf

Pont Neuf **3**

R Henri Robert

Pl Dauphine

13

9

11

16

1ER

Conciergerie; Palais de Justice

2 Conciergerie

Tribunal de Commerce

Cité Ⓜ

17

Q de Conti

R Dauphine

Q des Grands Augustins

Q des Orfèvres

Sainte-Chapelle **1**

Pl Louis Lépin

R de Lutèce

R de la Cité

Hôpital Hôtel Dieu

R des Grands Augustins

R Séguier

R Gît-le-Cœur

Pont St-Michel

Île de la Cité

Préfecture de Police

St-Michel – Notre Dame

R St-André des Arts

Pl St-Michel

Q du Marché Neuf

Parvis Notre Dame – Pl Jean-Paul II

St-Michel– Notre Dame Ⓜ

St-Michel Ⓜ

Q St-Michel

Petit Pont

Pont du Double

St-Michel Ⓜ

Pl St-André des Arts

6E

R Danton

Bd St-Michel

R de la Harpe

Église St-Séverin

Sq René Viviani

R Galande

R Lagrange

Pl H Mondor

Bd St- Germain

R de l'École de Médecine

Cluny–La Sorbonne Ⓜ

R St-Jacques

R Dante

5E

Pl Maubert

Maubert – Mutualité Ⓜ

R des Carmes

Sq et Place Paul Painlevé

R du Sommerard

Sorbonne (Universités Paris III & IV)

R des Écoles

For reviews see	
⚫ Top Experiences	p138
⊙ Sights	p144
✕ Eating	p146
🍷 Drinking	p148
🔒 Shopping	p149

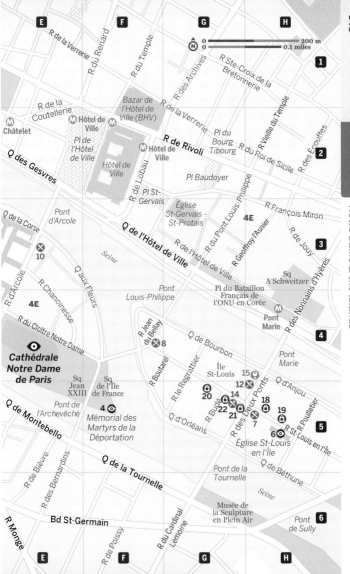

E F G H

R de la Verrerie
R du Renard
R du Temple
R des Archives
R Ste-Croix de la Bretonnerie

1

N 0   200 m
   0   0.1 miles

R de la Coutellerie
Bazar de l'Hôtel de Ville (BHV)
R de la Verrerie
Pl du Bourg Tibourg
R Vieille du Temple
R des Écouffes

M Châtelet
M Hôtel de Ville
Pl de l'Hôtel de Ville
M Hôtel de Ville
R de Rivoli
R du Roi de Sicile

2

Q des Gesvres
Hôtel de Ville
R de Lobau
Pl Baudoyer

Q de la Corse
Pont d'Arcole
Pl St-Gervais
Église St-Gervais - St-Protais
R du Pont Louis-Philippe
4E
R François Miron

Q de l'Hôtel de Ville
R de l'Hôtel de Ville
R Geoffroy l'Asnier
R de Jouy

3

✕ 10
Seine
Q aux Fleurs
Pont Louis-Philippe
Sq A Schweitzer
R des Nonnains d'Hyères

R d'Arcole
R Chanoinesse
4E
R du Cloître Notre Dame
Pl du Bataillon Français de l'ONU en Corée
M Pont Marie

4

O Cathédrale Notre Dame de Paris
Sq Jean XXIII
Sq de l'Île de France
R Jean du Bellay
✕ 8
R Boutarel
Q de Bourbon
Île St-Louis
R le Regrattier
Pont Marie

15 ⬀
12 ✕
Q d'Anjou
20 🔒
14
22 🔒
21
18 🔒
19 🔒
7
6
R St-Louis en l'Île
R des Deux Ponts
R Poulletier

5

Q de Montebello
Pont de l'Archevêché
4 ⊚
Mémorial des Martyrs de la Déportation
Q d'Orléans
Église St-Louis en l'Île
Q de Béthune

R de Bièvre
R des Bernardins
Q de la Tournelle
Pont de la Tournelle
Seine

Musée de la Sculpture en Plein Air

6

R Monge
Bd St-Germain
R de Poissy
R du Cardinal Lemoine
Pont de Sully

E F G H

The Winds of Change

The eventual rebuild of the city's fire-ravaged cathedral is not the only momentous change afoot on the ancient Parisian islands. The departure of the law courts and police HQ from Île de la Cité to the northern suburb of Batignolles – coupled with the agreed future redevelopment of part of historic **Hôpital Hôtel Dieu** (Map p142, D3; 01 42 34 82 32; www.aphp.fr; 7 rue de la Cité, 4e; Cité) into commercial offices, shops and restaurants – heralds a new era for the island.

Sights

Sainte-Chapelle

CHAPEL

 MAP P142, C3

Visit Sainte-Chapelle on a sunny day when Paris' oldest, finest stained glass (1242–48) is at its dazzling best. Enshrined within the city's original, 13th-century Palais de Justice (Law Courts), this gem-like Holy Chapel is Paris' most exquisite Gothic monument, completed in 1248. It was conceived by Louis IX to house his personal collection of holy relics, including the famous Holy Crown. (01 53 40 60 80, concerts 01 42 77 65 65; www.sainte-chapelle.fr; 8 bd du Palais, 1er; adult/child €11.50/free,

combined ticket with Conciergerie €17/free; 9am-7pm Apr-Sep, to 5pm Oct-Mar; Cité)

Conciergerie

MONUMENT

 MAP P142, C2

A royal palace in the 14th century, the Conciergerie later became a prison. During the Reign of Terror (1793–94) alleged enemies of the Revolution were incarcerated here before being brought before the Revolutionary Tribunal next door in the 13th-century Palais de Justice. Top-billing exhibitions take place in the beautiful, Rayonnant Gothic Salle des Gens d'Armes, Europe's largest surviving medieval hall. (01 53 40 60 80; www.paris-conciergerie.fr; 2 bd du Palais, 1er; adult/child €9.50/free, combined ticket with Sainte-Chapelle €17/free; 9.30am-6pm; Cité)

Pont Neuf

BRIDGE

3 MAP P142, A2

Paris' oldest bridge, misguidingly named 'New Bridge', has linked the western end of Île de la Cité with both riverbanks since 1607, when the king, Henri IV, inaugurated it by crossing the bridge on a white stallion. View the bridge's arches (seven on the northern stretch and five on the southern span), decorated with 381 *mascarons* (grotesque figures) depicting barbers, dentists, pickpockets, loiterers etc, from a spot along the river or afloat a boat. (Pont Neuf)

Mémorial des Martyrs de la Déportation MONUMENT

4 ⊙ MAP P142, F5

The Memorial to the Victims of the Deportation, erected in 1962, remembers the 200,000 French residents (including 76,000 Jews, of whom 11,000 were children) who were deported to and murdered in Nazi concentration camps during WWII. A single barred 'window' separates the bleak, rough-concrete courtyard from the waters of the Seine. Inside lies the Tomb of the Unknown Deportee. (📞01 46 33 87 56; Square de l'Île de France, 1er; admission free; ⊙10am-7pm Apr-Sep, to 5pm Tue-Sun Oct-Mar; Ⓜ Cité, Ⓡ RER St-Michel–Notre Dame)

Square du Vert-Galant PARK

5 ⊙ MAP P142, A2

Chestnut, yew, black walnut and weeping willow trees grace this picturesque park at the western-most tip of the Île de la Cité, along with migratory birds including mute swans, pochard and tufted ducks, black-headed gulls and wagtails. Sitting at the islands' original level, 7m below their current height, the waterside park is reached by stairs leading down from the Pont Neuf. It's romantic at any time of day, but especially so in the evening as the sun sets over the river. (place du Pont Neuf, 1er; Ⓜ Pont Neuf)

Stained-glass window in Sainte-Chapelle

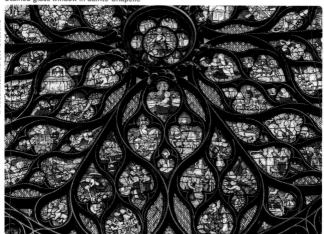

Île St-Louis: Two Islands in One

Today's Île St-Louis was originally, up to the early 17th century, two uninhabited islets called Île Notre Dame (Our Lady Isle) and Île aux Vaches (Cows Island). That was until building contractor Christophe Marie and two financiers worked out a deal with Louis XIII to create one island and build two stone bridges to the mainland. In exchange they could subdivide and sell the newly created real estate, and by 1664 the entire island was covered with fine houses facing the quays and the river, which remain today.

Église St-Louis en l'Île

CHURCH

6 MAP P142, H5

French Baroque Église St-Louis en l'Île, under renovation until 2022 (hence the veil of scaffolding outside), was built between 1664 and 1726. It hosts classical music and organ concerts, and offers a free guided tour of its interior (in French) one Sunday a month at 3pm; check the agenda online. (01 46 34 11 60; www.saintlouis enlile.catholique.fr; 19 rue St-Louis en l'Île, 4e; 9.30am-1pm & 2-7.30pm Mon-Sat, 9am-1pm & 2-7pm Sun; M Pont Marie)

Eating

Berthillon

ICE CREAM €

7 MAP P142, H5

Founded here in 1954, this esteemed *glacier* (ice-cream maker) is still run by the same family today. Its 70-plus all-natural, chemical-free flavours include fruit sorbets (pink grapefruit, raspberry and rose) and richer ice creams made from fresh milk and eggs (salted caramel, candied Ardèche chestnuts, Armagnac and prunes, gingerbread, liquorice, praline and pine kernels). Watch for tempting new seasonal flavours. (01 43 54 31 61; www.berthillon.fr; 29-31 rue St-Louis en l'Île, 4e; 1/2/3/4 scoops takeaway €3/4.50/6/7.50; 10am-8pm Wed-Sun, closed mid-Feb–early Mar & Aug; M Pont Marie)

Café Saint Régis

CAFE €

8 MAP P142, F4

Few addresses entice knowing locals across the river, but this vibrant all-rounder does. The international menu, served by waiters in long white aprons, offers tempting Parisian classics – garlicky snails, onion soup, fried-egg-topped *steak à cheval* – alongside breakfasts, burgers, club sandwiches and meal-sized salads. The retro decor, including glorious ceramic-tiled ceiling and distressed wall mirrors, is equally Paris-delicious. (01 43 54 59 41; www.lesaintregis-paris.com; 6 rue

Jean du Bellay, 4e; breakfast & snacks €3.50-15, mains €17-33; ☻7am-2am, kitchen 8am-midnight; ☞; M Pont Marie)

Sequana   MODERN FRENCH €€€

9 ✖ MAP P142, A2

At home in a chic steel-grey dining room with retro red-velour armchairs and 1950s-style turquoise banquet-seating on Île de la Cité's southwestern tip, fine-dining Sequana evokes the Gallo-Roman goddess of the River Seine. In the kitchen are well-travelled Philippe and Eugénie, whose childhood in Senegal finds its way into colourful combos such as mallard and butternut pumpkin or parsnip and black tea. (☎01 43 29 78 81; www.sequana.paris; 72 quai des Orfèvres, 1er; 2-/3-course lunch menus €24/32, 4-/6-course dinner menus €55/75; ☻noon-2.30pm & 7-10pm Tue-Fri, 7-10pm Sat; M Pont Neuf)

Boulangerie Huré   BAKERY €

10 ✖ MAP P142, E3

'Createur de plaisir' (creator of pleasure) is the enticing strapline of this contemporary *boulangerie* (bakery) where glass cabinets burst with feisty savoury quiches and pizza slices, jumbo salads, 26 types of *sables* (cookies), lavish fruit tarts (pear or banana and chocolate perhaps, or apple crumble?) and a rainbow of cakes. (www.facebook.com/hurecreaturde Plaisir; 1 rue d'Arcole, 4e; sandwiches €3.90-5.20, lunch menus €8.50-10.80;

☻6.30am-8pm Mon-Sat; M St-Michel Notre Dame, Châtelet)

Le Caveau du Palais   MODERN FRENCH €€

11 ✖ MAP P142, B2

Le Caveau's half-timbered dining areas and (weather permitting) alfresco terrace are invariably packed with diners tucking into bountiful fresh fare: pan-seared scallops with artichokes, mushroom ravioli in creamy chestnut sauce, or duck with roast figs. The divinely flaky *millefeuille maison* or crème brûlée are typically sweet Parisian ways to end any meal here. (☎01 43 26 04 28; www.caveaudupalais.fr; 19 place Dauphine, 1er; mains €21-26; ☻noon-2.30pm & 7-10pm; M Pont Neuf)

Les Fous de l'Île   FRENCH €€

12 ✖ MAP P142, H5

Families flock to this island bistro, which features a rustic cockerel theme celebrating the French national symbol and chef Steven Rouquier in the kitchen. Inventive French fare includes steak tartare with smoked duck, roast avocado and fried seaweed, followed perhaps by marinated sardines in chickpea cream and, for dessert, tangy Abondance cheese from the Alps and apple-cider ice-cream. (☎01 43 25 76 67; www.lesfousde lile.com; 33 rue des Deux Ponts, 4e; 2-/3-course menus lunch €21/26, dinner €29/36, mains €17-22; ☻noon-11pm; ☞; M Pont Marie)

The Hunchback of Notre Dame

The damage inflicted on Notre Dame during the French Revolution saw it fall into ruin, and it was destined for demolition. Salvation came with the widespread popularity of Victor Hugo's 1831 novel *The Hunchback of Notre Dame,* which sparked a petition to save it.

The novel opens in 1482 on the Epiphany (6 January), the day of the 'Feast of Fools', with the eponymous hunchback, Quasimodo, the deafened bell-ringer at Notre Dame, crowned the King of Fools. Much of the ensuing action (such as the scene where the dancer Esmeralda is being led to the gallows and Quasimodo swings down by a bell rope to rescue her) takes place in and around the cathedral, which effectively becomes another 'character' in the novel. Subsequently, in 1845, architect Eugène Emmanuel Viollet-le-Duc began the cathedral's grand-scale renovations.

Likewise, Hugo's novel has gone on to achieve immortality of its own, with numerous film, TV, theatre and ballet adaptations, including the hugely successful 1996 Disney animation incorporating faithfully recreated architectural detail.

Ma Salle à Manger
BISTRO €€

13 ✖ MAP P142, B2

Framed by a pretty blue-and-white striped awning, My Dining Room chalks its daily bistro menu on a blackboard. No-fuss dishes include French onion soup, bœuf bourguignon and a feather-light crème brûlée. It also cooks up sandwiches and crêpes to take away. (☎01 43 29 52 34; 26 place Dauphine, 1er; 2-/3-course menus €29.50/37.50, mains €21-23; ⊙9am-10.30pm; Ⓜ Pont Neuf)

L'Îlot Vache
FRENCH €€

14 ✖ MAP P142, G5

Named for one of the Île St-Louis' previous two islands and decorated with cow statuettes, this former butcher shop flickers with candles that give its exposed stone walls and dark wood beams a romantic glow. Traditional French classics range from Burgundy snails in parsley butter to bœuf bourguignon 'grandma-style', duck confit and a glorious homemade tarte Tatin (upside-down apple tart). (☎01 46 33 55 16; www.lilotvache. fr; 35 rue St-Louis en l'Île, 4e; menus €39, mains €24.50-35; ⊙7-11pm; ☎; Ⓜ Pont Marie)

Drinking

Quai de Bourbon
WINE BAR

15 🅗 MAP P142, H4

With its worn petrol-blue façade and decorative vintage ironwork (look for the bunch of grapes), Quai de Bourbon appears to be just another quintessential Parisian neighbourhood bar. But enter the fashionably minimalist interior lit by two giant naked lightbulbs, and descend to the basement to uncover the island's coolest music and cocktail bar. (☎ 01 40 51 05 05; www.quaidebourbon.fr; 1 quai de Bourbon; ⏰ 5pm-2am Tue-Sat; Ⓜ Pont Marie)

Le Bar du Caveau
WINE BAR

16 🚇 MAP P142, B2

The wine bar of neighbouring restaurant Le Caveau du Palais (p147) is an enchanting spot for a glass of wine from France's flagship regions accompanied by a light salad (€14.50 to €16), oh-so-Parisian Poilâne-bread *tartine* (€11 to €13; open-faced sandwich) or warming *croque monsieur* –

cheese and ham toastie. (www.caveaudupalais.fr; 17 place Dauphine, 1er; ⏰ bar 8am-6.30pm Mon-Fri, kitchen noon-4pm Mon-Fri; Ⓜ Pont Neuf)

Shopping

Marché aux Fleurs Reine Elizabeth II
MARKET

17 🔒 MAP P142, D3

Blooms have been sold at this quaint flower market since 1808, making it the oldest market of any kind in Paris. On Sunday, there's also the **Marché aux Oiseaux** (⏰ 8am-7pm Sun), a cacophonous bird market. (www.facebook.com/marche.aux.fleurs.reine.elizabeth.2; Place Louis Lépine et Quai de la Corse, 4e; ⏰ 9.30am-7pm Mon-Sat, 8am-7pm Sun; Ⓜ Cité)

Île St-Louis (p146)

The French Revolution

Beginnings

By the late 1780s, the extravagance of Louis XVI and his queen, Marie Antoinette, had alienated virtually every segment of society and the king grew increasingly isolated as unrest and dissatisfaction reached the boiling point. When he tried to neutralise the power of the more reform-minded delegates at a meeting of the États-Généraux (States-General), the masses took to the streets. On 14 July 1789, a mob raided the Hôtel des Invalides, seized 32,000 muskets and stormed the prison at Bastille. The French Revolution had begun.

Girondins vs Jacobins

At first the Revolution was in the hands of moderate republicans called the Girondins. France was declared a constitutional monarchy and reforms were introduced, including the adoption of the Déclaration des Droits de l'Homme et du Citoyen (Declaration of the Rights of Man and of the Citizen). But as the masses armed themselves against the external threat to the new government by Austria, Prussia and the exiled French nobles, patriotism and nationalism combined with extreme fervour to both popularise and radicalise the Revolution. It was not long before the Girondins lost out to the extremist Jacobins, who abolished the monarchy and declared the First Republic in 1792. The Assemblée Nationale (National Assembly) was replaced by an elected Revolutionary Convention.

End of the Monarchy

Louis XVI, who had unsuccessfully tried to flee the country, was convicted of 'conspiring against the liberty of the nation' and guillotined at today's place de la Concorde in January 1793. Marie Antoinette was executed in October 1793.

The Jacobins set up the notorious Committee of Public Safety to deal with national defence and to apprehend and try 'traitors'. This body had dictatorial control over the city and the country during the Reign of Terror (September 1793 to July 1794), which saw thousands beheaded, most religious freedoms revoked and churches closed to worship and desecrated.

After the Reign of Terror, moderate republicans set themselves up to rule the republic. A group of royalists bent on overthrowing them were led by Napoléon, whose victories would soon turn him into an independent political force.

38 Saint Louis
FOOD & DRINKS

18 🅰 MAP P142, H5

Not only does this contemporary, creamy white-fronted *fromagerie* (cheese shop) run by young, dynamic, food-driven duo Didier Grosjean and Thibault Lhirondelle have an absolutely superb selection of first-class French cheese; it also offers Saturday wine tastings, artisan fruit juices and prepared dishes to go such as sheep's-cheese salad with truffle oil, and wooden boxes filled with vacuum-packed cheese to take home. (🖉01 46 33 30 00; 38 rue St-Louis en l'Île, 4e; ⏲8.30am-10pm Tue-Sat, 9.30am-4pm Sun; Ⓜ Pont Marie)

Librairie Ulysse
BOOKS

19 🅰 MAP P142, H5

Stuffed to the rafters with antiquarian and new travel guides, *National Geographic* back editions and maps, this bijou boutique was the world's first travel bookshop when it was opened in 1971 by the intrepid Catherine Domaine. Hours vary, but ring the bell and Catherine will open up if she's around. (🖉06 27 31 35 95 01 43 25 17 35; www.ulysse.fr; 26 rue St-Louis en l'Île, 4e; ⏲2-8pm Tue-Fri, mornings & Sat by appointment; Ⓜ Pont Marie)

L'Îles aux Images
ART

20 🅰 MAP P142, G5

Original and rare vintage posters, photographs and lithographs dating from 1850 onwards from artists including Man Ray, Salvador Dalí, Paul Gauguin and Picasso are stocked at this gallery-boutique. Many depict Parisian scenes and make evocative home decorations. Framing can be arranged. (🖉01 56 24 15 22; www.vintage-photos-lithos-paris.com; 51 rue Saint-Louis en l'Île, 4e; ⏲2-7pm Mon-Sat & by appointment; Ⓜ Pont Marie)

Upper
CONCEPT STORE

21 🅰 MAP P142, G5

Part boutique, art gallery, cafe (serving coffee, tea, beer, wine and cocktails) and coworking space (where you pay by the hour or day), Upper spreads over three floors. Men's and women's fashion, hats, handbags, jewellery, sunglasses, stationery and homewares such as lamps and pot plant holders are displayed alongside works by Parisian, French and international artists. (🖉01 42 49 29 96; www.upperconcept.com; 19 rue des Deux Ponts, 4e; ⏲11am-7pm Tue-Sat; Ⓜ Pont Marie)

Clair de Rêve
TOYS

22 🅰 MAP P142, G5

Stringed marionettes made of papier mâché, leather and porcelain bob from the ceiling of this endearing little shop. It also sells wind-up toys and music boxes. (🖉01 43 29 81 06; www.clairdereve.com; 35 rue St-Louis en l'Île, 4e; ⏲11am-1pm & 2-7pm Mon-Sat; Ⓜ Pont Marie)

The Latin Quarter

So named because international students communicated in Latin here until the French Revolution, the Latin Quarter remains the hub of academic life in Paris. Centred on the Sorbonne's main university campus, graced by fountains and lime trees, this lively area is also home to lovely museums and churches, along with Paris' beautiful art deco mosque and botanic gardens.

The Short List

○ **Panthéon (p158)** *Paying homage to France's greatest thinkers at this neoclassical mausoleum.*

○ **Shakespeare & Company (p168)** *Browsing the shelves of Paris' most magical bookshop.*

○ **Institut du Monde Arabe (p158)** *Visiting the fascinating exhibits inside, then heading to the roof to admire the incredible panorama.*

○ **Jardin des Plantes (p159)** *Strolling around Paris' sprawling botanical gardens and visiting its historic greenhouses.*

○ **Caveau de la Huchette (p167)** *Lapping up the Latin Quarter vibe at a jazz gig in a mythical medieval cellar.*

Getting There & Around

Ⓜ St-Michel (line 4) and the connected St-Michel–Notre Dame (RER B and C) is the neighbourhood's gateway.

Ⓜ Cluny–La Sorbonne (line 10) and Place Monge (line 7) are also handy metro stations.

⛴ The hop-on, hop-off Batobus stops in the Latin Quarter opposite Notre Dame and near the Jardin des Plantes.

Neighbourhood Map on p156

Walking Tour 🥾

A Stroll along Rue Mouffetard

Originally a Roman road, rue Mouffetard acquired its name in the 18th century, when the now underground River Bièvre became the communal waste disposal for local tanners and wood-pulpers. The odours gave rise to the name mouffettes (skunks), which evolved into Mouffetard. Today the aromas on 'La Mouffe', as it's nicknamed, are infinitely more enticing, particularly at its market stalls.

Walk Facts

Start Marché Mouffetard;
Ⓜ Censier Daubenton

Finish Chez Nicos;
Ⓜ Place Monge

Length 500m; 30 minutes

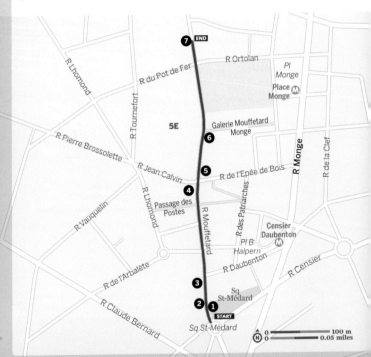

❶ Market Shopping

Grocers, butchers, fishmongers and other food purveyors set their goods out on street stalls along this sloping, cobbled street during the **Marché Mouffetard** (rue Mouffetard, 5e; ⊘8am-7.30pm Tue-Sat, to noon Sun; Ⓜ Censier Daubenton).

❷ Fine Cheeses

Don't let that robust Roquefort scare you off – at the *fromagerie* (cheese shop) **Androuet** (☎01 45 87 85 05; www.androuet.com; 134 rue Mouffetard, 5e; ⊘9.30am-1.30pm & 3.30-7.30pm Tue-Thu, 9.30am-7.30pm Fri & Sat, 9.30am-1.30pm Sun; Ⓜ Censier Daubenton) all of the cheeses can be vacuum-packed for free. (Be sure to look up to see the murals on the building's façade, too.)

❸ Delicious Deli

Marinated aubergines and stuffed olives and capsicums are among the picnic goodies at gourmet Italian deli **Delizius** (☎01 42 17 00 23; 134 rue Mouffetard, 5e; ⊘9.30am-8pm Tue-Sat, 9am-2pm Sun; Ⓜ Censier Daubenton), which also sells ready-to-eat hot meals, and fresh and dried pasta.

❹ Movie Time

Even locals find it easy to miss the small doorway leading to cinema **L'Epée de Bois** (☎08 92 68 75 35; www.cine-epeedebois.fr; 100 rue Mouffetard, 5e; adult/child €8.90/5; Ⓜ Censier Daubenton), which screens both art-house flicks and big-budget blockbusters.

❺ Sweet Treats

A mouth-watering range of chocolates are laid out like jewels at **Mococha** (☎01 47 07 13 66; www.chocolatsmococha.com; 89 rue Mouffetard, 5e; ⊘11am-8pm Tue-Sat, to 6pm Sun; Ⓜ Censier Daubenton). They are the creations of three *maîtres chocolatiers* (master chocolate makers) – Fabrice Gillotte, Jacques Bellanger and Patrice Chapoare.

❻ Caffeine Hit

Dip into Paris' blossoming craft-coffee scene with a serious espresso at **Dose** (www.dosedealerdecafe.fr; 73 rue Mouffetard, 5e; ⊘8am-6pm Tue-Fri, 9am-7pm Sat & Sun; 📶; Ⓜ Place Monge), a new-generation coffee shop and organic juice bar. Beans are supplied by Breton roastery Caffè Cataldi. Lounge over a newspaper on cushioned benches in a heated alley outside or with a line-up of digital creatives on their devices in the book-lined galley space.

❼ Crêpes at Chez Nicos

The signboard outside crêpe artist Nicos' unassuming little shop, **Chez Nicos** (☎01 45 87 28 13; 44 rue Mouffetard, 5e; crêpes €1.50-6; ⊘10am-2am; Ⓜ Place Monge), lists dozens of fillings. Ask by name for his masterpiece 'La Crêpe du Chef', stuffed with eggplant, feta, mozzarella, lettuce, tomatoes and onions. There's a handful of tables; otherwise, head to a nearby park.

The Latin Quarter

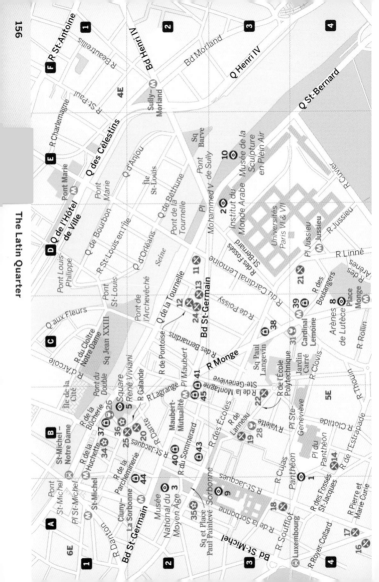

5

6

7

8

Jardin des ◉ 6
Plantes Pl
Valhubert

Gare
d'Austerlitz Ⓜ

Sq
Marie
Curie

Bd de l'Hôpital

R Buffon

St-Marcel Ⓜ

Hôpital de la
Pitié-Salpêtrière

R des Wallons

R Poliveau

For reviews see

◉	Sights	p158
✕	Eating	p161
✕	Drinking	p165
✿	Entertainment	p167
🛍	Shopping	p168

400 m
0.2 miles

Ⓜ E F

Ⓜ Campo
Formio

7 Muséum National
d'Histoire Naturelle

R Geoffroy-St-Hilaire

R Duméril

R Pirandelle

R du Banquier

R Lebrun

◉
4

32 ▢

R Larrey

Mosquée
de Paris

R Lacépède

R du Puits
de l'Ermite

R Daubenton

R Censier

R Scipion

R Fer-à-Moulin

Bd St-Marcel

23 ✕
R des Fossés
St-Marcel

Ⓜ Les
Gobelins

Bd Arago

D

Place
Monge Ⓜ

R Monge

R Mirbel

Censier ─
Daubenton Ⓜ

Pl B
Halpern

27 ▢

Sq
St-Médard

29

Av des Gobelins

R Pascal

Ⓜ Les
Gobelins

R Berbier du Mets

R de Cordelière

C

46 ▢

R Ortolan

R du Pot de Fer

R Tournefort

R Mouffetard

R Brossolette

R de l'Arbalète

R Vauquelin

R Rataud

R Claude-Bernard

R Broca

Bd de Port Royal

R St-Hippolyte

R de la Glacière

R Pascal

B

30 ▢

R Lhomond

R d'Ulm

Hôpital
Val de Grâce

Bd Arago

R de la Santé

A

42 ▢
R St-Jacques

R Gay Lussac

R des
Feuillantines

33 ✿

▼15

Hôpital
Cochin

14E

Bd Arago

7

8

5

6

7

8

Sights

Panthéon
MAUSOLEUM

1 ◉ MAP P156, A4

The Panthéon's stately neoclassical dome is an icon of the Parisian skyline. Its vast interior is an architectural masterpiece: originally an abbey church dedicated to Ste Geneviève and now a mausoleum, it has served since 1791 as the resting place of some of France's greatest thinkers, including Voltaire, Rousseau, Braille and Hugo. A copy of Foucault's pendulum, first hung from the dome in 1851 to demonstrate the rotation of the earth, takes pride of place. (☏01 44 32 18 00; www.paris-pantheon.fr; place du Panthéon, 5e; adult/child €9/free; ☉10am-6.30pm Apr-Sep, to 6pm Oct-Mar; Ⓜ Maubert-Mutualité, RER Luxembourg)

Institut du Monde Arabe
MUSEUM

2 ◉ MAP P156, E3

The Arab World Institute was jointly founded by France and 18 Middle Eastern and North African nations in 1980, with the aim of promoting cross-cultural dialogue. It hosts temporary exhibitions and a fascinating museum of Arabic culture and history (4th to 7th floors). The stunning building, designed by French architect Jean Nouvel, was inspired by latticed-wood windows (*mashrabiya*) traditional to Arabic architecture: thousands of modern-day photo-electrically sensitive apertures cover its sparkling glass façade. (Arab World Institute; ☏01 40 51 38 38; www.imarabe.org; 1 place Mohammed V, 5e; adult/child €8/free; ☉10am-6pm Tue-Fri, to 7pm Sat & Sun; Ⓜ Jussieu)

Musée National du Moyen Âge
MUSEUM

3 ◉ MAP P156, A2

The National Museum of the Middle Ages is undergoing renovations until at least early 2022. It will close completely for a minimum six months starting in June 2020; at other times it will be partially open. Check the website for updates. It showcases a series of sublime treasures, from medieval statuary, stained glass and objets d'art to its celebrated series of tapestries, *The Lady with the Unicorn* (1500). Other highlights include ornate 15th-century mansion Hôtel de Cluny and the *frigidarium* (cold room) of an enormous Roman-era bathhouse. (☏01 53 73 78 00; www.musee-moyenage.fr; 28 rue du Sommerard, 5e; adult/child €5/free, 1st Sun of month free; ☉9.15am-5.45pm Wed-Mon; Ⓜ Cluny–La Sorbonne)

Mosquée de Paris
MOSQUE

4 ◉ MAP P156, D5

Paris' central mosque, with a striking 26m-high minaret, was completed in 1926 in an ornate art deco Moorish style. You can visit the interior to admire the intricate tile work and calligraphy.

A separate entrance leads to the wonderful North African–style hammam, restaurant and tea-room, and a small souk (actually more of a gift shop). Visitors must be modestly dressed. (📞01 45 35 78 17; www.mosqueedeparis.net; 2bis place du Puits de l'Ermite, 5e; adult/child €3/2; 🕙9am-noon & 2-7pm Sat-Thu Apr-Sep, to 6pm Sat-Thu Oct-Mar; Ⓜ Place Monge)

Square René Viviani   PARK

5 ⊙ MAP P156, B1

Opened in 1928 on the site of the former graveyard of adjoining church Église St-Julien le Pauvre (p168), this picturesque little park is home to the oldest tree in Paris, a black locust (*Robinia pseudoacacia*). Royal gardener Jean Robin planted it here in 1602 following

a trip to the American colonies. It has been severely pruned back but, despite initial appearances, it is still alive. A fountain by Georges Jeanclos installed in 1995 depicts the legend of St Julien. (quai de Montebello, 5e; 🕙24hr; Ⓜ St-Michel)

Jardin des Plantes   PARK

6 ⊙ MAP P156, F5

Founded in 1626 as a medicinal herb garden for Louis XIII, Paris' 24-hectare botanic gardens – visually defined by the double alley of plane trees that runs the length of the park – are an idyllic spot to stroll around, break for a picnic (watch out for the automatic sprinklers!) and escape the city concrete for a spell. Three museums from the Muséum National

Jardin des Plantes

ATEL/ERCYPHER-BUDGET TRAVEL ©

The Latin Quarter Sights

d'Histoire Naturelle and a small zoo, **La Ménagerie** (Le Zoo du Jardin des Plantes; www.zoodujardindes plantes.fr; 57 rue Cuvier, 5e; adult/child €13/10; ⏰8am-6pm Mar-Oct, shorter hours Nov-Feb), add to its appeal. (📞01 40 79 56 01; www.jardindes plantes.net; place Valhubert & 36 rue Geoffroy-St-Hilaire, 5e; ⏰8am-7.30pm Apr-Sep, shorter hours winter; Ⓜ Gare d'Austerlitz, Censier Daubenton, Jussieu)

Muséum National d'Histoire Naturelle   MUSEUM

7 ◉ MAP P156, D6

Despite the name, the National Museum of Natural History is not a single building, but a collection of sites throughout France. Its historic home is in the Jardin des Plantes (p159), and it's here that you'll find the greatest number of branches: taxidermied animals in the excellent **Grande Galerie de l'Évolution** (📞01 40 79 54 79; www. grandegaleriedelevolution.fr; adult/ child €10/7, with Galeries des Enfants €12/9; ⏰10am-6pm Wed-Mon; 👶); fossils and dinosaur skeletons in the **Galerie de Paléontologie et d'Anatomie Comparée** (📞01 40 79 56 01; www.mnhn.fr; 2 rue Buffon, 5e; adult/child €9/free; ⏰10am-6pm Wed-Mon); and in the **Galerie de Minéralogie et de Géologie** (📞01 40 79 56 01; www.galeriede mineralogieetgeologie.fr; adult/child €7/free; ⏰10am-6pm Wed-Mon Mar-Oct, to 5pm Nov-Feb) you'll find meteorites and crystals. (www.mnhn. fr; place Valhubert & 36 rue Geoffroy-St-

Hilaire, 5e; Ⓜ Gare d'Austerlitz, Censier Daubenton, Jussieu)

Arènes de Lutèce   RUINS

8 ◉ MAP P156, C4

The 2nd-century Roman amphi-theatre Lutetia Arena once seated 10,000 people for gladiatorial combats and other events. Found by accident in 1869 when rue Monge was under construction, it's now used by locals playing football and, especially, boules (similar to lawn bowls). Hours can vary. (49 rue Monge, 5e; admission free; ⏰8am-8.30pm May-Aug, shorter hours rest year; Ⓜ Place Monge)

Sorbonne   UNIVERSITY

9 ◉ MAP P156, A3

The crème de la crème of aca-demia flock to this distinguished university, one of the world's most famous. Today 'La Sorbonne' embraces most of the 13 autono-mous universities – some 45,000 students in all – created when the University of Paris was reorgan-ised after the student protests of 1968. Visitors are not permitted to enter. (www.sorbonne.fr; 12 rue de la Sorbonne, 5e; Ⓜ Cluny–La Sorbonne, RER Luxembourg)

Musée de la Sculpture en Plein Air   SCULPTURE

10 ◉ MAP P156, E3

Along quai St-Bernard, this open-air sculpture museum (also known as the Jardin Tino Rossi) has more than 50 late-20th-century

1968: A Pivotal Year

The year 1968 was a watershed. In March a large demonstration in Paris against the Vietnam War gave impetus to protests by students of the University of Paris. In May police broke up yet another demonstration, prompting angry students to occupy the Sorbonne and erect barricades in the Latin Quarter. Workers quickly joined in, with six million people across France participating in a general strike that virtually paralysed the country.

But while workers wanted to reap greater benefits from the consumer market, the students supposedly wanted to destroy it. De Gaulle took advantage of this division and appealed to people's fear of anarchy. A 100,000-strong crowd of Gaullists marched in support for the government, quashing any idea of revolution.

Once stability was restored the re-elected government immediately decentralised the higher education system, and implemented a series of reforms throughout the 1970s – including lowering the voting age to 18 and enacting an abortion law – to create the modern society France is today.

unfenced sculptures. It could be a great picnic spot, but unfortunately is not always well maintained. (quai St-Bernard, 5e; admission free; M Gare d'Austerlitz)

Eating

Restaurant AT   GASTRONOMY €€€

 11 ⊗ MAP P156, D2

Trained by some of the biggest names in gastronomy (Pierre Gagnaire included), chef Atsushi Tanaka showcases abstract artlike masterpieces incorporating rare ingredients (charred bamboo, kohlrabi turnip cabbage, juniper berry powder, wild purple fennel, Nepalese Timut pepper) on stunning outsized plates in a blank-canvas-style dining space.

Reservations are essential. (☎01 56 81 94 08; 4 rue du Cardinal Lemoine, 5e; 6-course lunch menus €65, 12-course dinner tasting menus €115, with paired wines €185; ⊙12.30-1.30pm & 8-9.30pm Tue-Sat; M Cardinal Lemoine)

Baieta   FRENCH €€€

12 ⊗ MAP P156, C2

Baieta means 'little kiss' in the patois of Nice, the home town of culinary sensation Julia Sedefdjian, who at 21 was France's youngest Michelin-starred chef when she helmed Paris' Les Fables de La Fontaine. Opened in 2018, her timber- and charcoal-toned Latin Quarter premises showcase her Niçoise roots in creations like confit octopus with crab gnocchi, and smoked-quail *barbajuan*, ricotta-filled pastry. (01 42 02 59 19; www.restaurant-baieta-paris.fr; 5 rue de Pontoise, 5e; 2-/4-course weekday lunch menus €29/45, 7-course dinner menus €85, mains €29-42; noon-2.30pm & 7-10.30pm Tue-Sat; Maubert-Mutualité)

Kitchen Ter(re) GASTRONOMY €€

13 MAP P156, D2

William Ledeuil's third project, Kitchen Ter(re) showcases pasta dishes made from six varieties of ancient grains. But don't write it off as another tired riff on Italian cuisine: instead expect a marvellous procession of out-of-the-box flavour and colour combinations, ranging from citrusy girolette with pumpkin, peanut paste and a fourme d'Ambert cream, or conchiglioni with cockles, green curry and nori-roasted cabbage. (01 42 39 47 48; www.zekitchengalerie.fr; 26 bd St-Germain, 5e; 2-/3-course lunch menus €26/30, mains €21; 12.15-2pm & 7.15-10pm Tue-Sat; Maubert-Mutualité)

Café de la Nouvelle Mairie CAFE €

14 MAP P156, B4

Shhhh...just around the corner from the Panthéon (p158) but hidden away on a small, fountained square, this hybrid cafe-restaurant and wine bar is a tip-top neighbourhood secret, serving natural wines and delicious seasonal bistro fare, from oysters and ribs *(à la française)* to grilled lamb sausage

over lentils. It takes reservations for dinner but not lunch – arrive early. (01 44 07 04 41; 19 rue des Fossés St-Jacques, 5e; mains €11-18; 8am-midnight Mon-Fri, kitchen noon-2.30pm & 8-10.30pm Mon-Fri; Cardinal Lemoine)

La Bête Noire MEDITERRANEAN €

15 MAP P156, A7

A small, fashionably minimalist interior with open kitchen and funky music ensure bags of soul at this off-the-radar *cantine gastronomique,* a showcase for the sensational home cooking of passionate chef-owner Maria. Inspired by her Russian-Maltese heritage, she cooks just one meat and one vegetarian dish daily using seasonal ingredients from local farmers and small producers, washed down with Italian wines. (06 15 22 73 61; www.facebook.com/labetenoireparis; 58 rue Henri Barbusse, 5e; lunch mains €12-15, dinner menus €25-45, brunch €25; 8am-3pm Tue, 8am-3pm & 7-11pm Wed-Fri, 9am-5.30pm & 7-11pm Sat, 9am-5.30pm Sun;   RER Port Royal)

Les Papilles BISTRO €€

16 MAP P156, A4

This hybrid bistro, wine cellar and *épicerie* (specialist grocer) with a sunflower-yellow façade is one of those fabulous Parisian dining experiences. Meals are served at simply dressed tables wedged beneath bottle-lined walls, and fare is market driven: each weekday cooks up a different *retour du marché* (back-from-the-market menu). But what really sets it apart is its exceptional wine list. (☎01 43 25 20 79; www.les papillesparis.fr; 30 rue Gay Lussac, 5e; 2-/4-course menus €28/35; ☺noon-2pm & 7-10.30pm Tue-Sat; Ⓜ Raspail, RER Luxembourg)

Numéro 220   CAFE €

17 ⊗ MAP P156, A4

For a casual breakfast or vegetarian lunch, this cafe hits the spot. Temptations run from sweet-potato curry, salads and slices of quiche to sweet and savoury pancakes and French toast for breakfast. Coffee to go, too! (☎06 66 93 58 71; www.facebook.com/numero220; 220 rue St-Jacques, 5e; mains €7-14; ☺8.30am-6pm

Tue-Fri, 10.30am-5pm Sat; ✐; Ⓜ RER Luxembourg)

Croq' Fac   SANDWICHES €

18 ⊗ MAP P156, A3

Latin Quarter students pack out this *sandwicherie* (sandwich bar) at lunchtime and for good reason. Delicious, made-to-order sandwiches embrace dozens of bread types (wraps, ciabatta, panini, bagels, *pan bagnat* etc) and fillings (the world's your oyster). Arrive before noon to ensure a table – inside or on the people-watching pavement terrace – otherwise you can take away. (160 rue St-Jacques, 5e; sandwich menu from €4.50; ☺8am-7pm Mon-Fri; Ⓜ Cardinal Lemoine)

Les Papilles

Le Coupe-Chou
FRENCH €€

19 ✖ MAP P156, B3

This maze of candlelit rooms inside a vine-clad 17th-century townhouse is overwhelmingly romantic. Ceilings are beamed, furnishings are antique, open fireplaces crackle and background classical music mingles with the intimate chatter of diners. As in the days when Marlene Dietrich dined here, reservations are essential. Timeless French dishes include Burgundy snails, steak tartare and bœuf bourguignon. (📞01 46 33 68 69; www.lecoupechou.com; 9 & 11 rue de Lanneau, 5e; mains €22-36.50; ⏰7-10.30pm; Ⓜ Maubert-Mutualité)

Circus Bakery
BAKERY €

20 ✖ MAP P156, B2

Spectacular sourdough cinnamon rolls are the showstoppers at this bakery with a rustic dark-timber exterior and exposed stone and brick interior. Other treats include apple tarts and breads, such as chocolate-marbled varieties, and Parisian-roasted Hexagone coffee to take away. The wood-fired pita sandwiches are definitely pricey, but stuffed to bursting with scrumptious marinated veggies. (63 rue Galande, 5e; pastries €4-8.50, sandwiches €14; ⏰7am-8pm; Ⓜ Maubert-Mutualité)

Le Buisson Ardent
FRENCH €€

21 ✖ MAP P156, D4

Housed in a former coach house, this time-worn bistro (front-room murals date to the 1920s) serves classy, exciting French fare. The menu changes every week and includes varied dishes such as grilled tuna with capers and black olives, veal cutlets with candied ginger sauce and beef in porto. Stop by after 5pm for a happy-hour apéritif. (📞01 43 54 93 02; www.lebuissonardent.paris; 25 rue Jussieu, 5e; 2-/3-course lunch menus €19/24, mains €22-38; ⏰noon-2.30pm & 7.30-10.30pm; Ⓜ Jussieu)

Les Pipos
FRENCH €€

22 ✖ MAP P156, B3

Natural wines are the speciality of this *bar à vins* (wine bar), which it keeps in its vaulted stone cellar. First-rate food – served from noon onward – includes a fish of the day and oysters from Brittany, along with standards such as confit of duck and a mouthwatering cheese board, which includes all the French classics (Comté, Bleu d'Auvergne, Brie de Meaux, Rocamadour and St-Marcellin). (📞01 43 54 11 40; www.facebook.com/lespiposbaravins; 2 rue de l'École Polytechnique, 5e; 2-course weekday menus €14.50, mains €10.90-19.90; ⏰9.30am-midnight Mon-Fri, from noon Sat; Ⓜ Maubert-Mutualité)

L'Agrume
BISTRO €€

23 ✖ MAP P156, D7

Reserve a table in advance (online or by telephone) at this chic bistro where you can watch chefs work with seasonal products in the open kitchen while you dine at a table or the *comptoir* (counter). Lunch is magnificent value and a real gourmet experience. Evening dining is an exquisite, no-choice *dégustation* (tasting) medley of five courses that changes daily. (☎01 43 31 86 48; www.restaurant-lagrume.fr; 15 rue des Fossés St-Marcel, 5e; 2-/3-course lunch menus €23/26, dinner menus €48; ☺noon-2.30pm & 7.30-10.30pm Tue-Sat; Ⓜ Censier Daubenton)

Le Petit Pontoise
BISTRO €€

24 ✕ MAP P156, C2

Entering this tiny bistro with traditional lace curtains and simple wooden tables is like stepping into old-world Paris. And the kitchen lives up to expectation with fantastic old-fashioned classics including calf kidneys, veal liver cooked in raspberry vinegar, roast quail, *cassoulette d'escargots* (snail stew) and honey- and almond-baked camembert (out of this world). Everything is deliciously *fait maison* (homemade). (☎01 43 29 25 20; www.lepetitpontoise.fr; 9 rue de Pontoise, 5e; 2-/3-course weekday lunch menus €26/34, mains €23-36; ☺noon-2.30pm & 6.30-10.30pm; Ⓜ Maubert-Mutualité)

Odette
PATISSERIE €

25 ✕ MAP P156, B1

Odette's ground-floor space sells *choux* (pastry puffs) with seasonal flavoured cream fillings, such as coffee, lemon, green tea, salted caramel, pistachio and forest berries (nine on offer at a time).

Upstairs, its art deco tearoom plays 1920s music and serves *choux* along with tea, coffee and Champagne. The black-painted timber façade and a geranium-filled 1st-floor window box are charming. (☎01 43 26 13 06; www.odette-paris.com; 77 rue Galande, 5e; 1/6/12 pastry puffs €1.90/10.90/19.80; ☺9am-8pm Mon, Fri & Sat, 11am-8pm Tue-Thu; Ⓜ St-Michel)

Drinking

Shakespeare & Company Cafe
CAFE

26 ☕ MAP P156, B1

Instant history was made when this literary-inspired cafe opened in 2015 adjacent to magical bookshop Shakespeare & Company (p168), designed from long-lost sketches to fulfil late bookshop founder George Whitman's 1960s dream. Organic chai tea, turbo-power juices and specialist coffee by Parisian roaster **Café Lomi** (☎09 51 27 46 31; www.lomi.paris; 3ter rue Marcadet, 18e; ☺8am-6pm Mon-Fri, 10am-7pm Sat & Sun; Ⓜ Marcadet–Poissonnière) marry with soups, salads, bagels and pastries by Bob's Bake Shop. (www.shakespeareandcompany.com; 37 rue de la Bucherie, 5e; ☺9.30am-7pm Mon-Fri, to 8pm Sat & Sun; 🛜; Ⓜ St-Michel)

Le Verre à Pied
CAFE

27 ☕ MAP P156, C6

This *café-tabac* (cafe and tobacconist) is a pearl of a place where little has changed since 1870.

Its nicotine-hued mirrored wall, moulded cornices and original bar make it part of a dying breed, but it epitomises the charm, glamour and romance of an old Paris everyone loves, including stallholders from the rue Mouffetard market who yo-yo in and out. (☎01 43 31 15 72; 118bis rue Mouffetard, 5e; ◷9am-10pm Tue-Sat, to 4pm Sun; Ⓜ Censier Daubenton)

Pub St-Hilaire   PUB

28 🚇 MAP P156, B3

'Buzzing' fails to do justice to the pulsating vibe inside this student-loved pub. Generous happy hours last from 4pm to 9pm and the place is kept packed with a trio of pool tables, board games, music on two floors, hearty bar food and various gimmicks to rev up the party crowd, such as a metre of cocktails, 'be your own barman' etc). (☎01 46 33 52 42; www.face book.com/pubsthilaire; 2 rue Valette, 5e; ◷4pm-2am Mon-Thu, to 4am Fri & Sat; Ⓜ Maubert-Mutualité)

Cave La Bourgogne   BAR

29 🚇 MAP P156, C7

A prime spot for soaking up rue Mouffetard's contagious 'saunter-all-day' spirit, this neighbourhood hangout sits on square St-Médard, one of the Latin Quarter's loveliest, with flower-bedecked fountain, centuries-old church and market stalls spilling across one side. Inside, locals and their pet dogs meet for coffee around dark wood tables alongside a local wine-sipping set. In summer everything spills outside. (☎01 47 07 82 80;

Caveau de la Huchette

144 rue Mouffetard, 5e; ⏰7am-2am Mon-Sat, to 11pm Sun; Ⓜ Censier Daubenton)

Brewberry BAR

30 Ⓟ MAP P156, C5

If you're feeling homesick for your favourite IPA, there's a chance they might have it here, with 24 craft beers on tap from as far off as Colorado and Hawaii. (📞06 62 46 75 13; www.facebook.com/brewberrylebar; 11 rue du Pot de Fer, 5e; ⏰5pm-midnight Tue-Sat; Ⓜ Place Monge)

Strada Café COFFEE

31 Ⓟ MAP P156, C4

Beans from Parisian roastery L'Arbre à Café and Lyon's Mokxa roastery underpin the success of this sunlit corner cafe, strewn with an eclectic mix of armchairs and wooden-chair seating. Electrical sockets are plentiful (no laptops at weekends, however) and international baristas are passionate about their brews. There's breakfast, salad-and-soup lunches, weekend brunch and gluten-free cakes. (www.facebook.com/stradacafe94; 24 rue Monge, 5e; ⏰8am-6.30pm Mon-Fri, 9.30am-6.30pm Sat & Sun; 🛜; Ⓜ Cardinal Lemoine)

La Mosquée TEAHOUSE

32 Ⓟ MAP P156, D6

Sip a sweet mint tea and nibble on a *pâtisserie orientale* between trees and chirping birds in the courtyard of the tearoom of Paris'

beautiful mosque, the Mosquée de Paris (p158). (39 rue Geoffroy-St-Hilaire, 5e; ⏰noon-midnight; Ⓜ Censier Daubenton)

Entertainment

Café Universel JAZZ, BLUES

33 ⭐ MAP P156, A6

Café Universel hosts a brilliant array of live concerts with everything from bebop and Latin sounds to vocal jazz sessions (see its Facebook page for the schedule). Plenty of freedom is given to young producers and artists, and its convivial, relaxed atmosphere attracts a mix of students and jazz lovers. Concerts are free, but you should tip the artists when they pass the hat around. (📞01 43 25 74 20; www.facebook.com/cafeuniversel.paris05; 267 rue St-Jacques, 5e; ⏰cafe 7.30am-1am Tue-Sat, from 9.30am Sun; 🛜; Ⓜ Censier Daubenton, RER Port Royal)

Caveau de la Huchette JAZZ, BLUES

34 ⭐ MAP P156, B1

Housed in a medieval *cave* (wine cellar) used as a courtroom and torture chamber during the Revolution, this club is where many of the jazz greats (Count Basie, Art Blakey) have played since the end of WWII. It attracts its fair share of tourists, but the atmosphere can be more electric than at the more serious jazz clubs. Sessions start at around 9.30pm. (📞01 43 26 65 05; www.caveaudelahuchette.fr; 5 rue de la Huchette, 5e; admission €13-15; ⏱9pm-2am Sun-Thu, to 4am Fri & Sat; Ⓜ︎St-Michel)

Le Champo   CINEMA

35 ⭐ MAP P156, A2

This is one of the most popular of the many Latin Quarter cinemas, featuring classics and retrospectives looking at the films of such actors and directors as Alfred Hitchcock, Jacques Tati, Alain Resnais, Frank Capra and Tim Burton. One of the two *salles* (cinemas) has wheelchair access. (www.cinema-lechampo.com; 51 rue des Écoles, 5e; tickets adult/child €9/4; Ⓜ︎Cluny–La Sorbonne)

Église St-Julien le Pauvre   CLASSICAL MUSIC

36 ⭐ MAP P156, B1

Piano recitals (Chopin, Liszt) are staged at least two evenings a week in one of the oldest churches in Paris. Higher-priced tickets directly face the stage. Payment is by cash only at the door. (📞01 42 26 00 00; www.concertinparis.com; 1 rue St-Julien le Pauvre, 5e; hours vary; Ⓜ︎St-Michel)

Shopping

Shakespeare & Company   BOOKS

37 🔒 MAP P156, B1

Enchanting nooks and crannies overflow with new and second-hand English-language books. The original shop (12 rue l'Odéon, 6e;

closed by the Nazis in 1941) was run by Sylvia Beach and became the meeting point for Hemingway's 'Lost Generation'. Readings by emerging and illustrious authors regularly take place, and there's a wonderful cafe (p165) next door. (📞01 43 25 40 93; www.shakespeareandcompany.com; 37 rue de la Bûcherie, 5e; ⏱10am-10pm Mon-Sat, 12.30-8pm Sun; Ⓜ︎St-Michel)

Le Bonbon au Palais   FOOD

38 🔒 MAP P156, C3

Kids and kids-at-heart will adore this sugar-fuelled *tour de France*. The school-geography-themed boutique stocks rainbows of artisanal sweets from around the country. Old-fashioned glass jars brim with treats like *calissons* (diamond-shaped, icing-sugar-topped ground fruit and almonds from Aix-en-Provence), *rigolettes* (fruit-filled pillows from Nantes), *berlingots* (striped, triangular boiled sweets from Carpentras and elsewhere) and *papalines* (herbal liqueur-filled pink-chocolate balls from Avignon). (📞01 78 56 15 72; www.lebonbonaupalais.com; 19 rue Monge, 5e; ⏱10.30am-7.30pm Tue-Sat; Ⓜ︎Cardinal Lemoine)

Bières Cultes Jussieu   DRINKS

39 🔒 MAP P156, C4

At any one time this beer-lovers' fantasyland stocks around 500 different craft and/or international brews, along with four on tap to taste on the spot. Just some of its wares when you visit might include

US-brewed Alaskan Smoked Porter, German smoked Aecht Schlenkerla Rauchbier from Bamberg and New Zealand Monteith's. Check its website and Facebook page for events and seasonal releases. (☎09 51 27 04 84; www.bierescultes.fr; 44 rue des Boulangers, 5e; ⏱4-8pm Mon, 4-9.30pm Tue-Thu, 11am-2pm & 4-11pm Fri, 11am-2pm & 4-9.30pm Sat; Ⓜ Cardinal Lemoine)

Album
COMICS

40 🔒 MAP P156, B2

Album specialises in *bandes dessinées* (comic strips), which have an enormous following in France, with everything from Tintin and Babar to erotic comics and the latest Japanese manga. Serious comic collectors – and anyone excited by Harry Potter wands, *Star Wars*, *Superman* and other superhero figurines and T-shirts (you know who you are!) – shouldn't miss it. (☎01 53 10 00 60; www.album comics.com; 67 bd St-Germain, 5e; ⏱10am-8pm Mon-Sat, noon-7pm Sun; Ⓜ Cluny–La Sorbonne)

Fromagerie Laurent Dubois
CHEESE

41 🔒 MAP P156, C2

One of the best *fromageries* (cheese shops) in Paris, this cheese-lover's nirvana is filled with to-die-for delicacies, such as St-Félicien with Périgord truffles. Rare, limited-production cheeses include blue Termignon and Tarentaise goat's cheese. All are appropriately cellared in warm, humid or cold environments. Branches

Shakespeare & Company

Parisian Life

Within the Walls

Paris is defined by its former walls (now the Périphérique or ring road). *Intramuros* (Latin for 'within the walls'), the 105-sq-km interior has a population of about 2.2 million, while the greater metropolitan area (the Île de France *région*, encircled by rivers) has 12.5 million inhabitants, almost 19% of France's total population. This makes Paris – the capital of both the *région* and the highly centralised nation – in effect an 'island within an island' (or, as residents elsewhere might say, a bubble).

Communal Living

Paris isn't merely a commuter destination, however – its dense inner-city population defines city life. Paris' shops, street markets, parks and other facets of day-to-day living evoke a village atmosphere, and its almost total absence of high-rises gives it a human scale. Single-occupant dwellings make up around half of central Paris' households. And space shortages mean residential apartments are often minuscule. As a result, communal areas are the living and dining rooms and backyards of many Parisians, while neighbourhood shops are cornerstones of community life. This high concentration of city dwellers is why there are few late-night bars and cafes or inner-city nightclubs, due to noise restrictions. It's also why so many pet dogs live in Paris. Hefty fines for owners who don't clean up after them have meant the pavements are the cleanest they've ever been.

Beyond the Walls

The Grand Paris (Greater Paris) redevelopment project connects the outer suburbs with the city proper. This is a significant break in the physical and conceptual barrier that the Périphérique has imposed. Its crux is a massive decentralised metro expansion, with four new metro lines, the extension of several existing lines, and a total of 68 new stations, with a target completion date of 2030. The principal goal is to connect the suburbs with one another, instead of relying on a central inner-city hub from which all lines radiate outwards (the current model). Ultimately, the surrounding suburbs – Vincennes, Neuilly, Issy, St-Denis etc – will lose their autonomy and become part of a much larger Grand Paris governed by the Hôtel de Ville.

include one in the 15e. (📞01 43 54 50 93; www.fromageslaurent dubois.fr; 47ter bd St-Germain, 5e; 🕐8am-7.30pm Tue-Sat, 8.30am-1pm Sun; Ⓜ Maubert-Mutualité)

Nicolaï
PERFUME

42 🔒 MAP P156, A5

Established in Paris in 1986 by esteemed *parfumeuse* (perfume maker) Patricia de Nicolaï, whose great-grandfather Pierre-François Pascal Guerlain founded Guerlain 150 years earlier, Nicolaï remains a family-run business today. Fragrances include Cococabana (with notes of ylang-ylang, palm, vanilla and tonka flower), Kiss Me Tender (orange blossom, almond, jasmine and cloves) and Musc Monoï (lemon, magnolia, coconut and sandalwood). (📞01 44 55 02 00; www.pnicolai.com; 240 rue St-Jacques, 5e; 🕐10.30am-2pm & 3-6.30pm Mon-Sat; Ⓜ Place Monge)

Au Vieux Campeur
SPORTS & OUTDOORS

43 🔒 MAP P156, B2

This outdoor store has colonised the Latin Quarter, with some two dozen different boutiques scattered around its original shop that opened on rue St-Jacques in 1941 (actually a few doors down at No 38). Each space is devoted to a different sport: climbing, skiing, diving, camping, biking, water sports and so on. (📞01 53 10 48 48; www.auvieuxcampeur.fr; 48 rue des Écoles, 5e; 🕐11am-8pm Mon-Wed & Fri, 11am-9pm Thu, 10am-8pm Sat; Ⓜ Maubert-Mutualité)

Abbey Bookshop
BOOKS

44 🔒 MAP P156, A2

Inside 18th-century Hôtel Dubuisson, this chaotic but welcoming Canadian-run bookshop serves free coffee (sweetened with maple syrup) to sip while you browse thousands upon thousands of new and used books. Watch for occasional literary events. (📞01 46 33 16 24; https://abbeybookshop. wordpress.com; 29 rue de la Parcheminerie, 5e; 🕐10am-7pm Mon-Sat; Ⓜ Cluny–La Sorbonne)

Marché Maubert
MARKET

45 🔒 MAP P156, B2

Shop for fruit and veg (some organic), cheese, bread and so on at this welcoming, village-like food market that spills across place Maubert thrice weekly. (place Maubert, 5e; 🕐7am-2.30pm Tue & Thu, 7am-3pm Sat; Ⓜ Maubert-Mutualité)

Marché Monge
MARKET

46 🔒 MAP P156, C5

Open-air Marché Monge is laden with wonderful cheeses, baked goods and a host of other temptations. (place Monge, 5e; 🕐7am-2pm Wed, Fri & Sun; Ⓜ Place Monge)

Walking Tour 🥾

Southeastern Discovery

Spanning both banks of the Seine, Paris' southeast is an eclectic mix of quartiers (quarters) that makes for a fascinating stroll if you've stood in one tourist queue too many. But while it's an authentic slice of local life, there are plenty of big-hitting attractions here too, including France's national cinema institute and national library.

Getting There

This area stretches south from Gare de Lyon, 12e, to La Butte aux Cailles, 13e.

Ⓜ Gare de Lyon (lines 1 and 14) and Place d'Italie (lines 5, 6 and 7) are convenient start/end points.

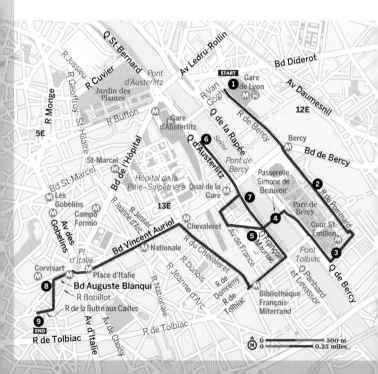

❶ Railway Splendour

Start your journey in style with a drink or classical fare at Belle Époque (beautiful era) showpiece **Le Train Bleu** (📞01 43 43 09 06; www.le-train-bleu.com; 1st fl, Gare de Lyon, 26 place Louis Armand, 12e; 2-/3-/6-course menus €49/65/110, mains €35-46; 🕐restaurant 11.30am-2.45pm & 7-10.45pm, bar 7.30am-10pm; 📶🚻; Ⓜ Gare de Lyon).

❷ Cinematic History

The **Cinémathèque Française** (📞01 71 19 33 33; www.cinematheque. fr; 51 rue de Bercy, 12e; adult/child €5/2.50, 1st Sun of month free, with film €8; 🕐noon-7pm Wed-Mon; Ⓜ Bercy) showcases the history of French cinema and screens films.

❸ Village Spirit

Bercy Village (www.bercyvillage. com; Cour St-Émilion, 12e; 🕐shops & cinema 10am-8pm, restaurants & bars 11am-2am; Ⓜ Cour St-Émilion) has more cinemas, along with shops, eateries and bars in its strip of former wine warehouses.

❹ Crossing the Bridge

The oak-and-steel foot and cycle bridge **Passerelle Simone de Beauvoir** (2006) links the Right and Left Banks.

❺ Hitting the Books

Topped by four sunlit glass towers shaped like open books, the **Bibliothèque Nationale de France** (📞01 53 79 59 59; www.bnf.fr; 11 quai François Mauriac, 13e; temporary exhibitions €9-11; 🕐9am-8pm Tue-Sat, 1-7pm Sun, closed 2 weeks in Sep; Ⓜ Bibliothèque François-Mitterrand) mounts exhibitions revolving around 'the word'.

❻ Dockside Fashion

Transformed warehouse **Les Docks** (Cité de la Mode et du Design; 📞01 76 77 25 30; www. citemodedesign.fr; 34 quai d'Austerlitz, 13e; 🕐10am-midnight; Ⓜ Gare d'Austerlitz) is the French fashion institute's HQ, with exhibitions and events.

❼ Swimming on the Seine

Splash at floating swimming pool **Piscine Joséphine Baker** (📞01 56 61 96 50; www.piscine-baker.fr; quai François Mauriac, 13e; adult/child from €4/2.20; 🕐7-9am & 10am-11pm Mon-Fri, 9am-8pm Sat & Sun Jun-Sep, shorter hours rest of year; Ⓜ Quai de la Gare).

❽ Bistro Dining

The pavement terrace of **La Butte aux Piafs** (📞09 83 51 07 50; www.labutteauxpiafs-paris.fr; 31 bd Auguste Blanqui, 13e; mains €15-19; 🕐noon-2.30pm & 7-10.30pm Mon-Fri, 7-10.30pm Sat; Ⓜ Place d'Italie) is great for savouring easygoing bistro dishes.

❾ Heading to the 'Hood

In the heart of the villagey La Butte aux Cailles *quartier*, retro bar **Le Merle Moqueur** (11 rue de la Butte aux Cailles, 13e; 🕐5pm-2am; Ⓜ Corvisart) is a local favourite.

Explore ⊚

Musée d'Orsay & St-Germain des Prés

Literary buffs, antique collectors and fashionistas flock to this legendary part of Paris, where the presence of writers such as Sartre, de Beauvoir and Hemingway still lingers in historic cafes. Despite gentrification there remains a startling cinematic quality to this part of the Left Bank.

The Short List

○ **Musée d'Orsay (p176)** *Revelling in a wealth of world-famous impressionist masterpieces and art nouveau architecture at this glorious national museum.*

○ **Jardin du Luxembourg (p178)** *Strolling through the chestnut groves and orchards, past ponds and statues, at the city's most popular park.*

○ **Les Catacombes (p186)** *Prowling the spine-prickling, skull-and-bone-packed subterranean tunnels of Paris' creepy ossuary.*

○ **Cimetière du Montparnasse (p186)** *Visiting the resting places of local luminaries.*

Getting There & Around

Ⓜ St-Germain des Prés (line 4), Mabillon (line 10) and Odéon (lines 4 and 10) are in the heart of the action.

Ⓜ Montparnasse Bienvenüe (lines 4, 6, 12 and 13) is Montparnasse's hub.

⚓ The hop-on, hop-off Batobus stops outside the Musée d'Orsay and at quai Malaquais in St-Germain des Prés.

Neighbourhood Map on p182

Plaza fronting Église St-Sulpice (p185) PAGE LIGHT STUDIOS/SHUTTERSTOCK ©

Top Experience 📷
Marvel at the Masters in the Musée d'Orsay

The home of France's national collection from the impressionist, postimpressionist and art nouveau movements spanning 1848 to 1914 is the glorious former Gare d'Orsay railway station – itself an art nouveau showpiece – where a roll-call of masters and their world-famous works are on display.

◎ MAP P182, C1

www.musee-orsay.fr

1 rue de la Légion d'Honneur, 7e

adult/child €14/free

🕑 9.30am-7pm Tue, Wed & Fri-Sun, to 8.45pm Thu

Ⓜ Assemblée Nationale, RER Musée d'Orsay

The Building

The Gare d'Orsay's platforms were built for the 1900 Exposition Universelle (World's Fair) – by 1939 they were too short for trains, and in a few years all rail services ceased. In 1962 Orson Welles filmed Kafka's *The Trial* in the then-abandoned building before the government set about transforming it into the country's premier showcase for art created between 1848 and 1914. Don't miss the panorama through the station's giant glass clockface and from the adjacent terrace.

Painting Collections

Masterpieces include Manet's *On the Beach*; Monet's gardens at Giverny and *Rue Montorgueil, Paris, Festival of June 30, 1878*; Cézanne's card players, *Green Apples* and *Blue Vase*; Renoir's *Ball at the Moulin de la Galette* and *Girls at the Piano*; Degas' ballerinas; Toulouse-Lautrec's cabaret dancers; Pissarro's *The Harvest*; Sisley's *View of the Canal St-Martin*; and Van Gogh's *Starry Night*.

Decorative Arts Collections

Household items from 1848 to 1914, such as hat stands, desks, chairs, bookcases, vases, water pitchers, decorated plates, goblets, bowls – and even kettles and cutlery – are true works of art and incorporate exquisite design elements.

Sculptures

Sculptures by Degas, Gauguin, Camille Claudel, Renoir and Rodin are magnificently displayed in the soaring building.

Graphic Arts Collections

Drawings and sketches from major artists are another of the Musée d'Orsay's highlights. Look for Georges Seurat's crayon on paper work *The Black Bow* (c 1882) and Paul Gauguin's poignant self-portrait (c 1902–03).

★ Top Tips

o Combined tickets with the Musée de l'Orangerie (p78) cost €18, while combined tickets with the Musée Rodin (p40) are €21; valid for a single visit to the museums within three months.

o The museum is busiest on Tuesday and Sunday.

✕ Take a Break

The ground-floor **Café de l'Ours** (⏱9.30am-4.45pm Tue, Wed & Fri-Sun, to 8pm Thu) overlooks Francois Pompon's sculpted *Polar Bear* (1923–33).

Alternatively, try the museum's orange-and-turquoise **Café Campana** (mains €14-19; ⏱10.30am-5pm Tue, Wed & Fri-Sun, to 9pm Thu) or dine at the Gare Orsay's original **Le Restaurant** (☎01 45 49 47 03; mains €17-29, lunch menus €24.50-31, dinner menus €49; ⏱11.45am-5.30pm Tue, Wed & Fri-Sun, 11.45am-2.45pm & 7-9.30pm Thu; ✏️👪).

Top Experience 📷
Relax in the Jardin du Luxembourg

This inner-city oasis of formal terraces, chestnut groves and lush lawns has a special place in Parisians' hearts. Napoléon dedicated the 23 gracefully laid-out hectares of the Luxembourg Gardens to the children of Paris, and many residents spent their childhood prodding little wooden sailboats with long sticks on the octagonal pond, watching puppet shows, riding the carousel or ponies or playing pétanque (similar to bowls)

◉ MAP P182, E5

www.senat.fr/visite/jardin

6e

🕐 hours vary

Ⓜ Mabillon, St-Sulpice, Rennes, Notre Dame des Champs, RER Luxembourg

Grand Bassin

All ages love the octagonal Grand Bassin, a serene ornamental pond where adults can lounge and kids can play with 1920s **toy sailboats** (www.lesvoiliersduluxembourg.fr; sailboat rental per 30min €4; ☉11am-6pm Apr-Oct). Nearby, littlies can take **pony rides** (☎06 07 32 53 95; www.animaponey.com; 600m/900m pony ride €6/8.50; ☉3-6pm Wed, Sat, Sun & school holidays) or romp around the **playgrounds** (adult/child €1.50/2.50; ☉hours vary) – the green half is for kids aged seven to 12 years, the blue half for under-sevens.

Puppet Shows

You don't have to be a kid or be able to speak French to be delighted by marionette shows, which have entertained audiences in France since the Middle Ages. The lively puppets perform in the Jardin du Luxembourg's little **Théâtre du Luxembourg** (☎01 43 29 50 97; www.marionnettesduluxembourg.fr; tickets €6.70; ☉Wed, Sat & Sun, daily during school holidays). Show times can vary; check the program online and arrive half an hour ahead.

Musée du Luxembourg

Prestigious temporary art exhibitions take place in the **Musée du Luxembourg** (☎01 40 13 62 00; www.museeduluxembourg.fr; 19 rue de Vaugirard, 6e; most exhibitions €13; ☉10.30am-7pm Tue-Sun, to 10pm Mon).

Around the back of the museum, lemon and orange trees, palms, grenadiers and oleanders shelter from the cold in the palace's orangery.

Palais du Luxembourg

The **Palais du Luxembourg** (www.senat.fr; rue de Vaugirard, 6e) was built in the 1620s and has been home to the Sénat (French Senate) since 1958. It's occasionally visitable by guided tour.

★ **Top Tips**

● Kiosks and cafes are dotted throughout the park.

● The elegantly manicured lawns are off-limits apart from a small wedge on the southern boundary. Do as Parisians do, and corral one of the iconic 1923-designed green metal chairs and find your own favourite part of the park.

✗ **Take a Break**

Polidor (www.polidor.com; 41 rue Monsieur le Prince, 6e; menus €22, mains €12-20; ☉noon-2.30pm & 7-10.30pm Mon-Sat, to 10pm Sun; Ⓜ Odéon) and its decor date from 1845 and it still serves family-style French cuisine.

Tearoom **Angelina** (☎01 46 34 31 19; www.angelina-paris.fr; 19 rue de Vaugirard, 6e; ☉10.30am-7pm; Ⓜ St-Sulpice) adjoins the Musée du Luxembourg.

Walking Tour 🥾

Left Bank Literary Loop

It wasn't only Paris' reputation for liberal thought and relaxed morals that lured writers in the early 20th century – Left Bank Paris was cheap and, unlike Prohibition-era America, you could drink to your heart's content. This walk through the area's long-gentrified streets takes in pivotal places from the era.

Walk Facts

Start Rue du Cardinal Lemoine; Ⓜ Cardinal Lemoine

Finish Rue Notre Dame des Champs; Ⓜ Vavin

Length 6.5km; three hours

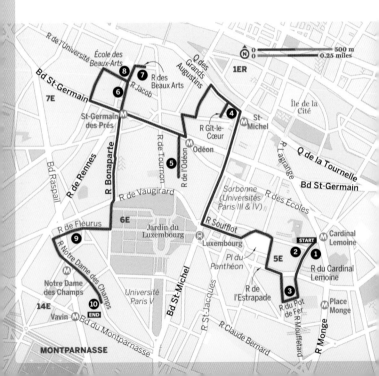

❶ Rue du Cardinal Lemoine

Walk southwest along rue du Cardinal Lemoine, peering down the passageway at No 71, where James Joyce finished *Ulysses* in apartment E. From 1922 to 1923, Ernest Hemingway lived at No 74.

❷ Rue Descartes

Hemingway wrote in the top-floor garret of a hotel at 39 rue Descartes – the same hotel where the poet Paul Verlaine died. Ignore the incorrect plaque.

❸ George Orwell's Boarding House

In 1928 George Orwell stayed in a **boarding house** (6 rue du Pot de Fer, 5e; Ⓜ Place Monge), which he called 'rue du Coq d'Or' in *Down and Out in Paris & London* (1933).

❹ Jack Kerouac's Hotel

The **Relais Hôtel du Vieux Paris** at 9 rue Gît le Coeur was a favourite of poet Allen Ginsberg and Beat writer Jack Kerouac in the 1950s.

❺ Shakespeare & Company

The original **Shakespeare & Company bookshop** (p168) stood at 12 rue de l'Odéon, where owner Sylvia Beach lent books to Hemingway and published *Ulysses* for Joyce in 1922. It was closed during WWII's Nazi occupation.

❻ Henry Miller's Room

Henry Miller stayed on the 5th floor of 36 rue Bonaparte in 1930; he wrote about the experience in *Letters to Emil* (1989).

❼ Oscar Wilde's Hotel

The former Hôtel d'Alsace, now **L'Hôtel** (☎ 01 44 41 99 00; www.l-hotel.com; 13 rue des Beaux Arts, 6e; Ⓜ St-Germain des Prés), is where Oscar Wilde died in 1900.

❽ Hemingway's First Night in Paris

Hemingway spent his first night in the city at the **Hôtel 'Angleterre** (☎ 01 42 60 34 72; www.hotel-dangleterre.com; 44 rue Jacob, 6e; d from €222; @ 🛜; Ⓜ St-Germain des Prés).

❾ Gertrude Stein's Home

Ezra Pound and Hemingway were among those entertained at 27 rue de Fleurus, where Gertrude Stein lived with Alice B Toklas.

❿ Rue Notre Dame des Champs

Pound lived at 70bis rue Notre Dame des Champs, while Hemingway's first apartment in this area was above a sawmill at No 113.

Musée d'Orsay & St-Germain des Prés

500 m
0.25 miles

R des Halles
R de Rivoli
R de Rivoli
1ER
Louvre
Rivoli
Pont
Neuf
Bouquinistes
Q de la
Mégisserie
Q de l'Horloge
Q de l'Horloge
Île de la
Cité
R de la Cité
Bd du Palais
Q des Orfèvres
St-Michel
Notre Dame
St-Michel–
Notre Dame
St-Michel
Cluny–
La Sorbonne
Bd St-Germain
R des Écoles
R St-Jacques
Sorbonne
Bd St-Michel
R Danton
Le Procope
R de l'École
de Médecine
R Monsieur-
le-Prince
R de l'Odéon
R de Médicis
Palais du
Luxembourg
R de Tournon
R Garancière
Église
St-Sulpice
R de Vaugirard
6E
R Madame
R Cassette
R de Rennes
R du Vieux
Colombier
R du
Regard
R du Cherche Midi
R de Sèvres
R Dupin
Sèvres–
Babylone
La Grande
Épicerie de
Paris
Le Bon
Marché
Vaneau
R de Babylone
R Oudinot
R de Sèvres
R Vaneau
Sq des
Missions
Étrangères
R de Babylone
R de Barbet de Jouy
R de Varenne
R de Grenelle
FAUBOURG
ST-GERMAIN
7E
R de Bellechasse
R de Grenelle
R de l'Université
R St-Dominique
Bd St-Germain
Assemblée
Nationale
Pl du Palais
Bourbon
Q d'Orsay
Musée
d'Orsay
Musée
d'Orsay
Parc Rives
de Seine
Q Anatole France
R de Lille
Solférino
Rue du Bac
R du Bac
R de Varenne
Bd Raspail
À la Petite
Chaise
R de Grenelle
R de Verneuil
R de Lille
Q Voltaire
Q Malaquais
Q de Conti
Pont
Royal
Pont du
Carrousel
Pont
des Arts
Q François Mitterrand
Q du Louvre
Musée
du Louvre
Pl du
Carrousel
Q des Tuileries
Pont
Neuf
Louvre
Rivoli
Monnaie de
Paris
Musée
National
Eugène
Delacroix
Église
St-Germain
des Prés
St-Germain
des Prés
Bd St-Germain
R de Seine
R Mazarine
R Dauphine
R Guénégaud
R de Buci
R Bonaparte
R de Seine
R Jacob
R des Sts-Pères
Magasin
Sennelier
R du Dragon
R du Four
R de l'Abbaye
Deyrolle
R de l'Échaudé
Poilâne
Mabillon
Odéon
St-Sulpice
Q des Grands
Augustins
R St-André des Arts
R Dauphine
Cité
R de Condé
R de l'Éperon

5
38
21
27
14
9
16
33
23
35
15
36
39
34
3
13
30
31
32
18
4
1
22
25
20
12
2
28
29
24
11
26
10
6

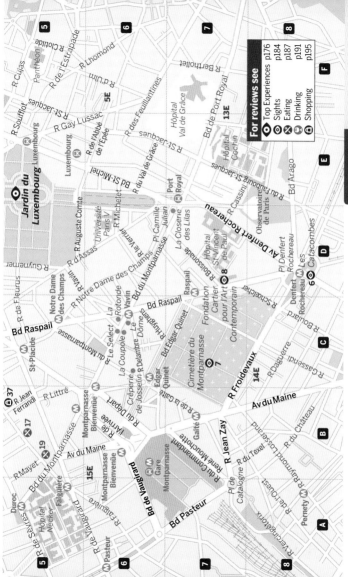

For reviews see
● Top Experiences   p176
● Sights   p184
⊗ Eating   p187
❶ Drinking   p191
⊟ Shopping   p195

Sights

Église St-Germain des Prés

CHURCH

1 MAP P182, D3

Paris' oldest standing church, the Romanesque St Germanus of the Fields, was built in the 11th century on the site of a 6th-century abbey and was the main place of worship in Paris until the arrival of Notre Dame. It's since been altered many times. The oldest part, Chapelle de St-Symphorien, is to the right as you enter; St Germanus (496–576), the first bishop of Paris, is believed to be buried there. (☑01 55 42 81 18; www.eglise-saintgermain despres.fr; 3 place St-Germain des Prés, 6e; ⏰9am-8pm; Ⓜ St-Germain des Prés)

Monnaie de Paris

MUSEUM

2 MAP P182, E2

The 18th-century royal mint, Monnaie de Paris, houses the Musée du 11 Conti, an interactive museum exploring the history of French coinage from antiquity onwards, plus edgy contemporary-art exhibitions. The impeccably restored, neoclassical building, with one of the longest façades on the Seine, stretching 116m long, squirrels away five sumptuous courtyards, the Hôtel de Conti designed by Jules Hardouin-Mansart in 1690, engraving workshops, the original foundry (now the museum boutique), Guy Savoy's **flagship restaurant** (☑01 43 80 40 61; www. guysavoy.com; lunch menus via online booking €250, 13-course tasting menus

Église St-Germain des Prés

JEROME LABOUYRIE/SHUTTERSTOCK ©

€478; ⊗noon-2pm & 7-10.30pm Tue-Fri, 7-10.30pm Sat) and fashionable **Frappé par Bloom** (🗂07 89 83 79 58; http://frappe.bloom-restaurant.fr; 2 rue Guénégaud, 6e; ⊗11am-7pm Tue-Sun) cafe. (🗂01 40 46 56 66; www.monnaiedeparis.fr; 11 quai de Conti, 6e; adult/child €12/free; ⊗11am-7pm Tue & Thu-Sun, to 9pm Wed; Ⓜ Pont Neuf)

Église St-Sulpice CHURCH

3 ◎ MAP P182, D4

In 1646 work started on the twin-towered Church of St Sulpicius, lined inside with 21 side chapels, and it took six architects 150 years to finish. It's famed for its striking Italianate façade with two rows of superimposed columns, its Counter Reformation–influenced neoclassical decor, its frescoes by Eugène Delacroix – and its setting for a murderous scene in Dan Brown's *The Da Vinci Code*. You can hear the monumental, 1781-built organ during 10.30am Mass on Sunday or the occasional Sunday-afternoon concert. (🗂01 42 34 59 98; www.pss75.fr/saint-sulpice-paris; place St-Sulpice, 6e; admission free; ⊗7.30am-7.30pm; Ⓜ St-Sulpice)

Musée National Eugène Delacroix MUSEUM

4 ◎ MAP P182, D3

In a courtyard off a tree-shaded square, this museum is housed in the romantic artist's home and studio at the time of his death in 1863. It contains a collection of his oil paintings, watercolours,

Start Up at Station F

Some 3000 resident entrepreneurs beaver away on ground-breaking ideas at the world's largest start-up campus, **Station F** (https://stationf.co; 5 Parvis Alan Turing, 13e; admission free; ⊗English-language tours by reservation 11.30am Tue & Thu; Ⓜ Chevaleret, Bibliothèque François-Mitterrand). Guided tours (English available; book well in advance) take visitors on a 45-minute waltz through the gargantuan steel, glass and concrete hangar – a railway depot constructed in 1927–29 to house new trains servicing nearby Gare de Austerlitz.

In its Chill Zone, gigantic restaurant La Felicità has five different kitchens, a vast pavement terrace, a bar, and dining in two train carriages.

pastels and drawings, including *L'Education de la Vierge* (1842) and his paintings of Morocco. (🗂01 44 41 86 50; www.musee-delacroix.fr; 6 rue de Furstenberg, 6e; adult/child €7/free; ⊗9.30am-5pm Wed-Mon; Ⓜ Mabillon)

Parc Rives de Seine PARK

5 ◎ MAP P182, B1

A breath of fresh air, this 2.5km-long expressway-turned-riverside-promenade on the Left Bank is a favourite spot in which to run,

Cruising the Bouquinistes

With some 3km of forest-green boxes lining the Seine – containing over 300,000 secondhand (and often out-of-print) books, rare magazines, postcards and old advertising posters – Paris' **bouquinistes** (Map p182, F2; quai Voltaire, 7e, to quai de la Tournelle, 5e, & Pont Marie, 4e, to quai du Louvre, 1er; ⏰11.30am-dusk) are as integral to the cityscape as Notre Dame. Many open only from spring to autumn (and many shut in August), but year-round you'll still find some to browse.

cycle, skate, climb (there's a climbing wall at pont des Invalides), play board games or take part in a packed program of events. It's also simply a great place to hang out – on the archipelago of floating gardens, or at the burgeoning restaurants and bars, some floating aboard boats and barges. (btwn Musée d'Orsay & Pont de l'Alma, 7e; ⏰information point noon-7pm Tue-Sun May-Sep, shorter hours Oct-Apr; Ⓜ Solférino, Assemblée Nationale, Invalides)

Les Catacombes   CEMETERY

6 ◉ MAP P182, D8

Paris' most macabre sight are these skull- and bone-lined underground tunnels. In 1785 it was decided to rectify the hygiene problems of Paris' overflowing cemeteries by exhuming the bones and storing them in disused quarry tunnels, and the Catacombes were created in 1810. After descending 20m (via 131 narrow, dizzying spiral steps), you follow dark, subterranean passages to the ossuary (about 1.5km in all). Exit up 112 steps via a 'transition space' with gift shop onto 21bis av René Coty, 14e. (☏01 43 22 47 63; www.catacombes.paris.fr; 1 av du Colonel Henri Rol-Tanguy, 14e; adult/child €14/free, online booking incl audioguide from €29/5; ⏰10am-8.30pm Tue-Sun, last admission 7.30pm; Ⓜ Denfert-Rochereau)

Cimetière du Montparnasse   CEMETERY

7 ◉ MAP P182, C7

This 19-hectare cemetery opened in 1824 and is Paris' second largest after Père Lachaise (p134). Famous residents include writer Guy de Maupassant, playwright Samuel Beckett, sculptor Constantin Brancusi, photographer Man Ray, industrialist André Citroën, Captain Alfred Dreyfus of the infamous Dreyfus Affair, legendary singer Serge Gainsbourg and philosopher-writers Jean-Paul Sartre and Simone de Beauvoir. (www.paris.fr; 3 bd Edgar Quinet, 14e; admission free; ⏰8am-5.30pm Mon-Fri, 8.30am-5.30pm Sat, 9am-5.30pm Sun; Ⓜ Edgar Quinet)

Fondation Cartier pour l'Art Contemporain

GALLERY

8 ⊙ MAP P182, D7

Designed by Jean Nouvel, this stunning glass-and-steel building is a work of art in itself. It hosts temporary exhibits on contemporary art (from the 1980s to today) in a diverse variety of media – from painting and photography to video and fashion, as well as performance art. Artist Lothar Baumgarten created the wonderfully rambling garden. (📞 01 42 18 56 50; www.fondation.cartier.com; 261 bd Raspail, 14e; adult/child €10.50/7; ⊙ 11am-10pm Tue, to 8pm Wed-Sun; Ⓜ Raspail)

Musée Maillol

MUSEUM

9 ⊙ MAP P182, C3

Located in the stunning 18th-century Hôtel Bouchardon, this splendid little museum focuses on the work of sculptor Aristide Maillol (1861–1944), whose creations primarily occupy several rooms on the 2nd floor, and also includes works by Matisse, Gauguin, Kandinsky, Cézanne and Picasso. All are from the private collection of Odessa-born Dina Vierny (1919–2009), Maillol's principal model for 10 years from the age of 15. Major temporary exhibitions (included in the admission price) regularly take place here. (Fondation Dina Vierny; www.museemaillol. com; 61 rue de Grenelle, 7e; adult/child €13.50/11.50; ⊙ 10.30am-6.30pm Sat-Thu, to 8.30pm Fri; Ⓜ Rue du Bac)

Visiting Rue Daguerre

Paris' traditional village atmosphere thrives along rue Daguerre, 14e.

Tucked just southwest of the Denfert-Rochereau metro and RER stations, this narrow street – pedestrianised between av du Général-Leclerc and rue Boulard – is lined with florists, *fromageries* (cheese shops), *boulangeries* (bakeries), patisseries (cake shops), greengrocers, delis (including Greek, Asian and Italian) and classic cafes where you can watch the local goings on.

Shops set up market stalls on the pavement; Sunday mornings are especially lively. It's a great option for lunch before or after visiting Les Catacombes, or packing a picnic to take to one of the area's parks or squares.

Eating

Bouillon Racine

BRASSERIE €€

10 ⊗ MAP P182, E4

Inconspicuously situated in a quiet street, this heritage-listed art nouveau 'soup kitchen', with mirrored walls, floral motifs and ceramic tiling, was built in 1906 to feed market workers. Despite the magnificent interior, the food – inspired by age-old recipes – is no afterthought and is superbly

Paris' Oldest Restaurant & Cafe

St-Germain claims both the city's oldest restaurant and its oldest cafe: **À la Petite Chaise** (Map p182, C3; ☎01 42 22 13 35; www.ala petitechaise.fr; 36 rue de Grenelle, 7e; lunch menus €26-34, dinner menus €37, mains €21; ☺noon-2pm & 7-11pm; ⓂSèvres-Babylone) hides behind an iron gate that's been here since it opened in 1680, when pioneering wine merchant Georges Rameau served food (to accompany his wares). Classical decor and cuisine (onion soup, venison terrine with hazelnuts) make it worth a visit above and beyond its history.

Le Procope (Map p182, E3; ☎01 40 46 79 00; www.procope.com; 13 rue de l'Ancienne Comédie, 6e; mains €22-37, menus €32-39; ☺noon-midnight Sun-Wed, to 1am Thu-Sat; ⓂOdéon) welcomed its first patrons in 1686, and was frequented by Voltaire, Molière and Balzac. Its chandeliered interior also has an entrance onto the 1735-built glass-roofed passageway Cour du Commerce St-André. House specialities include coq au vin, veal blanquette, and homemade ice cream.

executed (stuffed, spit-roasted suckling pig, pork shank in Rodenbach red beer, scallops and shrimps with lobster coulis). (☎01 44 32 15 60; www.bouillonracine.fr; 3 rue Racine, 6e; lunch menu €17.50, menu €35, mains €19-32; ☺noon-11pm; 🍴; ⓂCluny–La Sorbonne)

L'Avant Comptoir de la Mer

SEAFOOD €

11 ❌ MAP P182, E3

One of Yves Camdeborde's stunning line-up of St-Germain hors d'oeuvre bars – alongside **Le Comptoir** (☎01 44 27 07 97; 9 Carrefour de l'Odéon, 6e; mains €13-45; ☺noon-11pm; ⓂOdéon), **L'Avant Comptoir de la Terre** (3 Carrefour de l'Odéon, 6e; tapas €5-16; ☺noon-11pm; ⓂOdéon) and **L'Avant Comptoir du Marché** (15 rue Lobineau, 6e; tapas €5-21; ☺noon-11pm; ⓂMabillon) – serves succulent Cap Ferret oysters (straight, Bloody Mary–style or with chipolata sausages), herring tartine, cauliflower and trout roe, blood-orange razor clams, roasted scallops and salmon croquettes, complemented by fantastic artisanal bread, hand-churned flavoured butters, sea salt and Kalamata olives. (☎01 42 38 47 55; www.hotel-paris-relais-saint-germain.com; 3 Carrefour de l'Odéon, 6e; tapas €5-25, oysters per half-dozen from €19; ☺noon-11pm; ⓂOdéon)

Bistrot Ernest

BISTRO €

12 ❌ MAP P182, E2

An unpretentious yet characterful bistro with affordable mains in the heart of the 6e is an increasingly rare treat. A hot fave among art dealers and gallerists, Bistrot Ernest fulfils many a Francophile dream. Old-fashioned bookshelves and bistro tables, a curvy zinc bar and an affable patron, all give the place an essential Parisian buzz.

The cuisine is wholly simple but people come here to absorb the atmosphere. (☎01 56 24 47 47; www.facebook.com/bistroternest; 21 rue de Seine, 6e; mains €13-19; ⊗noon-3pm & 6-10pm Tue-Sun; Ⓜ Odéon)

Maison Mulot   PASTRIES €

13 ✖ MAP P182, E3

Fruit tarts (peach, lemon, apple), croissants, cakes and *amaryllis* (the house signature dessert) are among this celebrated pastry chef's specialities sold at his delightfully quaint patisserie (cake shop) with candyfloss pink-and-white striped canopy. Also sells quiches and gourmet sandwiches. (☎01 43 26 91 03; www.gerard-mulot.com; 76 rue de Seine, 6e; items from €1.80; ⊗7am-8pm; Ⓜ Odéon)

VGT Bowl   VEGETARIAN €

14 ✖ MAP P182, C2

V stands for 'Végétal', G for 'Gourmand' and T for 'Tonique' – this gives you an idea of what's on offer at this quirky, buzzy and colourful vegetarian den. Enjoy a bowl replete with healthy ingredients while sampling a delicious fruit cocktail. And there's nothing better than finishing on a sweet note with, say, an apple crumble. (☎01 47 03 92 07; https://vgt-bowl.business.site; 22 rue de Beaune, 7e; mains €12-18; ⊗11.30am-4pm Mon-Sat; 🖉; Ⓜ Rue du Bac)

Le Procope

PETR KOVALENKOV/SHUTTERSTOCK ©

'Little Brittany'

Gare Montparnasse links Paris with Brittany, and the station's surrounding streets, especially rue du Montparnasse and rue d'Odessa, 14e, are lined with dozens of authentic crêperies.

Breton savoury buckwheat-flour *galettes* and sweet crêpes, with traditional toppings such as *caramel au beurre salé* (salty caramel), are served on a plate and eaten using cutlery.

Try lace-curtain-screened **Crêperie Josselin** (Map p182, C6; 01 43 20 93 50; 67 rue du Montparnasse, 14e; crêpes €5-12; 11am-11pm Tue-Sun; Edgar Quinet).

La Cantine du Troquet

BISTRO €€

15 MAP P182, B4

One of six eateries run by chef Christian Etchebest in Paris, La Cantine du Troquet is a favoured spot for fans of bistro fare made with top-notch ingredients and sourced from the best producers around the country. Classics include pig loin and grilled razor clams. There are sturdy desserts such as *riz au lait* (milk rice) and a great wine list. (01 43 27 70 06; www.lacantinedutroquet.com; 79 rue du Cherche Midi, 6e; mains €19-25; noon-2pm & 7-10pm Mon-Fri; St-Placide)

Beaupassage

FOOD HALL €€

16 MAP P182, C3

Some of France's finest chefs, artisans and purveyors occupy this open-air 'mini district'. Look out for Yannick Alléno (with a restaurant, wine cellar and art gallery), Anne-Sophie Pic (gastronomy), Olivier Bellin (seafood), Thierry Marx (bakery-patisserie) and Pierre Hermé (pastries, including his signature macarons), as well as the eye-catching Coya, a Peruvian bar-restaurant in a former church, opened in 2019. (www.beaupassage. fr; 53-57 rue de Grenelle, 7e; passage 7am-11pm, individual hours vary; Sèvres-Babylone)

Anicia

FRENCH €€

17 MAP P182, B5

An advance online booking is essential at this glorious 'bistro nature', showcase for the earthy but refined cuisine of chef François Gagnaire who ran a Michelin-starred restaurant in Puy-en-Velay in the Auvergne before uprooting to the French capital. He still sources dozens of regional products – Puy lentils, meat from Haute-Loire, St-Nectaire cheese – from small-time producers in central France, to stunning effect. (01 43 35 41 50; www.anicia-bistrot. com; 97 rue du Cherche Midi, 6e; mains €18-42, lunch menus €26-35, dinner menus €69-85; noon-10.30pm Tue-Sat; Duroc, Vaneau)

Semilla
NEOBISTRO €€

18 MAP P182, E3

Stark concrete floor, beams and an open kitchen (in front of which you can book front-row 'chef seats') set the factory-style scene for edgy, modern, daily changing dishes such as grilled octopus scallops or hake fillet with mashed salsifis. Desserts are equally creative and irresistible. Be sure to book. (☑01 43 54 34 50; www.semillaparis.com; 54 rue de Seine, 6e; lunch menus €37-41, mains €32-42; ⏱12.30-2pm & 7-10.30pm Mon-Sat, to 10pm Sun; ⓂMabillon)

Chez Dumonet
BISTRO €€

19 MAP P182, B5

Fondly known by its former name, Joséphine, this lace-curtained, mosaic-tiled place with white-cloth tables inside and out is the Parisian bistro of many people's dreams, serving timeless standards such as beef tartare and grilled chateaubriand steak with Béarnaise sauce. Order its enormous signature Grand Marnier soufflé at the end of your meal. Mains, unusually, come in full or half-portion sizes. (Joséphine; ☑01 45 48 52 40; www.facebook.com/chezdumonetjosephine; 117 rue du Cherche Midi, 6e; mains €26-42; ⏱noon-2pm & 7.30-9.30pm Tue-Sat; ⓂDuroc)

Clover Green
BISTRO €€€

20 MAP P182, C2

Dining at hot-shot chef Jean-François Piège's casual bistro is like attending a private party: the galley-style open kitchen adjoining the 20 seats is part of the dining-room decor, putting customers at the front and centre of the culinary action. Expect a *cuisine du jour*, inspired by the chef's mood and what's available at the market. (☑01 75 50 00 05; www.clover-paris.com; 5 rue Perronet, 7e; lunch menus €37-47, dinner menus €58-68; ⏱12.30-2pm & 7-10pm Tue-Fri, 12.30-2.30pm & 7-10pm Sat; ⓂSt-Germain des Prés)

Les Climats
FRENCH €€€

21 MAP P182, C2

Like the neighbouring Musée d'Orsay, this is a magnificent art nouveau treasure. Once a 1905-built home for female telephone, telegram and postal workers, it features soaring vaulted ceilings and original stained glass, along with a lunchtime summer garden and glassed-in winter garden. Exquisite Michelin-starred dishes complement its 150-page list of wines, sparkling wines and whiskies purely from the Burgundy region. (☑01 58 62 10 08; www.lesclimats.fr; 41 rue de Lille, 7e; lunch/dinner menus €49/130, mains €56-65; ⏱12.15-2pm & 7-9pm Tue-Sat; ⓂSolférino)

Drinking

Les Deux Magots
CAFE

22 MAP P182, D3

If ever there was a cafe that summed up St-Germain des Prés' early-20th-century literary scene, it's this former hang-out of anyone who was anyone. You'll spend substantially more here to sip *un café* (coffee, €4.80) in a wicker chair on the pavement terrace shaded by dark-green awnings, but it's an undeniable piece of Parisian history. Also try its wicked hot chocolate. (☏01 45 48 55 25; www.lesdeux magots.fr; 6 place St-Germain des Prés, 6e; ⏱7.30am-1am; Ⓜ St-Germain des Prés)

Au Sauvignon
WINE BAR

23 Ⓜ MAP P182, C3

Grab a table in the evening light at this wonderfully authentic wine bar or head to the quintessential bistro interior, with original zinc bar, tightly packed tables and hand-painted ceiling celebrating French viticultural tradition. A *casse-croûtes au pain Poilâne* (gourmet sandwich) is the perfect accompaniment. (☏01 45 48 49 02; www.ausauvignon.com; 80 rue des Sts-Pères, 7e; ⏱8am-11pm Mon-Sat, 9am-10pm Sun; Ⓜ Sèvres-Babylone)

Augustin Marchand D'Vins
WINE BAR

24 Ⓜ MAP P182, E3

At a prime address in the 6e, Augustin is a trendy lair for chilled-out drinking. Enjoy the decor – dim lighting, stone walls and beamed ceilings – and the superb wines on offer, some of which are available by the glass (from €7). If you have the munchies, order a delicious platter of charcuterie or cheese

from €10. (☏09 81 21 76 21; www. facebook.com/augustinmarchand dvins; 26 rue des Grands Augustins, 6e; ⏱6-11pm Tue-Fri, from 11am Sat & Sun; Ⓜ Odéon)

Café de Flore
CAFE

25 Ⓜ MAP P182, D3

The red upholstered benches, mirrors and marble walls at this art deco landmark haven't changed much since the days when Jean-Paul Sartre and Simone de Beauvoir essentially set up office here, writing in its warmth during the Nazi occupation. (☏01 45 48 55 26; www.cafedeflore.fr; 172 bd St-Germain, 6e; ⏱7.30am-1.30am; Ⓜ St-Germain des Prés)

Castor Club
COCKTAIL BAR

26 Ⓜ MAP P182, E3

Discreetly signed, this superb underground cocktail bar has an intimate English gentleman's club–style upstairs bar with vintage wall lamps and slinky, red velour stools. But it's downstairs, in the 18th-century stone cellar with hole-in-the-wall booths, that the real cocktail-sipping action happens. Blues tracks add to the already cool vibe. (☏09 50 64 99 38; 14 rue Hautefeuille, 6e; ⏱7pm-2am Tue & Wed, to 4am Thu-Sat; Ⓜ Odéon)

La Cave des Climats
WINE BAR

27 Ⓜ MAP P182, C2

A wine-taster's fantasy, this upmarket and convivial *cave à manger* (wine shop where you can drink and dine) features a great variety of references, with an emphasis on Burgundy wines (by the bottle or full glass to suit all budgets). It also serves up inventive platters (from €12) in a warm atmosphere. Check the website for €50 tasting sessions. (☎01 42 33 87 94; www.lacavedesclimats.fr; 35 rue de Verneuil, 7e; ☺3-10.45pm Tue-Fri, from noon Sat; Ⓜ Rue du Bac)

La Palette CAFE

28 Ⓟ MAP P182, E2

In the heart of gallery land, this timeless fin-de-siècle cafe and erstwhile stomping ground of Paul Cézanne and Georges Braque attracts a grown-up set of fashion-industry professionals and local art dealers. Its summer terrace is beautiful but overcrowded. (☎01 43 26 68 15; www.lapalette-paris.com; 43 rue de Seine, 6e; ☺8am-2am Mon-Sat, from 10am Sun; 🛜; Ⓜ Mabillon)

Prescription Cocktail Club COCKTAIL BAR

29 Ⓟ MAP P182, E3

With bowler and flat-top hats as lampshades and a 1930s speakeasy New York air to the place, this cocktail club – run by the same mega-successful team as Experimental Cocktail Club (p84) – is very Parisian-cool. Getting past the doormen can be tough, but once in, it's friendliness and old-fashioned cocktails all round. (☎09 50 35 72 87; www.facebook.com/prescriptionparis; 23 rue Mazarine, 6e; ☺7pm-2am

La Rotonde (p194)

KAVALENKAVA/SHUTTERSTOCK ©

The Brasseries of Montparnasse

After WWI, avant-garde writers, poets and artists shifted from Montmartre to the area around bd du Montparnasse.

Artists Chagall, Modigliani, Léger, Soutine, Miró, Matisse, Kandinsky and Picasso, composer Stravinsky, and writers Hemingway, Ezra Pound and Cocteau were among those who hung out here. It remained a creative hub until the mid-1930s. Historic brasseries (restaurants) that recall their legacy include the following:

La Rotonde (Map p182, C6; ☏ 01 43 26 48 26; 105 bd du Montparnasse, 6e; mains €17-48, seafood platters €29.50-118.50, menu €48; ☺6am-2am, kitchen noon-3pm & 7-11pm; Ⓜ Vavin) Opened in 1911.

Le Select (Map p182, C6; www.leselectmontparnasse.fr; 99 bd du Montparnasse, 6e; ☺7am-2am Sun-Thu, to 3am Fri & Sat; ☏; Ⓜ Vavin) The first of the area's grand cafes to stay open late into the night; founded in 1923.

La Coupole (Map p182, C6; ☏ 01 43 20 14 20; www.lacoupole-paris.com; 102 bd du Montparnasse, 14e; lunch menus €20-30, mains €21-46; ☺8am-11pm Mon, 8am-midnight Tue-Fri, 8.30am-midnight Sat, 8.30am-11pm Sun; ☏; Ⓜ Vavin) This 450-seat, 1927-opened brasserie has muralled columns painted by artists including Chagall.

La Closerie des Lilas (Map p182, D7; ☏ 01 40 51 34 50; www.closerie deslilas.fr; 171 bd du Montparnasse, 6e; mains restaurant €28-55, brasserie €19-27, lunch menus from €52; ☺restaurant noon-2.30pm & 7-11.30pm, brasserie noon-12.30am, piano bar 11am-1.30am; Ⓜ Vavin, RER Port Royal) Hemingway's favourite (established 1847).

Le Dôme (Map p182, C6; ☏ 01 43 35 25 81; www.restaurant-ledome.com; 108 bd du Montparnasse, 14e; mains €22-60, seafood platters €85-159, menu €43-48; ☺noon-3pm & 7-11pm; Ⓜ Vavin) A shellfish specialist and a 1930s art deco extravaganza.

Mon-Thu, to 4am Fri & Sat, 8pm-2am Sun; Ⓜ Odéon)

Bar du Marché

BAR

30 🍷 MAP P182, E3

Yes, the waiters are dressed like *titis parisiens* (hat and overalls) in this busy place in the heart of the 6e. Far from being a tourist trap, this popular bar with a vintage feel attracts a mixed crowd and is a perfect spot to tipple happily on a beer or a glass of wine, which can be accompanied by bistro food if you like. (☏ 01 43 26 55 15; 75 rue de Seine, 6e; ☺8am-2am; Ⓜ Mabillon)

Tiger
COCKTAIL BAR

31 MAP P182, D3

Suspended bare-bulb lights and fretted timber make this split-level space a stylish spot for specialist gins (130 varieties), including a devilish Opposite Attraction (gin, chocolate, almonds and orange). Dedicated G&T aficionados can work their way through a staggering 1040 combinations. Gin aside, Tiger serves Japanese sake, wine and craft beer. DJs play certain evenings. (www.tiger-paris.com; 13 rue Princesse, 6e; ☺6.30pm-2am Mon-Sat; MMabillon)

Shopping

La Dernière Goutte
WINE

32 MAP P182, D3

'The Last Drop' is the brainchild of Cuban-American sommelier Juan Sánchez, whose tiny wine shop is packed with exciting, mostly organic French *vins de propriétaires* (estate-bottled wines) made by small independent producers. Wine classes lasting two hours (two white tastings, five red) regularly take place in English (per person €55); it also hosts free tastings with winemakers most Saturdays. (☑01 43 29 11 62; www.ldgparis.com; 6 rue du Bourbon le Château, 6e; ☺3-8pm Mon, 10.30am-8pm Tue-Sat, 11am-7pm Sun; MMabillon)

Fermob
HOMEWARES

33 MAP P182, C3

Fermob is famed for manufacturing iconic French garden furniture, including the Jardin du Luxembourg's signature sage-green chairs, actually available in a spectacular rainbow of colours for your own garden or terrace. It also sells lovely cushions and lamps. Fermob has another branch across the river near Bastille. (☑01 45 44 10 28; www.fermob.com; 17 bd Raspail, 7e; ☺10am-7pm Mon-Sat; MRue du Bac)

Café Pierre Hermé
FOOD

34 MAP P182, D3

Leading *pâtissier* (pastry chef) and chocolate maker Pierre Hermé has several boutiques and cafes in Paris, including this branch in the heart of St-Germain. It's a veritable feast of perfectly presented cakes, chocolates, *millefeuilles*, tarts, nougats, jams and dazzling macarons. Oh, and the hot chocolate is so thick. You can eat in or take away. (☑01 82 73 25 15; www.pierreherme.com; 61 rue Bonaparte, 6e; ☺9am-8pm; MOdéon)

Marché Raspail
MARKET

35 MAP P182, C4

A traditional open-air market on Tuesday and Friday, Marché Raspail is especially popular on Sunday, when it's filled with *biologique* (organic) produce. (bd Raspail, btwn rue de Rennes & rue du Cherche Midi,

St-Germain des Prés' Historic Shops

St-Germain des Prés is filled with antique and vintage dealers and a raft of historic small shops.

Cire Trudon (Map p182, E3; ☏ 01 43 26 46 50; www.trudon.com; 78 rue de Seine, 6e; ☺11am-7pm Mon, from 10am Tue-Sat; Ⓜ Odéon) Claude Trudon began selling candles here in 1643, and officially supplied Versailles and Napoléon with light. It is now the world's oldest candlemaker (look for the plaque to the left of the awning).

Au Plat d'Étain (Map p182, D3; ☏ 01 43 54 32 06; www.soldats-plomb-au-plat-etain.fr; 16 rue Guisarde, 6e; ☺10.30am-6.30pm Tue-Sat; Ⓜ Mabillon, St-Sulpice) Miniature tin and lead soldiers have been sold at this tiny shop since 1775.

Le Bon Marché (Map p182, C4; ☏ 01 44 39 80 00; www.24s.com; 24 rue de Sèvres, 7e; ☺10am-8pm Mon-Sat, 11am-7.45pm Sun; Ⓜ Sèvres-Babylone) Designed by Gustave Eiffel, this 1852-opened department store houses fashion, homewares and food hall **La Grande Épicerie de Paris** (Map p182, B4; ☏ 01 44 39 81 00; www.lagrandeepicerie.com; 38 rue de Sèvres, 7e; ☺8.30am-9pm Mon-Sat, 10am-8pm Sun; Ⓜ Sèvres-Babylone), with fantastical displays of chocolates, pastries, biscuits, cheeses and more.

Poilâne (Map p182, C4; ☏ 01 45 48 42 59; www.poilane.com; 8 rue du Cherche Midi, 6e; ☺7am-8.30pm Mon-Sat; Ⓜ Sèvres-Babylone) Pierre Poilâne opened his *boulangerie* (bakery) in 1932. Today his granddaughter runs the company, which still turns out wood-fired, rounded sourdough loaves made with stonemilled flour and Guérande sea salt.

Deyrolle (Map p182, C2; ☏ 01 42 22 30 07; www.deyrolle.com; 46 rue du Bac, 7e; ☺10am-1pm & 2-7pm Mon, 10am-7pm Tue-Sat; Ⓜ Rue du Bac) Overrun with creatures such as lions, tigers, zebras and storks, this taxidermist opened in 1831.

Magasin Sennelier (Map p182, D2; ☏ 01 42 60 72 15; www.magasin sennelier.net; 3 quai Voltaire, 7e; ☺2-6.30pm Mon, 10am-12.45pm & 2-6.30pm Tue-Sat; Ⓜ St-Germain des Prés) Cézanne and Picasso were among the artists who helped develop products for this 1887-founded art supplier, which retains exquisite original timber cabinetry and glass display cases.

6e; ⏰7am-2.30pm Tue & Fri, organic market 9am-1.30pm Sun; Ⓜ Rennes)

Le Bazar Français CONCEPT STORE

36 🔒 MAP P182, C4

All pieces – fashion, homewares, jewellery, accessories – are designed and made in France in this charming boutique that started as an e-shop. A great place to stock up on original, quality gifts. (📞07 56 80 33 90; www.lebazarfrancais.com; 24 rue de l'Abbé Grégoire, 6e; ⏰11am-7pm Mon-Sat; Ⓜ Sèvres-Babylone)

Smallable Concept Store CHILDREN'S CLOTHING

37 🔒 MAP P182, B5

'Dream big' is the inviting strapline of this Parisian-chic space, a one-stop-shop for accessories, fashion and homewares for babies, children and teens. It stocks regularly changing premium brands. You can also buy exquisite cushions and linens. (📞01 40 46 01 15; www.smallable.com; 81 rue du Cherche Midi, 6e; ⏰2-7.30pm Mon, from 10.30am Tue-Sat; Ⓜ Vaneau)

Galerie Teo Leo ANTIQUES

38 🔒 MAP P182, C2

Not your average antique shop, Galerie Teo Leo is a treasure trove of lovingly selected pieces from the 1940s to the present day. Items are all collected by gallerist Laurent di Benedetto and include groovy lamps, mirrors, furniture, ceramics and plenty of unique

EQROY/SHUTTERSTOCK ©

Poilâne

decorative objects. (📞01 42 61 64 01; www.teoleo-galerie.com; 37 rue de Verneuil, 7e; ⏰11.30am-7pm Tue-Sat; Ⓜ Rue du Bac)

Le Slip Français CLOTHING

39 🔒 MAP P182, D3

A great success story, this outlet in the heart of a chic neighbourhood began as a start-up a few years ago. The French Underwear is known for its instantly identifiable colours and patterns. All items – briefs, underwear, pyjamas, shorts, jerseys and accessories, for men and women – sold in this playful boutique are designed and made in France. (📞01 45 38 90 56; www.leslipfrancais.com; 20 rue du Vieux Colombier, 6e; ⏰10am-7.30pm Mon-Sat; Ⓜ Saint-Sulpice)

Worth a Trip 🔭

Dazzle at the Château de Versailles

The opulent-and-then-some Château de Versailles sits amid 900 hectares of fountain-graced gardens, pond-filled parks and woods. Louis XIV transformed his father's hunting lodge in the mid-17th century and the Baroque palace was the political capital and seat of the royal court from 1682 until the fateful events of 1789, when revolutionaries massacred the palace guard.

www.chateauversailles.fr

adult/child passport ticket incl estate-wide access €20/free, with musical events €27/free, palace €18/free except during musical events

🕙 9am-6.30pm Tue-Sun Apr-Oct, to 5.30pm Tue-Sun Nov-Mar

RER Versailles-Château–Rive Gauche

Château de Versailles in Numbers

Louis XIV ordered 700 rooms, 2153 windows, 352 chimneys and 11 hectares of roof for the 580m-long main palace. It housed the entire court of 6000 (plus 5000 servants). The finest talent of the day installed some 6300 paintings, 2000 sculptures and statues, 15,000 engravings and 5000 furnishings and objets d'art.

Hall of Mirrors

The palace's opulence peaks in its shimmering, sparkling Galerie des Glaces (Hall of Mirrors). This 75m-long ballroom has 17 giant mirrors on one side and an equal number of windows on the other.

King's & Queen's State Apartments

Luxurious, ostentatious appointments – frescoes, marble, gilt and woodcarvings, with themes and symbols drawn from Greek and Roman mythology – emanate from every last moulding, cornice, ceiling and door in the palace's Grands Appartements du Roi et de la Reine.

Guided Tours

To access areas that are otherwise off-limits and learn more about Versailles' history, take a 90-minute **guided tour** (📞01 30 83 77 88; tours €10, plus palace entry) of the Private Apartments of Louis XV and Louis XVI and the Opera House or Royal Chapel. Tours include access to the most famous parts of the palace; book online.

The Gardens

Celebrated landscape artist André Le Nôtre was commissioned by Louis XIV to design the château's magnificent **gardens** (free except during musical events; ⏰gardens 8am-8.30pm Apr-Oct, to 6pm Nov-Mar, park 7am-8.30pm Apr-Oct, 8am-6pm

★ Top Tips

○ Tuesday, Saturday and Sunday are the palace's busiest days.

○ Versailles is free on the first Sunday of every month from November to March.

✕ Take a Break

Restaurants within the estate include Alain Ducasse's **Ore** (📞01 30 84 12 96; www.ducasse-chateauversailles. com; breakfast menus €12-20, mains €26-39; ⏰9am-6.30pm Tue-Sun Apr-Oct, to 5.30pm Nov-Mar; 📶) inside the palace.

In the Louis XIV–created town of Versailles, rue de Satory is lined with restaurants and cafes. More local options can be found on and around rue de la Paroisse.

ⓘ Getting There

🚆 Versailles has several train stations; the most convenient is to take RER C5 (return €7.30, 40 minutes, frequent) from Paris' Left Bank RER stations.

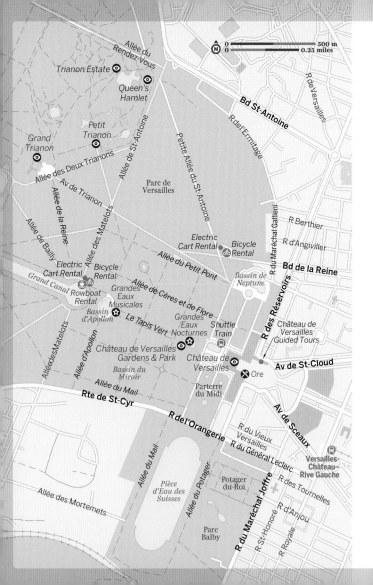

Allée du Rendez-Vous

Trianon Estate

Queen's Hamlet

Bd St-Antoine

R de Versailles

Petit Trianon

R de l'Ermitage

Grand Trianon

Allée de St-Antoine

Allée des Deux Trianons

Av de Trianon

Parc de Versailles

Petite Allée du St-Antoine

Allée de la Reine

Allée des Matelots

Allée de Bailly

R Berthier

R du Maréchal Gallieni

R d'Angiviller

Electric Cart Rental

Bicycle Rental

Bd de la Reine

Allée du Petit Pont

Grand Canal

Electric Cart Rental

Bicycle Rental

Allée de Cérès et de Flore

Bassin de Neptune

R des Réservoirs

Rowboat Rental

Grandes Eaux Musicales

Bassin d'Apollon

Le Tapis Vert

Grandes Eaux Nocturnes

Shuttle Train

Château de Versailles Guided Tours

Allée des Matelots

Allée d'Apollon

Château de Versailles Gardens & Park

Bassin du Miroir

Château de Versailles

Av de St-Cloud

Allée du Mail

Ore

Parterre du Midi

Rte de St-Cyr

R de l'Orangerie

R du Vieux Versailles

Av de Sceaux

R du Général Leclerc

Allée du Mail

Pièce d'Eau des Suisses

Allée du Potager

Potager du Roi

R du Maréchal Joffre

Versailles-Château–Rive Gauche

R des Tournelles

Allée des Mortemets

Parc Balby

R d'Anjou

R-St-Honoré

R Royale

0   500 m
0   0.25 miles

Nov-Mar). The best view over the rectangular pools is from the Hall of Mirrors. Pathways include the Royal Walk's verdant 'green carpet', with smaller paths leading to leafy groves.

The Canals

Oriented to reflect the sunset, the Grand Canal, 1.6km long and 62m wide, is traversed by the 1km-long Petit Canal, creating a cross-shaped body of water with a perimeter of more than 5.5km.

The Trianon Estate

Northwest of the main palace is the **Domaine de Trianon** (Trianon Estate; adult/child €12/free, with passport ticket free; noon-6.30pm Tue-Sun Apr-Oct, to 5.30pm Tue-Sat Nov-Mar). Tickets include the Grand and Petit Trianon palaces, and the Hameau de la Reine (Queen's Hamlet), a mock village of thatched cottages where Marie Antoinette played milkmaid. The pink-colonnaded Grand Trianon was built in 1687 for Louis XIV and his family as a place of escape from the rigid etiquette of the court, and renovated under Napoléon I in the Empire style. The ochre-coloured 1760s Petit Trianon was redecorated in 1867 by the consort of Napoléon III, Empress Eugénie, who added Louis XVI-style furnishings.

Musical Fountain Shows

Try to time your visit for the magical **Grandes Eaux Musicales** (www.chateauversailles-spectacles. fr; adult/child €9.50/8; 10am-7pm Sat & Sun Apr-Oct, also 10am-7pm Tue mid-May–mid-Jun) or the after-dark **Grandes Eaux Nocturnes** (www. chateauversailles-spectacles.fr; adult/ child €24/20; 8.30-11.30pm Sat mid-Jun–mid-Sep), 'dancing water' displays set to Baroque- and classical-era music.

Getting Around

The estate is so vast that the only way to see it all is to hire a four-person **electric cart** (01 39 66 97 66; car hire per hour €34; 10am-6.45pm Apr-Oct, to 5.30pm Feb & Mar, to 5pm Nov & Dec) or hop aboard the **shuttle train** (www.train-versailles. com; adult/child €8/6.10; every 20min 10.10am-6.50pm Apr-Oct, shorter hours Nov-Mar); you can also rent a **bike** (01 39 66 97 66; bike hire per hour/day €8.50/20; 10am-6.45pm Apr-Oct, shorter hours Nov-Mar) or a **rowboat** (01 39 66 97 66; boat hire per 30min/1hr €13/17; 10am-6.45pm Jul & Aug, shorter hours Mar-Jun & Sep–mid-Nov).

Survival Guide

Place de la Concorde (p79) GUILLAUME CHANSON/GETTY IMAGES ©

Before You Go

Book Your Stay

○ Paris has a wealth of accommodation for all budgets, but it's often *complet* (full) in advance. Reservations are recommended year-round and essential during the warmer months (April to October) and all public and school holidays.

○ Although marginally cheaper, accommodation outside central Paris is invariably a false economy given travel time and costs. Choose somewhere within Paris' 20 *arrondissements* (city districts) to experience Parisian life the moment you step out the door.

○ The city of Paris levies a *taxe de séjour* (tourist tax) on all accommodation, from €1 to €5 per person per night (normally added to your bill).

○ Breakfast is rarely included; cafes often offer better value.

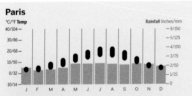

When to Go

○ **Winter (Nov–Feb)** Cold and dark, occasional snow. Museums are quieter and accommodation prices are lower.

○ **Spring (Mar–May)** Mild, sometimes wet. Major sights start getting busier; parks and gardens begin to come into their own.

○ **Summer (Jun–Aug)** Warm to hot, generally sunny. Main tourist season. Some businesses close for August.

○ **Autumn (Sep–Nov)** Mild, generally sunny. Cultural life moving into top gear after the summer lull.

Useful Websites

○ **Lonely Planet** (lonely planet.com/france/paris/hotels) Reviews of our top choices.

○ **Paris Attitude** (www.parisattitude.com) Thousands of apartment rentals, professional service, reasonable fees.

○ **Haven In** (www.haven in.com) Charming Parisian apartments for rent.

Best Budget

○ **Hôtel du Dragon** (www.hoteldudragon.com) Home-made jam is on the breakfast menu at this heart-warming spot.

○ **Les Piaules** (www.les piaules.com) Belleville hotspot to mingle with locals.

○ **Cosmos Hôtel** (www.cosmos-hotel-paris.com) Cheap, brilliant value and footsteps from the nightlife of the 11e's rue JPT.

○ **Generator Hostel** (www.generatorhostels.com) State-of-the-art hostel with a rooftop bar and basement club.

Best Midrange

○ **Hôtel Paris Bastille Boutet** (www.hotel-par is-bastille-boutet.com)

One-time chocolate factory with beautiful art deco tiling and a basement pool.

○ **Hôtel Banke** (www.hotelbanke.com) Magnificently set in a former bank.

○ **Familia Hôtel** (www.familiahotel.com) Sepia murals and flower-bedecked balconies in the Latin Quarter.

○ **Hôtel Georgette** (www.hotelgeorgette.com) Designer rooms inspired by the nearby Centre Pompidou.

Best Top End

○ **Les Bains** (www.lesbains-paris.com) Nineteenth-century thermal baths turned nightclub turned rockstar-hot lifestyle hotel.

○ **Hôtel Crayon** (www.hotelcrayon.com) Line drawings, retro furnishings and coloured-glass shower doors.

○ **Hôtel Molitor** (www.mltr.fr) Stunningly restored art deco swimming pool with gallery-style poolside rooms.

○ **Cour des Vosges** (www.courdesvosges.com) Intimate, five-star elegance on Paris' most beautiful square

Arriving in Paris

Charles de Gaulle Airport

Most international airlines fly to **Aéroport de Charles de Gaulle** (📞01 70 36 39 50; www.parisaeroport.fr; Roissy), 28km northeast of central Paris. In French the airport is commonly called 'Roissy' after the suburb in which it is located. Inter-terminal shuttle services are free. A high-speed train link between Charles de Gaulle and Gare de l'Est in central Paris is planned; when complete in 2024, the CDG Express will cut the current 50-minute journey to 20 minutes. A fourth terminal is due to open by 2028.

Train

Charles de Gaulle Airport is served by the RER B line (€11.40, children aged four to nine €7.90, approximately 50 minutes, every 10 to 15 min-

utes), which connects with central Paris stations including Gare du Nord, Châtelet–Les Halles and St-Michel–Notre Dame. Trains run from 4.50am to 11.50pm (from Gare du Nord 4.53am to 12.15am).

Bus

Noctilien buses 140 and 143 (€8 or four metro tickets) Part of the RATP night service. Noctilien has two hourly services that link the airport with **Gare de l'Est** (rue du 8 Mai 1945, 10e; Ⓜ Gare de l'Est) in northern Paris via nearby **Gare du Nord** (170 rue La Fayette, 10e; Ⓜ Gare du Nord): bus 140 (1am to 4am; from Gare de l'Est 1am to 3.40am) takes 80 minutes, and bus 143 (12.32am to 4.32am; from Gare de l'Est 12.55am to 5.08am) takes 55 minutes.

RATP bus 350 (€6 or three metro tickets, 80 minutes, every 15 to 30 minutes from 5.30am to 9.30pm) Links the airport with **Gare de l'Est** (www.ratp.fr; bd de Strasbourg, 10e; Ⓜ Gare de l'Est).

RATP bus 351 (€6 or three metro tickets, 90 minutes, every 15 to 30 minutes from 5.35am to 9.37pm) Links the airport with **place de la Nation** (2 av du Trône, 12e; M Nation) in eastern Paris.

Roissybus (€13.70, 75 minutes, from the airport every 15 to 20 minutes from 6am to 12.30am; from Paris every 15 to 20 minutes from 5.15am to 12.30am) Links the airport with **Opéra** (13-15 rue Scribe, 9e; M Opéra).

Taxi

A taxi to the city centre takes 40 to 80 minutes. Fares are standardised to a flat rate: €53 to the Right Bank and €58 to the Left Bank. The fare increases by 15% between 7pm and 7am and on Sundays.

Only take taxis at a clearly marked rank. Never follow anyone who approaches you at the airport and claims to be a driver.

Orly Airport

Aéroport d'Orly

(01 70 36 39 50; www. parisaeroport.fr; Orly) is 19km south of central Paris but, despite being closer than Charles de Gaulle, it is not as frequently used by international airlines, and public-transport options aren't quite as straightforward. That will change by 2027, when metro line 14 will be extended to the airport. A TGV station is due to arrive here in 2025.

Train

There is currently no direct train to/from Orly; you'll need to change halfway. Note that while it is possible to take a shuttle to the RER C line, this service is quite long and not recommended.

RER B (€12.10, children aged four to nine €6.05, 35 minutes, every four to 12 minutes) This line connects Orly with the St-Michel–Notre Dame, Châtelet–Les Halles and Gare du Nord stations in the city centre. In order to get from Orly to the RER station (Antony), you must first take the Orlyval automatic train. The service runs every five to seven minutes from 6am to 11.35pm and takes six minutes. You only need one ticket to take the two trains.

Tram

Tramway T7 (€1.90, 30 minutes, every eight to 15 minutes from 6am to 11.45pm) This tramway links Orly with Villejuif–Louis Aragon metro station in southern Paris; buy tickets from the machine at the tram stop as no tickets are sold on board.

Bus

OrlyBus (€9.50, 30 minutes, every eight to 15 minutes from 6am to 12.30am from Orly, 5.35am to midnight from Paris) Runs to/from **place Denfert-Rochereau** (www.ratp.fr; 3 place Denfert-Rochereau, 14e; M Denfert-Rochereau) in southern Paris.

Taxi

A taxi to the city centre takes roughly 30 minutes. Standardised flat-rate fares mean a taxi costs €32 to the Left Bank and €37 to the Right Bank. The fare increases by 15% between 7pm and 7am and on Sundays.

Beauvais Airport

Aéroport de Beauvais
(☎ 08 92 68 20 66; www.
aeroportparisbeauvais.
com; Beauvais) is
located 75km north of
Paris and is served by
a few low-cost flights.
Before you snap up
that bargain, though,
consider whether the
post-arrival journey is
worth it.

The Beauvais
navette (shuttle bus;
€17, 1¼ hours) links the
airport with **Parking
Pershing** (Gare Routière
Pershing; 22-24 bd Pershing;
17e; Ⓜ Porte Maillot) on
central Paris' western
edge; services are
coordinated with flight
times. See the airport
website for details and
tickets.

A taxi to central
Paris (around 1¾
hours) during the day/
night costs around
€170/210 (probably
more than the cost of
your flight!).

Gare du Nord

Gare du Nord (rue de
Dunkerque, 10e; Ⓜ Gare du
Nord) The terminus for
northbound domestic
trains as well as several
international services.

Located in northern
Paris.

Eurostar (www.euro
star.com) The London–
Paris line runs from St
Pancras International to
Gare du Nord. Voyages
take 2¼ hours.

Thalys (www.thalys.
com) Trains pull into
Paris' Gare du Nord
from Brussels, Amster-
dam and Cologne.

Other Mainline
Train Stations

o Paris has five other
stations for long-
distance trains, each
with its own metro sta-
tion: **Gare d'Austerlitz**
(bd de l'Hôpital, 13e;
Ⓜ Gare d'Austerlitz),
Gare de l'Est (place du
11 Novembre 1918, 10e;
Ⓜ Gare de l'Est), **Gare
de Lyon** (bd Diderot, 12e;
Ⓜ Gare de Lyon), **Gare
Montparnasse** (av du
Maine & bd de Vaugirard,
15e; Ⓜ Montparnasse
Bienvenüe) and **Gare St-
Lazare** (rue Intérieure, 8e;
Ⓜ St-Lazare). The station
used depends on the
direction from Paris.

o Contact Voyages SNCF
(www.voyages-sncf.
com) for connections
throughout France and
continental Europe.

Getting
Around

Metro & RER

Paris' underground
network is run by
RATP (www.ratp.
fr). It consists of
two separate but
linked systems: the
metro and the Réseau
Express Régional
(RER) suburban train
line. The metro has
14 numbered lines;
the RER has five
main lines (but you'll
probably only need
to use A, B and C).
When buying tickets
consider how many
zones your journey will
cover; there are five
concentric transport
zones rippling out
from Paris (zone 5 be-
ing the furthest); if you
travel from Charles de
Gaulle airport to Paris,
for instance, you will
have to buy a ticket for
zones 1 to 5.

o Metro lines are
identified by both their
number (eg ligne 1 – line
1) and their colour, listed
on official metro signs
and maps.

o Signs in metro and RER stations indicate the way to the correct platform for your line. The *direction* signs on each platform indicate the terminus. On lines that split into several branches (such as lines 7 and 13), the terminus of each train is indicated on the cars and on signs on each platform giving the number of minutes until the next and subsequent train.

o Signs marked *correspondance* (transfer) show how to reach connecting trains. At stations with many intersecting lines, like Châtelet and Montparnasse Bienvenüe, walking from one platform to the next can take a very long time.

o Different station exits are indicated by white-on-blue *sortie* (exit) signs. You can get your bearings by checking the *plan du quartier* (neighbourhood maps) posted at exits.

o Each line has its own schedule, but trains usually start at around 5.30am, with the last train beginning its run between 12.35am and 1.15am (2.15am on Friday and Saturday).

Bus

o Paris' bus system, operated by the RATP, runs from approximately 5am to 1am Monday to Saturday; services are drastically reduced on Sunday and public holidays. Hours vary substantially depending on the line.

o The RATP runs night-bus lines known as Noctilien (www.vianavigo.com), which depart hourly from 11.45pm to 6am. The services pass through the main train stations and cross the major axes of the city before leading out to the suburbs. Look for navy-blue N or Noctilien signs at bus stops.

Bicycle

o The **Vélib'** (☑ 01 76 49 12 34; www.velib-metropole.fr; day/week subscription €5/15, standard bike hire up to 30/60min free/€1, electric bike €1/2) bike-share scheme changed operators; check the website for the latest information. Thousands of bikes (30% of which are electric) are available at some 1400 stations throughout Paris, accessible around the clock.

o For longer rentals, places generally require a deposit (usually €150 for a standard bike, €300 for electric bikes). Take ID and your bank or credit card.

Freescoot (☑ 01 44 07 06 72; www.freescoot.fr; 63 quai de la Tournelle, 5e; 50/125cc scooters per 24hr from €65/75, bicycle/tandem/electric-bike hire per 24hr from €20/40/40; ⏱ 9am-1pm & 3-7pm Mon-Sat, closed late Jul-late Aug & late Dec-early Jan; Ⓜ Maubert-Mutualité)

Gepetto et Vélos (☑ 01 43 54 19 95; www.gepetto-velos.com; 28 rue des Fossés St-Bernard, 5e; bike rental per hour/day/weekend from €4/16/27; ⏱ 9am-7pm Tue-Sat, closed Aug; Ⓜ Cardinal Lemoine)

Paris à Vélo, C'est Sympa (☑ 01 48 87 60 01; www.parisavelo.fr; 22 rue Alphonse Baudin, 11e; half-/full day/24hr bike from €13/16/22, electric bike €33/40/50; ⏱ 9.30am-1pm & 2-6pm Mon-Fri, 9am-7pm Sat & Sun Apr-Oct, shorter hours Nov-Mar; Ⓜ Richard Lenoir)

Boat

Batobus (www.batobus.com; adult/child 1-day pass €17/8, 2-day pass €21/11; ⏱10am-9.30pm late Apr-Aug, shorter hours Sep-late Apr) Runs glassed-in trimarans that dock every 20 to 25 minutes at nine small piers along the Seine: Eiffel Tower, Invalides, Musée d'Orsay, St-Germain des Prés, Notre Dame/Latin Quarter, Jardin des Plantes, Hôtel de Ville, Musée du Louvre and place de la Concorde.

Buy tickets online, at ferry stops or at tourist offices. Two-day passes must be used on consecutive days. You can also buy a Pass+ that includes **L'Open Tour buses** (📞01 42 66 56 56; www.opentourparis.com; adult/child 1-day pass €35/18, night tour €27/17), to be used on consecutive days. A two-day pass per adult/child costs €47/21; a three day-pass is €51/21.

Taxi

o The *prise en charge* (flagfall) is €4.10. Within the city limits, it costs €1.07 per kilometre for travel between 10am and 5pm Monday to Saturday (*Tarif A;* white light on taxi roof and meter).

o At night (5pm to 10am), on Sunday from 7am to midnight, and in the inner suburbs the rate is €1.29 per kilometre (*Tarif B;* orange light).

o Travel in the city limits and inner suburbs on Sunday night (midnight to 7am Monday) and in the outer suburbs is at *Tarif C,* €1.56 per kilometre (blue light).

o The minimum taxi fare for a short trip is €7.30.

o There are flat-fee fares to/from the major airports (Charles de Gualle from €50, Orly from €30).

o A fifth passenger incurs a €4 surcharge.

o There's no additional charge for luggage.

o Flagging down a taxi in Paris can be difficult; it's best to find an official taxi stand.

o To order a taxi, call or reserve online with **Taxis G7** (📞from a French phone 3607, from an international phone 01 41 27 66 99; www.g7.fr) or **Alpha Taxis** (📞01 45 85 85 85; www.alphataxis.fr).

Essential Information

Accessible Travel

o Visit www.parisinfo.com/accessibility for a wealth of information.

o For information about which cultural venues in Paris are accessible to people with disabilities, visit Accès Culture (www.accesculture.org).

o **Mobile en Ville** (📞06 52 76 62 49; www.mobileenville.org; 8 rue des Mariniers, 14e) works hard to make independent travel within the city easier for people in wheelchairs. Among other things it organises wheelchair *randonnées* (walks) in and around Paris; those in wheelchairs are pushed by 'walkers' on roller skates; contact the association well ahead of your visit to take part.

o Download Lonely Planet's free *Accessible Travel Online Resources* from http://lptravel.to/AccessibleTravel for heaps more useful websites, including travel agents and tour operators.

Tickets & Passes

○ Paris is phasing out paper tickets by 2022.

○ A Navigo Easy contactless card (€2) allows infrequent transport users including visitors to prepay for journeys (single t+ tickets or banks of 10) by topping the card up; there is no expiry date, and cards can be shared between passengers.

○ The same RATP 'tickets' (loaded onto contactless cards) are valid on the metro, the RER (for travel within the city limits), buses, trams and the Montmartre funicular.

○ Individual t+ tickets cost €1.90 (half price for children aged four to nine years) if bought individually; a *carnet* (book, ie a bank) of 10 costs €14.90 for adults.

○ Navigo cards and top-ups are sold at all metro stations. Ticket windows accept most credit cards; however, machines do not accept credit cards without embedded chips (and even then, not all foreign chip-embedded cards are accepted).

○ One ticket lets you travel between any two metro stations (no return journeys) for a period of 1½ hours, no matter how many transfers are required. You can also use it on the RER for travel within zone 1, which encompasses all of central Paris.

○ Transfers from the metro to buses (or trams) or vice versa are not possible.

○ You will have to pay a fine if you don't have a valid ticket.

○ Mobilis day tickets and Paris Visite tourist passes cover transport.

Transport

○ Info Mobi (www.vianavigo.com/accessibilite) has detailed information about public transport in the Île-de-France region surrounding Paris, filterable by disability type.

○ Taxis G7 (📞 from a French phone 3607, from an international phone 01 41 27 66 99; www.g7.fr) has hundreds of low-base cars and 120 cars equipped with ramps, and drivers trained in helping passengers with disabilities. Guide dogs are accepted in its entire fleet.

Business Hours

The following list covers *approximate* standard opening hours. Many businesses close in August for summer holidays.

Banks 9am to 1pm and 2pm to 5pm Monday to Friday; some open on Saturday morning

Bars and cafes 7am to 2am

Museums 10am to 6pm; closed Monday or Tuesday

Post offices 8am to 7pm Monday to Friday, and until noon Saturday

Restaurants noon to 2pm and 7.30pm to 10.30pm

Shops 10am to 7pm Monday to Saturday; they occasionally close in the early afternoon for lunch and sometimes all day Monday; hours are longer for shops in defined ZTIs (international tourist zones)

Discount Cards

Paris Museum Pass (www,en.parismuseum pass.com; two/four/six days €48/62/74) Gets you into 50-plus venues in and around Paris; a huge advantage is that pass holders usually enter larger sights at a different entrance, meaning you bypass (or substantially reduce) ridiculously long ticket queues.

Paris Passlib' (www. parisinfo.com; two/ three/five days €119/139/165) Sold at the **Paris Convention & Visitors Bureau** (Paris Office de Tourisme; ☏ 01 49 52 42 63; www. parisinfo.com; 29 rue de Rivoli, 4e; ◷10am-6pm; 📶; M Hôtel de Ville) and on its website, this handy city pass

covers unlimited public transport in zones 1 to 3, admission to some 50 museums in the Paris region (aka a Paris Museum Pass), temporary exhibitions at most municipal museums, a one-hour **Bateaux Parisiens** (☏ 01 76 64 14 45; www.bateauxparisiens. com; Port de la Bourdonnais, 7e; adult/child €15/7; M Bir Hakeim or RER Pont de l'Alma) boat cruise along the Seine, and a one-day hop-on, hop-off open-top bus sightseeing service around central Paris' key sights with **L'Open Tour** (☏ 01 42 66 56 56; www.opentourparis.com; adult/child 1-day pass €35/18, night tour €27/17). There's an optional €20 supplement for a skip-the-line ticket to levels one and two of the Eiffel Tower.

Mobilis and **Paris Visite** As Paris is phasing out paper tickets, they will be available in contactless card form. Passes operate by date (rather than 24-hour periods), so activate them early in the day for the best value.

Mobilis Allows unlimited travel for one day and costs €7.50 (for

two zones) to €17.80 (five zones).

Paris Visite Allows unlimited travel as well as discounted entry to certain museums and other discounts and bonuses. The 'Paris+ Suburbs+ Airports' pass includes transport to/ from the airports and costs €25.25/38.35/ 53.75/65.80 for one/ two/ three/five days. The cheaper 'Paris Centre' pass, valid for zones 1 to 3, costs €12/19.50/ 26.65/38.35 for one/ two/ three/five days. Children aged four to 11 years pay half price.

Electricity

Type E
230V/50Hz

Emergencies

Ambulance (SAMU)	15
Fire	18
Police	17
EU-wide emergency	112
France's country code	33

Internet Access

o Wi-fi (pronounced 'wee-fee' in France) is available in most Paris hotels, usually at no extra cost, and in some museums.

o Many cafes and bars have free wi-fi for customers; you may need to ask for the code.

o Free wi-fi is available in hundreds of public places, including parks, libraries and municipal buildings; look for a purple 'Zone Wi-Fi' sign. To connect, select the 'PARIS_WI-FI_' network. Sessions are limited to two hours (renewable). For complete details and a map of hot spots, see www.paris.fr/wifi.

o Co-working cafes have sprung up across Paris; you typically pay for a set amount of time, with wi-fi, drinks and snacks included.

Money

o France uses the euro (€). For updated exchange rates, check www.xe.com.

o Visa is the most widely accepted credit card, followed by MasterCard. American Express and Diners Club cards are accepted only at more exclusive establishments. Some restaurants don't accept credit cards.

o Many automated services, such as ticket machines, require a chip-and-PIN credit card (even some foreign chip-enabled cards won't work). Ask your bank for advice before you leave.

Public Holidays

A *jour férié* (public holiday) is celebrated strictly on the day on which it falls. If it falls on a Saturday or Sunday, no provision is made for an extra day off.

New Year's Day (Jour de l'An) 1 January

Easter Sunday & Monday (Pâques & Lundi de Pâques) Late March/April

May Day (Fête du Travail) 1 May

Victory in Europe Day (Victoire 1945) 8 May

Ascension Thursday (L'Ascension) May, celebrated on the 40th day after Easter

Whit Monday (Lundi de Pentecôte) Mid-May to mid-June on the seventh Monday after Easter

Bastille Day/National Day (Fête Nationale) 14 July

Assumption Day (L'Assomption) 15 August

All Saints' Day (La Toussaint) 1 November

Armistice Day/ Remembrance Day (Le Onze Novembre) 11 November

Christmas (Noël) 25 December

Responsible Travel

There are plenty of options to travel responsibly in Paris.

o Travel off-season, ideally in October and November, as well as in March and June. August is also a great month, when Parisians are on holidays.

o Avoid staying in central Paris and opt for hotels

Dos & Don'ts

Overall, communication tends to be formal and reserved, but this shouldn't be mistaken for unfriendliness.

Greetings Always greet/farewell anyone you interact with, such as shopkeepers, with '*Bonjour* (*bonsoir* at night)/*Au revoir*'.

Shops Particularly in smaller upmarket boutiques, staff may not appreciate your touching the merchandise until you have been invited to do so, nor taking photographs.

Speech Parisians don't speak loudly – modulate your voice to a similarly low pitch.

Terms of address *Tu* and *vous* both mean 'you', but *tu* is only used with people you know very well, children or animals. Use *vous* until you're invited to use *tu*.

Conversation topics Discussing financial affairs (eg salaries or spending outlays) is generally taboo in public.

Waitstaff Never use '*garçon*' (literally 'boy') to summon a waiter, rather 'Monsieur' or 'Madame'.

○ Common 'distraction' scams include would-be pickpockets pretending to 'find' a gold ring, brandishing fake petitions, dropping items, and tying 'friendship bracelets' to your wrist.

○ Metro stations best avoided late at night include Châtelet–Les Halles, Château Rouge, Gare du Nord, Strasbourg St-Denis, Réaumur Sébastopol, Stalingrad and Montparnasse Bienvenüe. Marx Dormoy, Porte de la Chapelle and Marcadet–Poissonniers can be sketchy day and night.

○ *Bornes d'alarme* (alarm boxes) are located in the centre of metro/RER platforms and some station corridors.

located in the *Première Couronne* (the adjoining suburbs), which is easily accessible from Paris by bus or metro.

○ Explore Paris' secret spots and villages. Some great areas include Butte Aux Cailles and Cité Florale in the 13e arrondissement (city district), Pernety Plaisance in the 14e arrondissement, the Mouzaïa in the 19e arrondissement and

Batignolles in the 17e arrondissement.

Safe Travel

Overall, Paris is well lit and safe, and random street assaults are rare.

○ Stay alert for pickpockets and take precautions: don't carry more cash than you need, and keep credit cards and passports in a concealed pouch.

Toilets

○ Public toilets in Paris are signposted *toilettes* or *WC*. On main roads, *sanisettes* (self-cleaning cylindrical toilets) are open 24 hours and are free of charge. Look for the words *libre* ('available'; green-coloured) or *occupé* ('occupied'; red-coloured). Locations are mapped at www.parisinfo.com.

○ Cafe owners do not appreciate you using their facilities if you are not a paying customer (a coffee can be a good investment); however, if you have young children they may make an exception (ask first!). Other good bets are big hotels and major department stores (the latter may incur a charge).

○ There are free public toilets near the Arc de Triomphe, down the steps at Sacré-Cœur (to the east and west) and at the northwestern entrance to the Jardins des Tuileries.

Tourist Information

Information desks are located at Charles de Gaulle and Orly airports.

Paris Convention & Visitors Bureau (Paris Office de Tourisme; ☑ 01 49 52 42 63; www.parisinfo. com; 29 rue de Rivoli, 4e;

⊙ 10am-6pm; ☎; Ⓜ Hôtel de Ville) Paris' main tourist office is at the Hôtel de Ville. It sells tickets for tours and several attractions, plus museum and transport passes.

Gare du Nord Welcome Desk (www. parisinfo.com; 18 rue de Dunkerque, 10e; ⊙ 9am-5pm Mon-Sat; Ⓜ Gare du Nord) Inside Gare du Nord station, under the glass roof of the Île-de-France departure and arrival area (eastern end of station).

Visas

○ Citizens or residents of EU and Schengen countries have no entry restrictions.

○ From 1 January 2021, non-EU nationals who don't require a visa for entry to the Schengen area need prior authorisation to enter under the new European Travel Information and Authorisation System

(ETIAS; www.etias.com). Travellers can apply online; the cost is €7 for a three-year, multi-entry authorisation.

○ With ETIAS pre-authorisation, travellers who require it can stay for 90 days out of 180 days.

○ Nationals of other countries should check with a French embassy or consulate about applying for a Schengen visa.

○ A visa for any Schengen country should be valid throughout the Schengen area, but it pays to double-check with the embassy or consulate of each country you intend to visit. Note that the UK and Ireland are not Schengen countries.

○ Check www.diplomatie.gouv.fr for the latest visa regulations and the closest French embassy to your current residence.

Language

The sounds used in spoken French can almost all be found in English. There are a couple of exceptions: nasal vowels (represented in our pronunciation guides by 'o' or 'u' followed by an almost inaudible nasal consonant sound 'm', 'n' or 'ng'), the 'funny' u sound ('ew' in our guides) and the deep-in-the-throat r. Bearing these few points in mind and reading our pronunciation guides below as if they were English, you'll be understood just fine. The markers (m) and (f) indicate the forms for male and female speakers.

To enhance your trip with a phrasebook, visit **lonelyplanet.com**. Lonely Planet iPhone phrasebooks are available in the Apple App store.

Basics

Hello.
Bonjour.   bon·zhoor

Goodbye.
Au revoir.   o·rer·vwa

How are you?
Comment   ko·mon
allez-vous?   ta·lay·voo

I'm fine, thanks.
Bien, merci.   byun mair·see

Please.
S'il vous plaît.   seel voo play

Thank you.
Merci.   mair·see

Excuse me.
Excusez-moi.   ek·skew·zay·mwa

Sorry.
Pardon.   par·don

Yes./No.
Oui./Non.   wee/non

I don't understand.
Je ne comprends   zher ner kom·pron
pas.   pa

Do you speak English?
Parlez-vous   par·lay·voo
anglais?   ong·glay

Eating & Drinking

..., please.
..., s'il vous plaît.   ..., seel voo play

A coffee	un café	un ka·fay
A table for two	une table pour deux	ewn ta·bler poor der
Two beers	deux bières	der bee·yair

I'm a vegetarian.
Je suis   zher swee
végétarien/   vay·zhay·ta·ryun/
végétarienne. (m/f) vay·zhay·ta·ryen

That was delicious!
C'était délicieux!   say·tay day·lee·syer

The bill, please.
L'addition,   la·dee·syon
s'il vous plaît.   seel voo play

Shopping

I'd like to buy ...
Je voudrais   zher voo·dray
acheter ...   ash·tay ...

I'm just looking.
Je regarde.   zher rer·gard

How much is it?
C'est combien?   say kom·byun

It's too expensive.
C'est trop cher.   say tro shair

Can you lower the price?
Vous pouvez voo poo·vay
baisser le prix? bay·say ler pree

Emergencies

Help!
Au secours! o skoor

Call the police!
Appelez la police! a·play la po·lees

Call a doctor!
Appelez un a·play un
médecin! mayd·sun

I'm sick.
Je suis malade. zher swee ma·lad

I'm lost.
Je suis perdu/ zher swee
perdue. (m/f) pair·dew

Where are the toilets?
Où sont les oo son lay
toilettes? twa·let

Time & Numbers

What time is it?
Quelle heure kel er
est-il? ay til

It's (eight) o'clock.
Il est (huit) il ay (weet)
heures. er

It's half past (10).
Il est (dix) heures il ay (deez) er
et demie. ay day·mee

morning	*matin*	ma·tun
afternoon	*après-midi*	a·pray·mee·dee
evening	*soir*	swar
yesterday	*hier*	yair
today	*aujourd'hui*	o·zhoor·dwee
tomorrow	*demain*	der·mun

Monday	*lundi*	lun·dee
Tuesday	*mardi*	mar·dee
Wednesday	*mercredi*	mair·krer·dee
Thursday	*jeudi*	zher·dee
Friday	*vendredi*	von·drer·dee
Saturday	*samedi*	sam·dee
Sunday	*dimanche*	dee·monsh

1	*un*	un
2	*deux*	der
3	*trois*	trwa
4	*quatre*	ka·trer
5	*cinq*	sungk
6	*six*	sees
7	*sept*	set
8	*huit*	weet
9	*neuf*	nerf
10	*dix*	dees
100	*cent*	son
1000	*mille*	meel

Transport & Directions

Where's ...?
Où est ...? oo ay ...

What's the address?
Quelle est l'adresse? kel ay la·dres

Can you show me (on the map)?
Pouvez-vous poo·vay·voo
m'indiquer mun·dee·kay
(sur la carte)? (sewr la kart)

I want to go to ...
Je voudrais zher voo·dray
aller à ... a·lay a ...

Does it stop at (Amboise)?
Est-ce qu'il es·kil
s'arrête à sa·ret a
(Amboise)? (om·bwaz)

I want to get off here.
Je veux zher ver
descendre day·son·drer
ici. ee·see

Behind the Scenes

Send Us Your Feedback

We love to hear from travellers – your comments help make our books better. We read every word, and we guarantee that your feedback goes straight to the authors. Visit **lonelyplanet.com/contact** to submit your updates and suggestions.

Note: We may edit, reproduce and incorporate your comments in Lonely Planet products such as guidebooks, websites and digital products, so let us know if you don't want your comments reproduced or your name acknowledged. For a copy of our privacy policy visit lonelyplanet.com/privacy.

Acknowledgements

Cover photograph: View towards the Eiffel Tower, Jan Christopher Becke, AWL Images ©

Photographs pp32/3: compass andcamera/ACQUIA ©, joe daniel price/ACQUIA ©

Jean-Bernard Carillet's Thanks

Heaps of thanks to the commissioning and production team at Lonely Planet, especially Sandie, for their trust and support, and to the editorial and cartography teams. In Paris, a special mention goes to my friends Didier, Sarah, Elodie, Marie and many more, who happily shared their passion of Paris. And how could I forget my daughter Eva, who is a *Parisienne par excellence*?

Catherine Le Nevez's Thanks

Merci mille fois first and foremost to Julian, and to the innumerable Parisians who provided insights, inspiration and great times. Huge thanks too to my Paris co-writers, and to Sandie Kestell, Genna Patterson and everyone at Lonely Planet. As ever, a heartfelt *merci encore* to my family for sustaining my lifelong love of Paris.

Christopher Pitts' Thanks

Special thanks to my three great co-writers for their advice and input and to all the crew at LP who have put so much hard work into making this book what it is. *Bises* as always to the Pavillard clan, and my dearest partners in crime: Perrine, Elliot and Céleste.

Nicola Williams' Thanks

Many thanks as always to the many good friends and savvy Paris professionals who pulled out all the stops to ensure I tracked down the best of Paris, including street-smart local in the 13e Mary Winston-Nicklin, New Yorker-in-Paris Kasia Dietz, adopted-Parisian-in-London Daisy of the Louvre's fabulous ThatMuse, and the ever-dedicated Elodie Berta at the Paris Convention & Visitors Bureau. On the home front, *bisou* as always to my tireless, trilingual travel and support team Matthias, Niko, Mischa and Kaya.

Acknowledgements

Cover photographs: (front) Eiffel Tower and cafe, Jan Christopher Becke/AWL Images ©; (back) cheeses at Marché d'Aligre, Premier Photo/Shutterstock ©

This Book

This 7th edition of Lonely Planet's *Pocket Paris* guidebook was researched and written by Jean-Paul Carillet, Catherine Le Nevez, Christopher Pitts and Nicola Williams. The previous two editions were also written by Catherine, Christopher and Nicola. This guidebook was produced by the following:

Senior Product Editors Sandie Kestell, Amy Lynch

Regional Senior Cartographers Mark Griffiths, Alison Lyall

Product Editors Barbara Delissen, Genna Patterson, Amanda Williamson

Book Designers Hannah Blackie, Brooke Giacomin

Assisting Editors Andrea Dobbin, Ali Lemer

Assisting Cartographer Valentina Kremenchutskaya

Cover Researchers Gwen Cotter, Brendan Dempsey-Spencer

Thanks to James Appleton, Fergal Condon, Melanie Dankel, Karen Henderson, Jelena Huber, Abbie Hunt, Fraser Hunt, Amy Lysen, Genna Patterson, Rachel Rawling, Kirsten Rawlings, Himanshu Talan

Index

See also separate subindexes for:

Eating p221
Drinking p221
Entertainment p222
Shopping p222

Sights 000
Map Pages **000**

W

🛇 Eating

🍷 Drinking